Praise for *The Solution Revolution*

"We know that governments can't afford to do everything these days, but fortunately there's a revolution in how we tackle social needs. Citizens and businesses are creating a 'solution economy' that blends market forces and altruism to get good things done. This book shows the beauty of harnessing innovation for the public good. Watch out. It may inspire you to join the revolution!"
—Walter Isaacson, President and CEO, Aspen Institute; author, *Steve Jobs*

"Today the world's biggest problems are the world's biggest market opportunities. Want to become a billionaire? Solve a billion-person problem. *The Solution Revolution* shows you how."
—Peter H. Diamandis, Chairman and CEO, XPRIZE Foundation; Chairman, Singularity University; coauthor, *Abundance: The Future Is Better Than You Think*

"If the writing weren't already on the wall, Eggers and Macmillan have put it there. Too often, we are trying to address the big challenges of our day with models and institutions that don't scale. *The Solution Revolution* explores how the intersections of the sectors can unlock the potential we'll need to face the realities of the twenty-first century."
—Jennifer Pahlka, Deputy US CTO; founder and Executive Director, Code for America

"*The Solution Revolution* shows how today's corporations are increasingly measuring outcomes rather than output, and societies are

judging business success not solely by the profits they make but also by the difference they make—a difference that can only be made through working across sectors."
—Robert Collymore, CEO, Safaricom

"*The Solution Revolution* is a practical guide to multisector problem solving and provides a powerful framework to address the many global challenges society currently faces. It reminds us that the collective action of people and organizations can have the most effective impact."
—Kathy Calvin, President and CEO, United Nations Foundation

"*The Solution Revolution* is a wise reminder that global problems shouldn't be left to government alone to solve. Whether we're in business, government, or the social sector, we can find solutions together if we cross boundaries and find mutual interests with stakeholders. Read this book and join today's 'solution economy.'"
—John Mackey, co-CEO and cofounder, Whole Foods Market; coauthor, *Conscious Capitalism: Liberating the Heroic Spirit of Business*

"With a global population approaching nine billion and governments so indebted that their only answer is to beggar succeeding generations, the current path is clearly unsustainable. Eggers and Macmillan seek a better way. *The Solution Revolution* is well worth reading."
—The Right Honourable Paul Martin, former Prime Minister of Canada

"Read this book if you want to understand how the 'solution revolution' will create a trillion-dollar market for social good by unlocking the value of underutilized resources in ways and on a scale never possible before."
—Rachel Botsman, coauthor, *What's Mine Is Yours: The Rise of Collaborative Consumption*

"Eggers and Macmillan vividly describe creative solutions that break the boundaries between the public and private sectors and civil society. They show just how much is possible—in everything from mining open data to turning social outcomes into an asset class."
—Geoff Mulgan, CEO, Nesta; author, *The Locust and the Bee: Predators and Creators in Capitalism's Future*

"*The Solution Revolution* is a pioneering book exploring the fascinating transition underway as social innovation moves to the 'third rail' ecosystems outside of government. Eggers and Macmillan's revolution will be improvised!"
—Peter Sims, author, *Little Bets: How Breakthrough Ideas Emerge from Small Discoveries*

"The old African saying, 'it takes a village to raise a child,' is truer now than ever. With a rapidly expanding youth population, Africa is at a turning point. It will need to leverage innovative solutions to sustain the well-being of its population by tapping into all players: government, businesses, nonprofits, and individual communities. *The Solution Revolution* is a timely guide to how to get this done."
—Omari Issa, CEO, Investment Climate Facility for Africa

"*The Solution Revolution* is a needed guide to accelerate the innovative solutions required to address the economic and social challenges we face as a consequence of unsustainable models of growth."
—Roberto Artavia, Chairman, Viva Trust; CEO, Social Progress Imperative

"How can businesses and governments work together with innovative 'citizen changemakers' and social entrepreneurs? *The Solution Revolution* spotlights individuals and institutions that 'get it,' and offers a perfect jumping-off point for those seeking real social impact."
—Premal Shah, President, Kiva

The
SOLUTION
REVOLUTION

The
SOLUTION
REVOLUTION

How BUSINESS, GOVERNMENT,

and SOCIAL ENTERPRISES Are Teaming Up

to Solve Society's Toughest Problems

WILLIAM D. EGGERS AND PAUL MACMILLAN

Harvard Business Review Press • Boston, Massachusetts

Copyright 2013 Deloitte Global Services Limited
For more information, contact Deloitte Touche Tohmatsu Limited.

The opinions of this book are those of the co-authors and not of Deloitte. Deloitte refers to one or more of Deloitte Touche Tohmatsu Limited, a UK private company limited by guarantee, and its network of member firms, each of which is a legally separate and independent entity. Please see www.deloitte.com/about for a detailed description of the legal structure of Deloitte Touche Tohmatsu Limited and its member firms.

The web addresses referenced in this book were live and correct at the time of the book's publication but may be subject to change.

Library of Congress Cataloging-in-Publication Data

Eggers, William D.
   The solution revolution : how business, government, and social enterprises are teaming up to solve society's toughest problems / William D. Eggers, Paul Macmillan.
     pages cm
   ISBN 978-1-4221-9219-1 (hardback)
   1. Social entrepreneurship.   2. Social responsibility of business.   3. Social problems—Economic aspects.   4. Economics—Sociological aspects.   I. Macmillan, Paul.   II. Title.
   HD60.E337 2013
   361.8—dc23

                                                                    2013018709

The paper used in this publication meets the requirements of the American National Standard for Permanence of Paper for Publications and Documents in Libraries and Archives Z39.48-1992.

ISBN: 9781422192191
eISBN: 9781422192207

Contents

The
SOLUTION
REVOLUTION

Introduction: The Power of the Solution Economy

The new trillion-dollar market for public good

Shel Silverstein's wildly popular children's book *The Giving Tree* has been translated into more than thirty languages since its initial publication in 1964. The story chronicles a tree's enduring devotion to a boy. At first, the tree provides the simple comforts of shade and refreshment. But as it meets the boy's continuing demands, it relinquishes everything, down to its apples, branches, and trunk. Eventually, all that remains is a humble stump, which even then is put to use.

Like the tree in Silverstein's story, governments are finding the problems they've agreed to address to be truly insatiable.

During the twentieth century, the need to tackle massive public problems such as public health epidemics and large infrastructure development meant that government became the center of solving big problems. From building the Hoover Dam to eradicating smallpox, from economic development in Africa to education worldwide, government was the place to be for those who wanted to change the world for the better. The Great Society's war on poverty, an unlimited war against want, was perhaps the zenith of this identification of government with great achievement—or at least great aspiration.

There is very little that we *haven't* asked from government in modern times. We ask it to keep us safe from terrorists and to protect our privacy; to prevent global economic meltdowns and stop the contagion of failing states; to bail out banks and contain the spiraling costs of an array of competing vital interests, from health care to education.

The sheer range and variety of these goals mean that government agencies often find themselves working at cross-purposes. Public health agencies fund obesity programs while the U.S. Department of Agriculture subsidizes sugar. Transportation departments fight traffic congestion on the one hand while subsidizing road use on the other. International development agencies provide aid to farmers in the developing world while trade barriers keep foreign agricultural goods out of Western markets.

Developing countries may lack such an ambitious public sector, but neither can they afford to produce one—at least not the same model as the West. For these countries, it would take decades for GDP growth to grow fast enough to support industrial-age government, with its soaring costs in health care and education. Consider India. Per-capita health-care spending in India would have to increase thirty-seven-fold to match Canadian spending levels. At current rates of growth, this wouldn't happen until 2070—much too late, considering India's rapidly growing middle class. India simply can't afford to take the high-cost Western route.

Increasingly, the West can't, either. The defining feature of Western-style government—its success in catering to a wide variety of citizen needs—has become its greatest liability. Governments are going broke while contorting themselves into ever-stranger positions to satisfy often contradictory constituent demands.

In Colorado Springs, for instance, tight budgets led to reduced city services and, ultimately, a system in which community residents made à la carte purchases. If a neighborhood wanted its street lamps to light up at dusk, it could pay the city a $125 fee. Keep the nearby park maintained? $2,500.[1]

In Europe and North America, the great recession forced governments on a path of austerity, causing them to reduce their police forces and close schools, libraries, and hospitals they could simply no longer afford. And with debt growing at a rate of roughly $4 billion per day in the United States and more in Europe, fiscal constraints have become the new normal.

So at both the low end and the high end of spending, governments have a desperate need for an alternative to a traditional top-down service model.

Fortunately, government is no longer the only game in town when it comes to societal problem solving. Society is witnessing a step change in how it deals with its own problems—a shift from a government-dominated model to one in which government is just one player among many. Over the last decade or so, a dizzying variety of new players has entered the societal problem-solving arena. Acumen and Ashoka, Kiva and Kaggle, Zipcar and Zimride, Recyclebank and RelayRides, SpaceX and M-Pesa, Branson and Bloomberg, Omidyar and Gates—the list is long and growing briskly. They operate within what we call a solution economy. These new innovators are closing the widening gap between what governments provide and what citizens need. This approach promises better results, lower costs, and the best hope we have for public innovation in an era of fiscal constraints and unmet needs.

The Economy in Eliminating Problems

In the 1970s and 1980s, governments provided for the public good while the private sector largely stuck with Milton Friedman's admonition that the social responsibility of business was to increase its profits.[2] Thinking beyond the bottom line was viewed as unfocused or, even worse, a disservice to shareholders. Meanwhile, because outside the United States civil society tended to be relatively small and highly localized, individual citizens and communities were only able to organize with limited scope and scale, placing a heavy dependency on government.

Many problems went unsolved. The solutions that did emerge didn't spread easily. Citizen needs, particularly those of the poor in the developing world, went unmet.

Today, the landscape has changed dramatically. Citizens, businesses, entrepreneurs, and foundations often turn to each other rather than relying solely on the public sector to coordinate solutions to every problem. This is blurring, if not eliminating, decades old divisions of public and private sector responsibilities.

Whereas the twentieth century was a time of sector specialization, the twenty-first century has boundaries too fluid for, say, a public nutrition issue to be the sole province of government.

A new economy has emerged at the borderlands where traditional sectors overlap. This economy trades in social outcomes; its currencies include public data, reputation, and social impact. Untapped markets are developed and drive financial returns. The business models are unusual, and the motivations range from new notions of public accountability to moral obligation to even shareholder value.

New problem-solving innovators and investors power the solution economy. These wavemakers assume many forms, including edgy social enterprises with the mentality of a Silicon Valley start-up, megafoundations, and *Fortune* 500 companies that now deliver social good on the path to profit. They range from Ashoka, which deploys three thousand citizen changemakers in sixty countries, to the global pharmaceutical giants that annually give away billions of dollars in medicine to low-income citizens anywhere, from Africa to the United States.

Just how big are the contributions of these new players? Unlike government spending figures, this data has not been systematically tracked. Their impacts translate only tenuously into dollar terms. However, even a rough estimate suggests trillions of dollars in impact.

Consider just a few data points. In 2009, private US philanthropy to developing countries exceeded official US government aid by almost $9 billion.[3] In one survey of 184 global companies, the average company contributed about $22 million to philanthropy, with the group total exceeding $15 billion in just one year. Even institutional investors have started funding groups that create public value. Socially responsible investing has grown into a $1 trillion industry.[4]

The solution economy represents not just an economic opportunity, but a new manner of solving entrenched societal problems. Equipped with new business models and lightweight technologies, the new problem solvers are less impeded by sectorial divides. Whether a problem is public or private, social or commercial, economic or political is not what drives the design. Rather, the ability and energy to reach the previously unreachable, raise funds from untapped sources, and leverage social networks is fueling new markets for solving entrenched societal problems.

These multi-billion-dollar markets are forming around some of the world's toughest problems, from fighting malaria to providing low-cost housing to educating the poorest of the poor. In these *solution markets* businesses, social entrepreneurs, nonprofits, and multinational companies compete, coordinate, and collaborate to solve megaproblems. Instead of trying to patch a market failure, they create a market for the solution. Foundations, venture philanthropists, governments—and, often, private businesses themselves—act as funders, investors, and market makers. Unlike most government-driven programs that are limited by political borders, these emerging solutions spread nimbly across the globe. In less than a decade, Unilever's Project Shakti microloan program for women in rural Indian villages expanded from seventeen saleswomen to forty-five thousand, serving three million Indian households; it is now spreading to Sri Lanka and Bangladesh.[5]

This all might inspire a touch of skepticism. You might be thinking something like this: We have markets in shoes, in homes, and in automobiles, but markets in societal outcomes? It seems illogical. Weren't these big, wicked problems the very areas where we've experienced market failure in the first place—where government was forced to step in? Take something like human trafficking. It's easy to see how there can be a market in engaging in this awful practice, but can a market be constructed to help stop it?

In this book, we assert that yes, you can create markets—or at least market mechanisms—around problems like environmental cleanup, transitioning from welfare to work, and even fighting human trafficking. In fact, markets and economic ecosystems are developing around all manner of societal problems. The buyers in these markets purchase impacts or outcomes: healthier communities, kids who can read, reduced recidivism. Sellers provide the outcomes for the buyer: they design and sell cheap, solar-powered lights; write the code that tracks salmonella outbreaks using government data; and build the cross-sector networks to fight scourges like human trafficking.

Government's role has changed dramatically just in the past decade or two. Sometimes it is a funder, but usually not the only funder; sometimes it integrates all the players; sometimes it's the market maker; sometimes it's just one of many contributors to the solution; and sometimes all it has to do is get out of the way to let these solution markets work.

Creating Mutual Advantage

We spent two years intensely studying this phenomenon, traveling to dozens of hotspots around the world, and interviewing hundreds of problem solvers both big and small. The experience made it clear that success stories like Project Shakti were anything but an isolated example. Almost invisibly, a large and growing global movement has developed around delivering better societal outcomes.

Converging factors have made this kind of social innovation more attainable. Technology and greater access to venture capital and other funding enable organizations with innovative business models to scale rapidly. Powerful collaboration tools enable citizens to work directly with peers to solve problems. Greater corporate social awareness enables changemakers to more easily connect their firm's resources to wider problems.

The common thread across these initiatives is that of mutual advantage: the unprecedented alignment of financial and social incentives toward a greater public good. Private enterprise for public gain no longer need be an oxymoron. A growing army of societal problem solvers are rewarded for successfully tackling big, hard problems. Trillions of dollars in value potentially lies largely untapped at the intersection of the public, private, and nonprofit sectors. *The Solution Revolution* is about how to unlock this value.

Contrary to some of the hype, this doesn't mean that social entrepreneurs will ride in and solve all of society's problems. Instead, we argue that the role of the major contributors is changing and that those contributors can gain significant mutual advantage not only by working together to solve problems, but also by doing so in new ways.

The motivations go well beyond mere economic considerations. Visit almost any large company today and you'll find individuals in executive suites whose goals match those of someone leading a social enterprise or impact investing fund—and they are beginning to speak the same language. This makes for a fundamentally more substantive conversation. Changes in the larger culture are also aligning interests. Employees, customers, and graduating MBAs that aspire to run top companies all expect higher returns than merely pure profit. That allows for more sustained interest in seeking win-win scenarios between profit and purpose.

This book builds on earlier research. Other important books have ably documented the new wave of billionaire philanthropists (*Philanthrocapitalism*); the rise in corporate social responsibility (*SuperCorp* and *The Market for Virtue*); and the rapid growth in social entrepreneurs (*How to Change the World*).[6] Such books have greatly informed our thinking, but our task here is different in several respects. First, rather than focus on a few categories of players, we intend to provide a detailed picture of the space that hosts their interaction. Second, in just the few years since those books were published, the landscape has evolved greatly. We can now be much clearer about how to conceptualize and accelerate this movement while maximizing its effectiveness in solving society's toughest problems.

In some ways, the solution economy resembles a traditional one. In fact, like the wider economy, the solution economy incorporates supply and demand, goods and services, trade and distribution, capital markets, and government regulation. What has evolved are the participants and how they interact.

Understanding how the solution economy works requires looking beyond traditional divisions and removing entrenched mental silos. New players dynamically react to unmet needs, and the players we *think* we know take on new roles; for example, Walmart assuming a major role in the fight against obesity. The contributors trade in unorthodox currencies: data, results, and reputation. They measure their bottom lines in social value. They invent imaginative new business models. Cutting-edge technical and social developments translate into remedies for old human obstacles. International borders are eventually bridged. And just as in the private sector, the pool of entrants expands as traditional barriers to entry decline.

The solution economy is powered by six principal features (figure I-1):

- Wavemakers, who solve problems
- Disruptive technologies
- Business models that scale
- Impact currencies
- Public-value exchanges
- Solution ecosystems

Each of the six central elements is powerful in its own right. However, the real breakthroughs come from deftly weaving the elements together—doing so can make even the thorniest problems solvable. The best way to understand this is to observe how they come together

FIGURE I-1

The solution economy

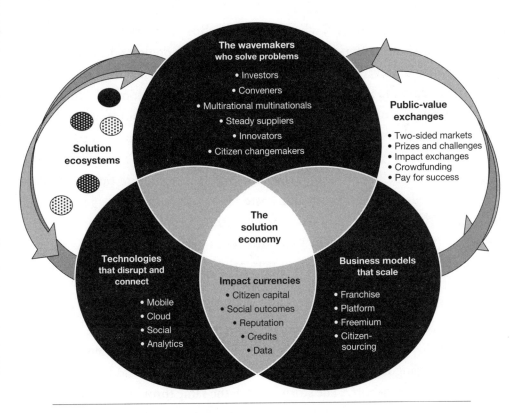

in solving an actual public problem—in this case, a really difficult problem that heretofore has escaped a solution: traffic gridlock.

Innovating for the Public Good

A crowd of twentysomethings gathers in the heart of San Francisco's Mission District. It's 10 a.m. Google shuttles have been scooping up workers across the city for four hours already. An unmarked white bus with tinted windows pulls to the curb. Workers stream on. Some sleep while others open their laptops to get a jumpstart on their frenzied workday as they barrel toward Mountain View in the fast lane. Engineers who could probably afford Porsches are taking the bus.

"There's really no question for me," says a twenty-five-year-old engineer, Noah Stevens, who rides the "G-Bus" to work every day.

The shuttle offers a total win—for Stevens, Google, and the wider public. For Stevens, it saves time and gas. For Google, it lowers worker stress, cuts the need for parking lots, and allows the company to attract talent. For the public, it reduces fuel demand, emissions, and traffic. It's a clockwork-smooth system, creating both private and public good.

It's a small dent in an intractable problem: commute times continue to drain productivity and waste resources. For decades, governments have tried in vain to come up with solutions by adding high-occupancy vehicles (HOV) lanes to roads and spending billions on elaborate public transportation networks. Yet, traffic congestion and the cost of commuting continue to grow.

Today, 77 percent of Americans drive to work alone. Only 5 percent use public transit. A meager 10 percent share rides, down from about 20 percent in 1970.[7] Those numbers are also miserably low in the United Kingdom; just 3 percent of commuters carpool, and 13 percent use public transport.[8] The story is much the same throughout much of the West. Every day, neighbors steer largely empty cars down parallel routes.

In the United States, the average commuter loses thirty-four hours a year to congestion delays; that's 4.76 billion hours among all American commuters.[9] The economic opportunity cost is staggering: $429 million daily or about $160 billion every year.[10]

But that's just the cost to individuals. Every twenty-mile commute costs government a dollar, and those costs add up.[11] If you include the cost of congestion, air pollution, or even lost property value near roadways, the total estimated external cost of driving runs between $0.27 and $0.55 per mile.[12]

As government coffers drain and as oil prices continue to climb, approaches to reducing traffic are multiplying like bubbles in a swamp.

Municipal budgets have limited the expansion of public transit, but communities of cyclists have found a workaround. These problem solvers have requested law changes to encourage a safer bike commute and promoted bike sharing services as an alternative to driving. New technology allows Car2Go and Zipcar to rent cars by the hour, easing the viability of car-free life.

One abundant and underutilized resource offers another potential solution to the gridlock problem: the empty seats in cars. The rideshare component of problem solvers teems with ideas to turn lone commuters into a secondary public transit system. Ridesharing apps like Zimride, Avego, RelayRides, and Carpooling.com herald the revolution. Smaller, community ridesharing programs, though they never make national news, similarly carve out a piece of the solution.

Innovation in ridesharing is growing organically. Entrepreneurs and nonprofits are using clever business models and technology to backfill public services. Reward Ride awards points to riders and drivers who can trade points for rides of their own, creating a micro-economy in the process. Meanwhile, the Avego app displays a driver's routes to passengers, who can search for rides in their direction. The app works in real time. Wherever a passenger waits, the app alerts drivers, pulling up a profile of the prospective rider. A driver can then survey the profile at a red light or another stopping point. Both a driver's trip progress and a rider's journey are logged via GPS. When the ride ends, Avego transfers a fee ($1.00, plus $0.20 per mile) from the passenger's Avego account to the driver's, with Avego taking a cut.[13] Users then rate each other.

"We are making the private car part of the public transit network," says Avego founder Sean O'Sullivan, echoing an increasingly common refrain of people pushing this new model of grassroots public transportation system. "The consumer is making [his or her] asset, empty seats, usable."[14]

Technology is reshaping society's ability to solve its problems. As with ridesharing, many of the successes profiled in the book have taken advantage of a combination of new technologies such as cloud computing, data analytics, social media, geospatial analysis, and mobile computing.

The new ridesharing programs track progress through digital currencies. Amovens serves as a message board where travelers with profiles post where they hope to travel and how much they'll pay to do so, allowing dollar prices to fluctuate freely. Users trust each other according to a person's accumulated social credit—user ratings thus form a currency to increase the odds of finding a willing driver.

The ridesharing innovations demonstrate just one of many ways the new solutions beyond traditional government spending are being fueled. They may come in the form of a loan to a promising social entrepreneur, a scientific formula for an immunization, or sharing your car with strangers. *Impact currencies* are a means of paying for social impacts. They determine how resources are allocated across the rapidly growing and evolving solution economy.

This is a central idea behind the solution revolution: social impact becomes a form of currency with real value to millions—from foundations to governments to venture philanthropists to individual citizens. Its form is limited only by the creativity of those who make and exchange it.

Another key feature of the solution economy is *public-value exchanges,* platforms created by entrepreneurs, companies, and governments to spread social impact. These exchanges range from crowdfunding platforms like Kiva that enable socially conscious citizens to invest in social entrepreneurs to prizes and pay-for-success systems that connect large funders to problem solvers.

Returning to the ridesharing example, changing commuter behavior requires that ridesharing offer an easy, comfortable, safe alternative to driving alone. The business models of the various ridesharing exchanges are predicated on the idea that the more participants, the greater the reliability that rides will be available and on time.

Such exchanges, if successful, can potentially have an outsized social impact. By our calculations, doubling the number of rideshare commuters (which would simply bring the percentage back up to

1970 levels) and shifting 10 percent of drivers to car sharing could take nearly sixteen million cars off the road and save 757 million wasted hours in congestion per year in the United States. The country's carbon dioxide emissions would decline by nearly 2 percent.[15]

If the government tried to match these savings by building new public transit, the bill would run around $27.5 billion, roughly the amount dedicated to repairing the country's crumbling roads and bridges as part of the American Recovery and Reinvestment Act in 2009.[16] In contrast, ridesharing costs the public sector almost nothing. In fact, government saves more than $8 billion in road maintenance costs.[17]

The last element of the solution economy is the *solution ecosystems*—the collaboration networks that come together to solve a specific problem. For example, companies, social entrepreneurs, foundations, and individual citizens are collaborating to revolutionize education and find low-cost solutions to housing the billions of poor people worldwide who live in slums. Wavemakers and the other elements of solution ecosystems are distributing vaccines. They are combating human trafficking on a more coordinated level than ever before. And they are solving society's big problems through unique convergences of resources and uncommon alliances.

Working to avoid the shackles or apathy of the past, the solution revolution is almost the antithesis of how society's toughest public challenges have traditionally been approached by large institutions. In no other space do we see such diverse resources—volunteer time, crowdfunding, capabilities of multinational corporations, entrepreneurial capital, philanthropic funding—aligned around common objectives such as reducing congestion, providing safe drinking water, or promoting healthy living.

Of course, transforming something as ingrained as someone's commuting habits isn't necessarily easy, but it's possible. After landing the job at Google, Stevens the engineer noticed that his Triumph Thunderbird was staying on its kickstand. "I used to take my bike everywhere," says Stevens. "But I guess I just got used to being along for the ride."[18]

Nurturing the Solution Economy

Throughout human history, new forms of economic value production created new economic structures and new political structures. The shift from hunter-gatherer to agriculture prompted the rise of the city-state. The growth of international trade in the eighteenth century made it critical to extend the rule of law to the high seas and put an end to the piracy and smuggling that had come before. With the industrial revolution, patent laws and other protections of intellectual property rights became essential parts of a functioning economy in ways they weren't in the sixteenth century. Stock exchanges took off in the nineteenth and twentieth centuries as large corporations took on greater importance as wealth generators. New means of production required new legal, political, and economic infrastructure.

Similarly, the solution economy is spawning new exchanges, ecosystems, and currencies that are collectively creating entirely new forms of economic organization and shifting the focus away from a government-only model. In countries where the solution economy is strong, a mix of providers and sustainable business models is creating social innovations with greater transparency and more public trust. The market infrastructure for investing in social impacts is becoming more robust. And more and more of the nation's best and brightest graduates are marrying their vocation with their passion for larger social good.

We're still learning how government, business, investors, and philanthropists can best create and expand flourishing markets in the solution economy. In India, the government has created a $1 billion "inclusive innovation fund" to spur private-sector solutions to some of the country's knottiest problems. Meanwhile, the Cameron government in the United Kingdom launched a £600 million fund in 2012 to help fund new societal problem solvers.[19]

Across the Atlantic, the Obama administration introduced a bevy of initiatives to support a growing solution sector, including a $50 million social innovation fund and a new Office of Social Innovation.[20]

"President Obama wanted to take the ideas of social entrepreneurship and bring them into the oval office," says Jonathan Greenblatt, who drives these efforts as the director of the White House office. "We're trying to find new ways to solve old problems and do so at scale." The White House even established a new Presidential Innovation Fellowship to pair top innovators in the business, nonprofit, and academic sectors with top innovators in government. The teams work together on key public policy issues in six-month sprints.[21] "We believe cross-sector leadership is fundamental to the future of America," exclaims federal Chief Technology Officer Todd Park, the force behind the initiative.[22]

Meanwhile, the US State Department and US Agency for International Development (USAID) have begun to pivot away from traditional aid in favor of public-private partnerships that support the growth of businesses that produce both financial and social returns.[23] At the same time, changes in state laws encourage new hybrid corporate forms like the benefit corporation (B corporation, or B corp), in which a corporation can legally justify a bottom line in terms of social good, not just shareholder return.[24]

Despite their benefits, these positive developments are still a far cry from what could be done to take full advantage of the solution movement. The stakes are high because the potential impact is so immense—tens of thousands of lives saved, millions of poor children educated, and health dramatically improved worldwide at lower cost.

For an individual citizen, civil servant, or employee at a large firm, these kinds of problems might seem daunting—even impenetrable. Where would you even start? In the pages that follow, we show myriad ways regular people can participate in the solution revolution through everything from crowdfunding to impact investing to peer-to-peer learning to citizen science. And we show the critical part changemakers in government and large companies can play in pivoting their organization's focus toward a bigger role in the solution economy.

A quick guide to the organization of the book: in chapter 1, we'll look more closely at the different categories of wavemakers and how they are changing conventional beliefs and practices. Chapters 2 and 3 explore the disruptive technologies and business models that are enabling radically new solutions to old problems. In chapters 4 and 5, we delve into the new currencies propelling the solution economy and the novel exchanges where they are traded. Chapter 6 looks at how these pieces can be brought together in the form of problem-solving ecosystems that do everything from fighting human trafficking to providing radically low cost housing for the very poor. Lastly, in chapter 7 we outline six strategies you can use to create your own solution revolution.

Along the way, we'll address the big questions involved in this movement. What's working? What's not? How can government facilitate the solution economy? How is this movement different from traditional nonprofit efforts to deliver public good? What are the implications of these myriad efforts on existing structures and institutions? How do we judge success and failure in this new, multisector approach to governance?

We begin by looking at the growing universe of wavemakers that are at the very heart of the solution revolution.

ONE

The Wavemakers

The rising new players engaged in delivering societal solutions

The modern flush toilet was invented in the eighteenth century. The substantial amount of water and sewer infrastructure needed to operate one hasn't changed much since. Consequently, about 2.5 billion people in the world rely on unsafe toilets or do their "business" out in the open. It's a crappy situation that the Bill & Melinda Gates Foundation decided to clean up. In 2011, the foundation awarded eight universities grants of about $400,000 to catalyze the technology of waterless, hygienic, and affordable toilets for people in the developing world.

A year later, teams gathered at the foundation's headquarters in Seattle for the heady, two-day Reinvent the Toilet fair, where innovators enthusiastically showcased their prototypes and pet projects. These included a urine-diversion system that recovers water (for flushing) and a solar-powered toilet that generates hydrogen and electricity. The audience in the room—a mix of researchers, designers, investors, advocates, and representatives of the communities in need—brimmed with enthusiasm.[1]

Not long ago, the idea of a philanthropic foundation's funding product development would have sounded really strange. Even stranger: that a foundation would invest the capital and technical support to help position the product to scale. But it's happening. Today's philanthropic foundations, like that of Bill and Melinda Gates, strategically invest to grow the solution economy.

The Bill & Melinda Gates Foundation is the single most influential philanthropic organization in the world. Its mission is audacious: to pursue the breakthroughs in health, education, and development that will create the most profound improvements in people's lives. "Private money can take risks in a way that government money often isn't willing to," explains Bill Gates.[2]

The sheer size of the foundation commands attention. With $37 billion in assets as of 2010, the foundation dwarfs even the largest traditional foundations such as the Ford Foundation, the Rockefeller Foundation, and the Carnegie Endowment for International Peace.[3] The thousand-plus staff that maintains ongoing projects in more than one hundred countries ensures that the foundation's footprint is both wide and deep.[4] Compare the Bill & Melinda Gates Foundation's annual grant-making budget of $3.21 billion with Denmark's entire overseas-development budget of $2.76 billion to understand the foundation's power.[5]

Its size and innovative approach make the Gates Foundation extraordinarily influential—able to wrestle with problems that historically have been strictly the province of government. The enormous impact and breadth of the foundation has been chronicled in detail elsewhere.[6] What's important here is that the foundation is a leader in today's new breed of *wavemakers,* that is, for-profit, nonprofit, and governmental organizations or individuals that revolutionize how the world approaches thorny social challenges. The wavemakers of the solution economy see old problems with new eyes.

Perhaps nowhere is this change clearer than international development. During the 1970s, 1980s, and early 1990s, governments dominated international aid. The results were less than ideal. Corrupt kleptocrats often intercepted funds. When aid did reach the local level, grandiose projects often failed to produce their intended life-changing benefits.

Today, private philanthropy to the developing world surpasses the monetary contributions of all governments combined (and no, that's not a typo).[7] Just as important, entrepreneurial-spirited pioneers are embracing innovative solutions. The Gates' foundation, for example, relies on a highly data-driven funding model. Rather than funding the most elegantly written grant—or, worse, the politically favored one— the foundation underwrites solutions that actually move the needle. The result has been a dramatic increase in small revolutions that have a large impact on those living in poverty—things like mosquito nets or better toilets. The new wave of deep-pocketed philanthropists places its faith, and its dollars, in metric-driven governance.[8]

Wavemakers can use their influence through direct and indirect means, funding compelling solutions, delivering the solutions, or congregating the various players in an ecosystem to progress toward their chosen social agendas. In each capacity, the wavemaker can amplify the capabilities of other players and promote collaboration across the ecosystem. Wavemakers do more than dent the problems society faces; they change the battlefield on which people face the problems.

Part of a wavemaker's role is to redefine a sphere, typically with new approaches that over time become standard practice. The Bill & Melinda Gates Foundation shaped behavior by bringing business discipline to the field. In business, outcomes can be measured through readily quantifiable indicators such as profit margins and units sold. Social impacts, by contrast, historically have been much less quantifiable. When the Gates Foundation first entered the development arena, the metrics for measuring social impacts were fairly immature. So the foundation developed its own guidelines for connecting inputs to social impacts. In the few years since Bill Gates committed to it full-time, the foundation has rapidly expanded its reach, quadrupling its staff and increasing its giving, thanks in part to Warren Buffett's contribution of billions to the endowment.[9]

While a giant in the philanthropy world, the Bill & Melinda Gates Foundation is just one of many wavemakers solving big problems and improving social outcomes. But you don't have to be a billionaire to make a big difference. The impact of Ashoka's thousands of fellows—all citizen changemakers in the fullest sense—is not through monetary contributions but through their ability to assemble cross-sector ecosystems to solve tough problems.

A complex, interconnected web of various wavemakers—investors, conveners, multinationals, innovators, suppliers, and citizen changemakers—has emerged (figure 1-1). Each of these players has its own role to play in the solution economy. When these capabilities converge around a shared objective, the effects are truly transformative. From funding research that assesses root problems in their full complexity, to accepting the early-stage risk innate in new approaches, to embracing a growing array of collaboration tools, wavemakers provide greater potential to solve even the thorniest challenges.

FIGURE 1-1

Wavemakers in the solution revolution

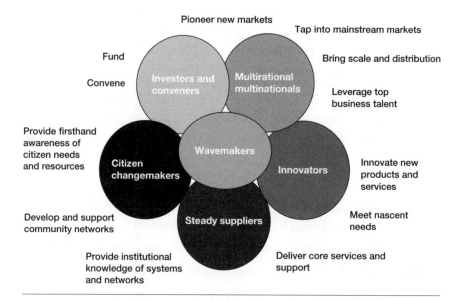

The Investors: Mobilizing Private Capital for Public Gain

A hospital chain in India delivers three hundred thousand cataract surgeries a year for an average of $25 per patient. A maker of mosquito nets aims to prevent the 18 million new cases of malaria and 100,000 deaths that occur in Tanzania each year. An entrepreneurial water company provides clean, affordable water to two hundred towns and villages in south central India—locales that previously had no sources of clean water.[10]

What do these disparate companies have in common? For one thing, their business models are focused on market solutions that provide basic infrastructure and services for the poor in developing countries. Second, they share a key investor: the New York City–based Acumen.

Founded in 2001, Acumen, a fund that invests in businesses that serve the poor, pioneered the rapidly expanding field of impact investing, which applies models from venture capital finance and business management to social goals. Acumen is not alone. Other dominant players in this space include the Omidyar Network, founded by eBay founder Pierre Omidyar and his wife, Pam; Root Capital; New Schools Venture Fund; and Elevar Equity. Because many of these funds and their peers source their capital from philanthropic donations, they have more freedom to focus on social impact. At the same time, by investing much of this capital in debt and equity, the funds help launch more scalable and sustainable businesses that can attract financing from commercial investors.

The initial investments from these investors typically fall below what a blue-chip venture capital (VC) firm might invest in a start-up.[11] Yet, hundreds of successful enterprises, including many that serve over a million people, owe their present scale in part to the foresight and support of these early-stage investors.

Just as a traditional VC firm seeds investments across numerous start-ups in the hopes of a megahit, venture philanthropists and impact investors hope to reap impressive *social returns* from investments.

In the same way that profits validate a traditional investment, social returns, which investors calculate from a combination of factors like the number of people served or innovative solutions developed, help validate impact investments. That is how Acumen, with a humble annual operating budget of a little more than $10 million a year, has transformed millions of lives.[12] It funds businesses in Africa, India, and Pakistan. After having identified six sectors where lack of access to basic goods and services keeps low-income households from escaping poverty, the company invests in those sectors to translate its invested capital into social impact. With expanded access to agricultural inputs, crop yields improve, which provides financial breathing room for families to educate their children. When water quality is improved, health-care costs fall with the reduced incidence of diarrhea and other waterborne illnesses.

Founder Jacqueline Novogratz launched Acumen to reinvent philanthropy in developing countries. It began with a deep, nagging belief that existing philanthropic efforts, often in place for decades, simply weren't working. Instead of providing aid to corrupt governments or funding charities that remain highly dependent on Western donations, Acumen focuses instead on developing markets to serve the poor. "The poor are willing to pay for services they value and can afford," argues Novogratz. Acumen makes debt or equity investments in companies over a period of five to fifteen years. By doing so, says Novogratz, it supports "entrepreneurs who see the poor as customers who can make choices for themselves rather than as recipients of aid."[13]

Today, more than 3.5 billion poor people around the world are formally excluded from traditional consumer markets. They participate only in informal economies. Acumen is trying to change this by investing in entrepreneurs who can create markets in which the poor can participate.[14] Although Acumen has been a pioneer in this mission, a growing number of organizations now commit to this strategy, each with its own variations of how it empowers local entrepreneurs, many of which will be explored in this book.

Sizing the Solution Economy

CORPORATE PHILANTHROPY

Contributions by listed companies in 2012 were estimated to be $41 billion globally. Among *Fortune* 500 companies, contributions have grown at a CAGR of 10 percent since 2007.

Not all good works can turn a profit, but profits can be directed toward good. As Warren Buffett explains, "I've worked in an economy that rewards someone who saves the lives of others on a battlefield with a medal, rewards a great teacher with thank-you notes from parents, but rewards those who can detect the mispricing of securities with sums reaching into the billions."[15] As one of those billionaires, Buffett has pledged to give more than 99 percent of his wealth to philanthropy. Buffett's philanthropic commitment began in 2006, when he pledged all of his Berkshire Hathaway stock to good causes. In 2010, he, Bill and Melinda Gates, and representatives of other large fortunes pledged to give "the majority of their wealth to philanthropy."[16] Almost ten years after Ted Turner announced his $1 billion donation to the United Nations, Buffett changed the game by giving $1.52 billion in stock to the Bill & Melinda Gates Foundation.

To date, more than one hundred ninety billionaires have committed to Buffett's and Gates' "giving pledge," two-thirds of them from the *Forbes* list of the four hundred richest Americans, demonstrating unprecedented coordination and scale of philanthropy. Many of these philanthropists are profiled in *Philanthrocapitalism*, mentioned in the previous chapter. Many target specific goals, such as George Lucas's $4 billion commitment to education. The giving pledge unleashes billions of dollars of capital toward public good, much of it in unexpected soil.[17]

Megagiving is not unique to the West, of course. The first addition to the giving pledge from Africa was Patrice Motsepe, South Africa's richest man. Motsepe's fortune, which comes from the mining industry, will be deployed to serve marginalized populations in South Africa and beyond.[18]

Meanwhile, mobile communications mogul Mo Ibrahim set out on a mission to rebrand Africa—by its good leaders and governance, not just by its headline-grabbing failures.[19] He sold his company, Celtel, for $3.4 billion in 2005 and is using the proceeds for philanthropic purposes. His foundation offers $5 million lifetime awards to former African heads of state who used the tools of democracy and commerce to lift their countries up. As a powerful rejoinder to critics who question the impact of wealthy philanthropists throwing money at complex problems without bringing their own intellectual capacity and networks into the problem solving, the Ibrahim Index of African Governance is seen as a global indicator of progress for the fifty-six developing countries the index evaluates.[20] No less impactful, Nigerian banker and investor Tony O. Elumelu has committed his extensive largesse and business acumen to increasing the competitiveness of Africa's private sector. Elumelu's catalytic philanthropy is allowing Africans to overcome, and prosper from, their unique challenges.

It's not just billionaires like Buffett and Ibrahim and funds like Acumen, Skoll Foundation, and Omidyar Network that drive the solution economy. Key investors in the solution economy take many shapes and forms, from governments to impact investors, and from multilateral institutions to traditional foundations.

American foundations, for example, gave away $190 billion in 2010.[21] Between the diversity of regions that philanthropy now draws from and new options for less-wealthy individuals to launch their own donor-advised funds, global philanthropy is far more influential today than it was just a decade ago. In fact it has doubled in assets from the late 1990s to the 2000s.[22] The greatest increases have occurred in Europe, where the number of foundations increased more than sixfold.[23] Moreover, new technologies, bottom-up business models, and a proliferating number of crowdfunding sites are enabling the democratization of philanthropy, where money from the masses is bundled together to make large impacts. Socially responsible and environmental investment, for instance, accounted for 11 percent of all US assets under management in 2012, a 22 percent increase from 2010.[24]

The Conveners

The lights dim, conversation subsides, and all eyes turn toward a blue spotlight on an empty stage. As about twelve hundred people in the room await the master of ceremonies, attendees sneak side-glances around the room at their fellow attendees. Investor Warren Buffett, Goldman Sachs CEO Lloyd Blankfein, PepsiCo's Indra Nooyi, YouTube cofounders Chad Hurley and Steve Chen, and other executives and entrepreneurs pack the room. So do key government power brokers such as former Secretary of State Madeleine Albright and Colombian President Juan Manuel Santos, and celebrity activists such as Muhammad Ali and Angelina Jolie. The meeting has been blocked out on crowded calendars for months.[25]

The man responsible for convening them strides across the stage, settles into his seat, and acknowledges the audience with a warm, recognizable smile. Deafening applause erupts for former President Bill Clinton.

The annual meeting of the Clinton Global Initiative (CGI) symbolizes dedication to social problem solving on the grandest scale. The ability to connect so many movers and shakers is a power in itself. Just as the concentration of high-tech entrepreneurs in Silicon Valley encourages innovation, the collection of so many wavemakers promises a multiplier effect.

The conversation at a CGI meeting quickly pushes into questions of great gravity: How do we effectively promote sustainable consumption? What opportunities for women in the developing world are most transformative?[26] The brain trust assembled at each table maintains an ongoing discourse between scheduled panels.

Attendees are expected to make—and live up to—specific pledges of action on pressing social issues. Throughout the meeting, power brokers announce these commitments or deliver status updates on prior years' commitments. Richard Branson boldly pledges that all of Virgin's profits from Virgin Airlines and its other travel-related businesses over the next decade will be dedicated to developing environmentally friendly fuels. Yum! Brands CEO Dave Novak reports that his company's 2008 commitment to address world hunger in partnership with the World Food Program is 80 percent completed. Microsoft promises to deliver high-speed broadband to a hundred thousand educators and one million low-income households within three years.[27]

The CGI is a *convener*. It assembles leaders from the most remote locales and the largest cities, leaders who span an equally varied array of careers and capabilities. By uniting them, CGI spotlights solutions that transcend country lines and individual expertise. It is up to attendees, though, to hold to their commitments when the lights dim and business-as-usual activities beckon.

CGI is hardly alone in this capacity. Whereas government agencies such as The World Bank and their UN counterparts formerly dominated this role, now an increasing number of global conversations ponder big problems. Both TED Conferences and the Davos World Economic Forum (WEF) convene political, private-sector, and nonprofit contributors to tackle entrenched social problems. WEF actions, such as a 1988 Davos agreement to avert war between Greece and Turkey or the annual release of the Global Competitiveness Report, make international headlines.[28]

Meanwhile, TED talks featuring many of the world's most dynamic changemakers have garnered more than 500 million online views.[29] TED acknowledges the power of its network and makes networking part of the reward for its annual TED Prize. When health-food guru Jamie Oliver received a TED Prize in 2010, he invited supporters to join his food revolution and to sign a petition in favor of healthier food options in schools. To date almost eight hundred thousand have signed.[30]

Critics label CGI, Davos, TED, and some other big conveners as just gabfests for the rich, famous, and powerful. But such criticism belies the real impact they're having. In all, CGI summits have resulted in more than twenty-three hundred commitments, totaling $73 billion. These commitments are expected to improve more than 400 million lives, a striking contribution from a couple thousand attendees.[31]

Moreover, not all conveners target the global elite. The Aspen Network of Development Entrepreneurs brings together local groups and large-scale funders alike, as well as companies, academic and research institutions, and government bodies to cultivate small businesses in more than 130 developing countries for sustainable development.[32] Across a network of urban hubs, WEF also convenes what it calls its Global Shapers Community, groups of young, influential changemakers who passionately tackle local and global challenges.[33]

Some conveners focus their efforts around a specific region of the world or an issue. For instance, Fundación Avina centers its sustainability efforts on Latin America. As the world's most built-up developing region (75 percent of its citizens live in urban areas), Latin America risks destroying the rare biodiversity supported by this biologically rich region. To address this challenge, Avina forges partnerships between foundations like Skoll, the Ford Foundation, the Coca-Cola Foundation, and grassroots groups, with the goal of creating fifty "sustainable cities" in Latin America.[34] In parallel, Avina works with a consortium of corporate partners and national governments as part of the Latin American Climate Platform, which is dedicated to slowing the effects of climate change.

For the convener, the multiplier effect is the critical tool: good ideas catch fire and expand globally.[35] Many conveners now carry unprecedented reach, which is critical since the solution revolution relies on new governance models that allow the spread of ideas to link (and thus empower) key influencers. Conveners are an important piece of the puzzle. Not only do they bring key participants together, but they also have broken the monopoly on the conversation from the traditional institutions that "owned" the big global challenges in the past.

Multirational Multinationals: The Shifting Business Ethos

Dean Kamen is one of the world's great inventors. His arsenal of 440 patents runs the gamut from the Segway scooter to irrigation equipment to implantable insulin pumps.[36] Kamen's success derives in no small part from his technical genius, and he has an uncanny ability to promote the usefulness of his inventions.

To demonstrate a prosthetic arm Kamen designed for the Defense Advanced Research Projects Agency, he showed a wearer overcoming daily inconveniences—peeling a banana and sipping coffee—to display the enhanced motor skills.[37] His gravelly Long Island frankness emphasizes the intuitiveness of his designs, belying their full complexity. Kamen knows how to be understood.

Yet, igniting interest in a solution to water scarcity has been an uphill climb for Kamen. His team prototyped a water purification unit, the Slingshot, back in 2003. The Slingshot is capable of churning out a thousand liters of purified water daily while running on a variety of energy sources, including cow manure. Kamen and the rest of the team hope the unit will provide safe drinking water to more than a billion people. The purifier produces drinkable water out of even the murkiest contents, as Kamen once demonstrated on *The Colbert Report*, when Stephen Colbert skeptically poured a bag of spicy, bright-red Doritos into the Slingshot and produced colorless water. Kamen said it would yield purified water from ocean water, a "50-gallon drum of urine," and even toxic waste.[38]

Entertaining antics aside, the Slingshot stands to prevent 3.4 million deaths annually attributed to waterborne disease.[39] Kamen has personally invested $50 million in the solution. Unfortunately, finding a buyer for the Slingshot has proven difficult, eliciting waves of gracious declines or unresponsiveness from big players such as the

United Nations and large nongovernmental organizations (NGOs). The negative responses prompted Kamen to realize that "the NGOs aren't the ones who can help us get the machine into production, scale it up, [and] bring down the cost curve."[40]

Struck by its global reach across even the most rural regions of more than 150 countries, Kamen set his sights on Coca-Cola instead. In 2005, he developed a vending machine serving custom blends of carbonated beverages for Coca-Cola in the hope of building a future partnership.[41] Now Coca-Cola is distributing the Slingshot, beginning in rural Ghana, as part of the company's extensive water stewardship efforts.[42] The company targets numerous aspects of water use, beginning with its own production practices. Thanks to improved water stewardship, Coca-Cola's water use has remained flat even as production rises steadily.[43]

Partnering with Kamen to expand access to clean water supports Coca-Cola's already far-reaching clean-water initiatives. Coca-Cola also partners with organizations like The Nature Conservancy and USAID to improve water management.[44] Meanwhile, Coca-Cola's Safe Water for Africa program supplies water to areas of West Africa where water resources have deteriorated.[45]

Multinational corporations like Coca-Cola can scale social innovations faster and more widely than other institutions can. This capability magnifies the significance of those global companies that are elevating social causes from a footnote to a primary consideration in business decisions.

The concept of pursuing a *double bottom line,* in which companies seek to maximize financial *and* social impacts, or even a *triple bottom line,* with environmental benefits added to the equation, has gained traction among large, established firms and fledging enterprises alike. Corporate responses vary, from beefing up corporate social responsibility (CSR) initiatives to reinvesting profits back into a company's social mission. In recent years, CSR has taken off. Contrast the mere seventy CSR reports published in 1990 to the thousands produced today.[46] In 2006, only 25 percent of *Fortune* 500 companies produced

CSR reports. Today that figure has climbed to 80 percent.[47] While an increase in CSR reporting does not necessarily correspond to an increase in overall social impact, a rise in reporting does signal a mind shift—a realization that corporate profits aren't the only meaningful product of a *Fortune* 500 company.

A few decades ago, Kamen's idea of partnering with a large multinational corporation to wipe out waterborne disease would have struck many as bizarre. The widely held notion of businesses' role in society was succinctly captured in the title of Milton Friedman's famous 1970 *New York Times* piece: "The Social Responsibility of Business Is to Increase Its Profits."

Recent years, however, have seen many business leaders rethinking this basic premise. John Mackey, the founder of Whole Foods Market, is at the forefront of this evolution. A proud libertarian, Mackey strongly and unapologetically champions the free market. Nonetheless, his central idea, which he writes about in his book *Conscious Capitalism,* is that investors are only one of multiple constituencies with which a company must engage.[48] Customers, employees, vendors, and the community at large represent other important stakeholders. Since a company's choices can affect each stakeholder, it should pursue value for *all* constituents to create lasting financial and social returns.[49]

This concept at the core of the Whole Foods Market mission has caught on. Each year, Mackey's Conscious Capitalism Institute draws executives from dozens of large firms, including REI, the Container Store, and Trader Joe's, to discuss how they can bring the ethos to their own companies.

In a similar vein, Harvard Business School professor Michael Porter and Mark Kramer, founder of the social-impact consulting firm FSG, have evolved Jed Emerson's concept of "blended value" into a related concept they call "shared value." The idea "involves creating economic value in a way that also creates value for society by addressing its needs and challenges."[50] Businesses that practice shared value connect company success with wider social progress.

TABLE 1-1

Sample initiatives of multirational multinationals

Company	Target issue	Campaign, year started	Impact to date
Coca-Cola	Access to clean water	Safe Water for Africa, 2005	382 community water projects in 2012; 1.6 million people benefit
Whole Foods Market	Poverty	Annual Prosperity Campaign, 2009	Supported over one million people with microcredit; $5.6 million raised in 2012
Shell	Poverty	Shell Foundation, 2000	Invested over $1.2 billion in solving developmental issues by creating scalable enterprise-based solutions
Zappos	Urban revitalization	Downtown Project, 2011	Investing $350 million in real estate, education, small businesses, and tech start-ups to help transform downtown Las Vegas
P&G	Health	Tetanus vaccines, 2006	Immunized ~300 million expectant mothers
Unilever	Sanitation	Project Shakti, 2000	45,000 entrepreneurs in 135,000 villages, 15 Indian states, by 2009
Walmart	Access to quality food	Stores in USDA-designated food deserts, 2011	To add 275–300 stores in food deserts by 2016; to produce 40,000 jobs; to give 800,000 people access to healthy groceries
Microsoft	internet access	High-speed broadband, 2011	Committed to deliver high-speed broadband to one million low-income households within three years
Yum! Brands	Hunger	The World Hunger Relief Program, 2007	In United States, 148 million pounds of food donated (worth $650 million) to needy
GE	Cancer and environment	Ecomagination, 2004	Launched natural gas turbines that can replace coal plants and offset 2.6 million tons of carbon emissions per year
Virgin	Environment	Environment-friendly fuels	Uses Airbus A320 aircrafts, each of which emits 3,600 fewer tons of carbon per year

"We can make market forces work better for the poor," explains Bill Gates, "if we can develop a more creative capitalism—if we can stretch the reach of market forces so that more people can make a profit, or at least make a living, serving people who are suffering from the worst inequities."[51]

What Mackey, Gates, Emerson, Porter, and Kramer have in common is the belief that business should no longer solely cede the solving of social problems to government and nonprofits. The specific terms may vary, but the concepts converge around the idea that caring solely about profits is simply not *rational* anymore and in the long run is actually a liability. The ripples of business decisions across ecosystems, cultural and environmental, are too wide to ignore. If a company ignores the social impacts—both positive and negative—of its mainline operations, it does so at its own long-term peril. For this reason, a business must increasingly consider multiple factors, both internal and external, in its decisions. Hence the term *multirational multinational.*

A growing body of research supports the notion that such an expansive view of a company's role can boost profitability. Paul Griffin and Yuan Sun of the University of California Davis and Berkeley studied a group of companies that have issued CSR reports. The researchers found that the companies' shareholder perceptions improved and that the aggregate market value of the companies rose by $10 billion after the reports were released. Surprisingly, smaller companies benefited the most from reporting. A 2007 study from the Wharton School of Business demonstrated that companies striving to address the best interests of *all* stakeholders rather than just shareholders outperform the S&P 500 by a significant margin.[52]

Many mature companies' first involvement with the solution revolution is via corporate philanthropy. While companies have always invested in their communities, the sheer size of today's contributions and their global impact is unprecedented. In a study by the Committee Encouraging Corporate Philanthropy, 214 respondent companies reported collectively giving more than $15.5 billion in 2010, billions more than the UN Development Program's annual spending. Fully 82 percent of the respondent companies run their own foundation or trust.[53]

But philanthropic action alone runs counter to the premise of a multirational multinational. Instead, companies are increasingly applying their competitive capabilities and expertise to challenges that nonprofit organizations have struggled with for decades. Cincinnati-based Procter & Gamble is partnering with UNICEF to wipe out tetanus in Africa by 2015. Profits from the sales of Pampers diapers contribute to free vaccines for expectant mothers and newborn babies, through a program that has immunized over 300 million to date and raised widespread awareness about the issue.[54]

Unilever is another corporate trailblazer. Since 2000, it has partnered with NGOs, banks, and governments to sell cleaning products in parts of rural India where sanitation is a constant concern. Unilever employs women in rural villages to sell the products, lifting them and their families from poverty as they strive to address the sanitation needs of more than 600 million underserved Indians.[55] This base of the pyramid approach, discussed in more depth later in the book, introduces a brand-new market segment to Unilever—and underscores that doing good can often also be good business.

There is no shortage of skeptics of the corporate push into social innovation. On the one hand, many conservatives and libertarians argue that companies best serve larger societal interests not by focusing on social good but by employing workers and meeting consumer demand. On the other hand, some liberals remain skeptical of business intentions, viewing CSR and other efforts as merely self-serving exercises in corporate PR, as some of these efforts are. Still others assess the impacts of CSR and corporate social innovation initiatives as greatly overblown. In *The Market for Virtue*, political scientist David Vogel argues that while there might be a market for firms that do good, there is also one for less virtuous firms and "the size of the former does not appear to be increasing relative to the latter."[56]

ROBIN HOOD REDISTRIBUTORS

The linking of a company's giving directly to revenues demonstrates a bold commitment to social values. It's a company's way of saying, "My gain is your gain," through what we call the Robin Hood redistribution model.

TOMS Shoes donates a pair of shoes for each pair sold—having given more than two million pairs so far.[a] For every one of its items purchased at accessible chains like Starbucks, the healthy-snacks company KIND donates to the NGO PeaceWorks. This NGO approaches the Israel-Palestine dispute at the grassroots level, offering training, town hall meetings, and polling to mobilize the region's moderates in favor of a peaceful two-state solution.

Patagonia disperses 1 percent of all sales to environmental groups grappling with a diverse array of ecological challenges, from damaged coral reefs and deforestation to the preservation of natural landmarks.[b] Company founder Yvon Chouinard often refers to environmental giving as simply a cost of doing business. In 2002, he created a nonprofit called 1% for the Planet to draw other companies into the movement.[c] In recent years, at least one company a day has committed to the movement, with membership topping twelve hundred companies. While 1 percent of revenues might appear insignificant, collectively the participating companies have donated $70 million to nonprofits in forty countries. Moreover, annual giving in 2010 rose by 40 percent.[d]

a. http://www.toms.com/our-movement/.

b. "What We Do: Why Eyeglasses," VisionSpring, accessed February 6, 2013, www.visionspring.org/what-we-do/why-eyeglasses.php.

c. "About Us," 1% for the Planet, accessed February 6, 2013, www.onepercentfortheplanet.org/en/aboutus/.

d. Kailee Bradstreet, "1% for the Planet Grows Donations by 40% in 2010," *Transworld Business*, March 7, 2011, http://business.transworld.net/58894/news/1-for-the-planet-grows-donations-by-40-in-2010/.

Each perspective has a modicum of truth to it. What they all tend to miss, however, is the growing alignment of financial and social incentives that is pushing companies to move beyond traditional CSR. When larger societal problems are seen not as just charity but as actual market opportunities, then actions by business are more scalable and viable over the long term.

As a result, corporate contributions often align with each company's unique capabilities and objectives (table 1-1). Health-care companies tend to focus on health causes. Large technology firms with highly sophisticated educational requirements often contribute to higher education. Internationally, contributions to education and health account for more than half of corporate giving, dwarfing all other categories, including the arts and disaster relief.[57]

Many companies, then, are becoming multirational, integrating their corporate and social missions. Mark Kramer says that "social change becomes part of the competitive equation—companies have to compete around their ability to improve social conditions and achieve social outcomes."[58] Consumers are helping drive this trend. In an Edelman global survey, the majority of consumers viewed corporate donations as insufficient, instead urging companies "to integrate good causes into their day-to-day business."[59]

The Innovators: Private Enterprise, Public Benefit

Innovators that mix profit making and social missions fall into two broad categories. First are those whose societal mission is front and center, but for which the market is their instrument of change. These innovators are known as *social enterprises.*[60]

For the second type of innovator, the *market innovator,* profit is indeed the main motivation. But this innovator also fervently wants to carve out new space in markets for innovative, socially responsible products and services that disrupt the status quo, in the process fulfilling unmet needs. Providing fee-based health and education for the poorest of the poor, or enabling commuters to rideshare, or developing sustainable energy all look to the market innovator like untapped sources of profit and social return. Smaller than the behemoth multirational multinationals, the innovators bring their dynamism, passion, and entrepreneurial spirit to gaps in existing markets and the needs of marginalized populations, crafting new solutions to persistent problems.

The Social Enterprise Revolution

An altruistic agenda doesn't preclude sound business savvy. FareStart in Seattle, for example, with its inviting, reclaimed-wood tables and genial staff, has earned a reputation for good food and good service. Its catering company and restaurant have flourished, supporting the delivery of more than five million meals to the disadvantaged.

The cooks behind these celebrated meals are working through a job placement program. "I feel like a completely different person now," reflects Kat, a FareStart barista now enrolled in community college after overcoming bouts of clinical depression. FareStart launched its café to train young baristas like Kat, combating the city's high rates of youth unemployment and homelessness via Seattle's seemingly insatiable appetite for coffee.[61]

Recruits often arrive at FareStart from stints in prison or from struggles with substance abuse. They not only develop cooking skills but also gain much-needed stability and self-esteem.

Many restaurants across the globe are similarly striving to equip the underemployed with marketable skills and work experience, perhaps most notably Jamie Oliver's trendy London restaurant Fifteen. The model has extended beyond the culinary domain. Jerr Boschee, former head of the Social Enterprise Alliance and one of the architects of this sector in the United States, estimates that around two-thirds of social enterprises concentrate on creating social value by providing employment opportunities for the disadvantaged.[62]

Social enterprises often respond to local challenges, as with Seattle's FareStart. Other social enterprises scale to meet national or even

Sizing the Solution Economy

SOCIAL ENTERPRISES

Globally, social enterprises generated $2.1 trillion in revenue in 2012. In recent years this number has grown by 15.1 percent annually.

global needs. Bryson, Northern Ireland's largest social enterprise, delivers twenty-four thousand services throughout Northern Ireland each day, including care for the elderly, energy utilities, and waste management. In a country where the average private company brings in £5 million annually, Bryson generates more than £30 million.[63]

Social enterprises such as Samasource and Digital Data Divide transcend national borders to offer skill-building job opportunities that deliver fair wages and safe work conditions to individuals struggling to find employment. "We're a different kind of technology company," says Leila Jana, founder of Samasource. "We build tools to connect the world's poorest people to income via the internet using a concept called microwork. Microwork refers to any small task a person can do with a computer and an internet connection . . . Workers can digitize books for Google; they can transcribe receipts for Intuit during tax time; they can make sense of conflicting user data submitted by LinkedIn."[64]

Samasource's model is poised to grow as digital connectivity spreads globally. According to a report by our Monitor Deloitte colleagues and the Rockefeller Foundation, business process outsourcing to individuals at the base of the pyramid will employ 780,000 economically disadvantaged people and reach $20 billion in sales by 2015.[65]

While social enterprises are expanding globally, in some regions the growth has been particularly notable. We estimate that there are more than 650,000 active social enterprises in the United States. Across the pond, the United Kingdom has 62,000 social enterprises. In the European Union, estimates of the number of social enterprises range from our low-end estimate of about 400,000 all the way to 2.3 million, employing anywhere from 4 to 11 million workers.[66] In Australia, where the concept is still gaining steam, 20,000 social enterprises currently operate.[67]

While the term *social enterprise* is still unfamiliar to many in India, grassroots NGOs that meet social needs abound, numbering more than 3.3 million. These social entrepreneurs are a powerful force in India. Khosla Impact Ventures, Unitus, and LGT Venture Philanthropy are among eighteen India-based funds dedicated to funding social ventures domestically.[68]

The complications in quantifying social enterprises in India mirror the wider world's. We estimate that more than 5.6 million social enterprises are operating globally employing more than 56 million people.[69] Other analysts might make equally plausible, but higher or even slightly lower estimates. "It's definitely an ongoing challenge to estimate how many social enterprises are out there globally, since [social enterprise] means different things to different people," says Randall Kempner, executive director of the Aspen Network of Development Entrepreneurs.[70] If definitions vary (in some areas, social enterprises must cover specific percentages of operational costs through earned income to merit the label), legal structures under which social enterprises register span the spectrum as well, including for-profits, nonprofits, limited-liability corporations, community development corporations, and so forth.

Even in the United States, an official designation for social enterprises is a recent development. Since 2010, when some US states began to officially recognize benefit corporations, or B corps, many established for-profits and start-ups originally seeking nonprofit status have opted for this status. More than 650 US companies have now registered as B corps, together producing over $3 billion in annual revenues across sixty diverse industries.[71]

Already, this promising new sector has spawned classes on social enterprise in more than 150 business schools in twenty-four countries.

The Social Enterprise Club is perennially the most popular club at Harvard Business School.

Time will tell how the zeal for social enterprise rivals the ultimate impact, but already the creative problem solving emerging from the sector indicates a dramatic departure from how more traditional institutions have approached entrenched social issues. Numerous examples profiled throughout this book will highlight how, step-by-step, social enterprises are advancing the field of societal problem solving.

The Market Innovator

What happens when an organization's social and financial purpose are one and the same? Meet the market innovator.

Unlike carefully calculated strategic investments that drive profits, social responsibility initiatives often are funded in arbitrary increments. This is a product of what Kevin Jones, a prominent investor in social enterprises, calls the two-pocket problem—"I invest and put the money in one pocket, then I put some of the excess in another pocket and give it away."[72] The giving-away part of the equation can become an optional activity, subject to various discretionary funds and social interests. Unfortunately, these funds often are in shortest supply when demand for public services is highest. Jones and others are striving to shift thinking around the two-pocket problem, but it persists as an innate weakness of voluntary giving.

Profit-making companies that find ways to advance social objectives through their mainline businesses remove this element of variability. Unlike most multirational multinationals that enter from the business side by making a sudden, big shift toward more marginal ends of the market or gradually move in this direction, market innovators start with the thorny social issue, but keep the profitability of a solution as baseline criteria.

Start-ups such as M-Pesa, to be discussed later in the book, serve the banking needs of millions of the rural poor. In the United States, where more than 15 percent of the population is uninsured, Minute-

Shaffi Mather started his career as a successful young entrepreneur who, with his brothers, built the leading real estate company in his home state of Kerala, India. Mather then went on to work with two of India's biggest businessmen. Yet, he abandoned this promising career after a series of near-death experiences among his family and friends made it obvious to him that India was in dire need of a reliable emergency medical ambulance service.

With the help of three other entrepreneurs, Mather founded 1298 for Ambulance—since renamed Ziqitza Healthcare Limited (ZHL)—in 2005, with the goal of providing a world-class, financially self-sustainable, universally accessible ambulance service available to anyone in need. With a handful of ambulances and a twenty-four-hour call center, the company began operations in Mumbai. The business is built on a cross-subsidy model based on what the customer can afford: wealthier customers pay more, poorer customers pay less, and all accident victims receive the service free of charge.

In 2007, Acumen made a $1.5 million investment in ZHL to help the business purchase more ambulances (Acumen invested another $1.1 million in 2009). ZHL quickly expanded operations to six states within India. By charging to transport higher-income patients to private hospitals, it subsidized—or reduced to zero—the cost of bringing poorer patients to public hospitals. The company now has nearly a thousand ambulances and over twenty-seven hundred employees. ZHL serves the poorer population in association with the Ambulance Access for All Foundation. To date, this partnership has served more than 16 million people, most of them with daily incomes of less than $4.[a] Most notably, ZHL was the first ambulance service to arrive at the scene during the 2008 terror attacks at the Taj and Trident Hotels in Mumbai. The company has held fast to its commitment to making high-quality emergency care available to all who need it, regardless of income level.

a. "Touching Lives! Ambulance Access for All Foundation," Ziqitza Health Care Limited, accessed March 1, 2013, http://zhl.org.in/aaa_foundation.html.

Clinics have emerged in drugstores to treat basic ailments at low cost.[73] Applications designed for smartphones allow individuals to take responsibility for their health by tracking diet, workouts, and health indicators, with an estimated forty-four million health apps downloaded in 2012.[74]

Such transformative companies can be categorized as market innovators. Two interrelated trends are spurring their growth. First, markets are widening to include previously marginalized segments of the population. Philanthropic infusions from organizations like Acumen, Omidyar, and social entrepreneurs stabilize and bring basic resources like savings accounts and revenue streams to populations that can then afford much-needed fee-based services that market innovators can deliver. Second, innovative business models and enabling technologies are making the provision of public services a more financially appealing prospect. (These new methods and models will be covered more extensively in the next two chapters.)

One previously marginalized population capturing significant interest is the world's 4 billion people at the "base of the pyramid." This group collectively represents $5 trillion in purchasing power.[75] Unilever recognized the buying power of this segment of the population when the company opened up a new market in parts of rural India. Other firms are quickly following suit.

In *The Fortune at the Bottom of the Pyramid*, C. K. Prahalad notes that if the private sector can figure out how to profitably serve this population, the sector is positioned to tap this $5 trillion market, as a market of both buyers and suppliers. Jaipur Rugs, for example, employs more than fifty thousand people across villages in northern India to create rugs sold throughout the world. Part of the company's central philosophy is to merge profit and public value. Its business model not only supports communities of talented artisans, but also empowers them to find greater financial and social stability. The Jaipur Rugs Foundation facilitates literacy and vocational training for its network of artisans and provides health-care services through a series of village doctor visits. The foundation hopes to double its efforts and reach a hundred thousand artisans.[76]

Despite such successes, however, overall the record is distinctly mixed when it comes to business attempts to develop the base of the pyramid market. For one thing, the distribution costs in rural areas can capsize an already low-margin business. It often costs more to reach those who have least. Moreover, the high penetration rates needed to make these markets profitable requires the ability to absorb losses on the way there.

While the situation is no walk in the park, the bottom of the pyramid still has promise. Large companies, including Nestlé and ITC, combine their supply-chain expertise with local knowledge to obtain vital inputs for their products across vast rural areas. "The private sector cannot solve all problems but can bring technical and financial resources [as well as] the disciplines of organization, accountability, and entrepreneurial drive to bear on the problems," writes Prahalad.[77] In fact, extensive research from our Monitor Deloitte colleagues demonstrates that national and multinational companies are the key to the successful scaling of bottom-of-the-pyramid innovations.[78]

The Steady Suppliers: Always There

As scores of new entrants and innovative business models join the solution economy, it's easy to overlook the nongovernmental players that have quietly, consistently delivered public services for decades. These players, which we call *steady suppliers,* include both organizations that address community needs independently and those with government contracts to do so. Although the steady suppliers span a diverse spectrum of industries and services, they are seldom considered collectively.

The mix of nonprofit and for-profit suppliers varies enormously by sector and country. In the United States, nonprofits account for most hospitals, the majority of higher education institutions and social service providers, and one-third of nursing homes. In Australia and the United Kingdom, governments have helped catalyze the development of a larger civil sector, shifting everything—from offender management to welfare-to-work programs—to private providers.

In Asia, citizens are accustomed to fewer state and nonprofit services and have lower rates of volunteerism.[79] For example, China spends 5.5 percent of its GDP on health care; in contrast, the United States and other G8 members spend about 18 percent.[80] Stepping in to fill the gap in Asia are a number of organizations scaling successful models nationally or internationally.

The Bangladesh Rural Advancement Committee (BRAC) offers a prime example. BRAC began in the aftermath of Bangladesh's 1971 war for independence, when refugees flooded back to the nation, whose government hardly existed at the time. Now, BRAC employs or organizes more than 120,000 people. It provides human services, responds to natural disasters, and expands microlending. Operating completely separate from the government, BRAC has expanded throughout the Indian subcontinent and sub-Saharan Africa. The organization offers a host of public services, including a network of more than thirty-seven thousand schools that have educated almost five million students, representing the world's largest private school system. BRAC's tuberculosis program reaches eighty million Bangladeshis.[81]

BRAC quietly serves an enormous population, specializing in "taking an idea, testing it, perfecting it and then expanding it rapidly to national scale cost-effectively and without compromising quality." As its founder, Sir Fazle Hasan Abed, likes to say, "Small is beautiful . . . but big is necessary."[82]

Steady suppliers may lack the buzz of social entrepreneurs or flashy corporate initiatives, but their low profile belies their true impact. For centuries, unmet local needs have elicited action. The YMCA, for instance, began in London in 1844 as a neighborhood health and recreation center and continues its mission today in more than ten thousand locations. The Red Cross, founded in 1881, still handles a variety of emergency and humanitarian needs, rapidly deploying hundreds of thousands of trained volunteers where needed.[83]

The civil society sector amounts to 5 percent of GDP annually—on par with finance and construction—across thirty-five countries evaluated by Johns Hopkins University and the United Nations.[84] This staggering figure equates to the world's seventh-largest economy. The study also found that between 1995 and 2000, the sector generated expenditures of $1.3 trillion and engaged a workforce 45.5 million strong.[85] And the sector is growing rapidly. In the fallout of the 2008 financial crisis, college graduates streamed into nonprofits and social enterprises. A year after the crisis in the United States, 11 percent more graduates worked for nonprofits than in the year before. The popular two-year teaching fellowship, Teach for America, saw applications rise by a third; AmeriCorps applications tripled in just two years.[86]

Additionally, at every level of government, private providers support the delivery of vital services. Cities and states engage with private companies to haul waste, support or provide public transit, and deliver much-needed infrastructure improvements. Government contracting is a big component of this. Between 2000 and 2009, twenty-five of thirty-four OECD (Organisation for Economic Co-operation and Development) countries reported spending more on government outsourcing to deliver services.[87]

A host of problems face the way government currently engages with steady suppliers.[88] Even with such flaws, however, contracting relationships offer considerable benefits. One of the biggest is the cross-pollination of ideas among participating organizations.

With private organizations now delivering government services across the globe, the organizations can collect and disseminate useful ideas among public agencies worldwide. UK-based Serco Group, for example, runs a diverse portfolio of services, including detention centers and prisons in the United Kingdom, driver licensing in Canada, and air traffic control services in the United Arab Emirates. The *Guardian* calls Serco "the largest company you've never heard of."[89]

Sizing the Solution Economy

NONPROFITS

Nonprofits contributed an estimated $1.7 trillion to the global GDP in 2012.

Such global providers can rapidly transfer innovations from one jurisdiction to another. This worldwide transfer of innovation is very different from the classical pattern, in which government officials in different jurisdictions operate in isolation and make independent decisions about new ideas.

A willingness to revise existing models can be critical to a steady supplier's ongoing success. Pearson, for example, has long been one of the world's biggest textbook publishers. In a digital age, however, textbook publishing is being disrupted. In response, Pearson is reinventing itself, acquiring companies such as eCollege and SchoolNet to expand its digital capabilities and moving toward a model in which it advises teachers on how to incorporate and use the latest technology in the classroom.

Scott Drossos, head of Pearson's K-12 technology solutions, is quick to acknowledge the company's evolution: "We recognize that Apple computers, Google search features, and Khan Academy online courses all play very different but important roles in education, and we are one player among many in that ecosystem. When it comes to sharing best practices in the classroom around how to use these tools, though, that's something Pearson can do very well."[90]

Citizen Changemakers: The Rising Class of Citizens Who Engineer Social Impact

Arguably the most disruptive presence in the solution economy is its greatest beneficiary: the citizen. Never before have individuals been able to converge around common objectives with such speed and effectiveness, catapulting social issues into global recognition in a matter of hours.

Witness how Invisible Children's campaign, albeit ill-fated, against Ugandan warlord Joseph Kony generated one hundred million views online within six days.[91] In 2011, Arab Spring uprisings quickly toppled long-standing authoritarian regimes. Citizens collaborate over vast distances through social media now more than ever before, connecting over 80 percent of the world's population, compared with roughly half the population in 2007.[92]

By drawing on advances in technology, individuals can now contribute to the public good from the cubicle. Citizens who start initiatives themselves can raise money for their causes on sites such as Network for Good or Crowdrise. They can match volunteer requests to their skills on the website Sparked. In seconds, their perspectives can reach a global audience. (In chapter 2, we will explore the technologies driving these opportunities and how citizens and other players in the solution economy are creatively employing them.)

In 2006, *Wired* editor Jeff Howe coined the term *crowdsourcing* to describe "the act of a company or institution taking a function once performed by employees and outsourcing it to an undefined (and generally large) network of people in the form of an open call."[93] Since then, citizens have supported numerous public efforts via crowdsourcing.

To digitize content for its national library, for instance, Finland created a central "game" platform to persuade ordinary citizens to provide free labor. Participants have completed more than 4.1 million small projects, or "microtasks," to date.[94]

The nonprofit Code for America asks tech-savvy US citizens to help build web apps that connect citizens, local government, and neighbors so that these players can better coordinate civic tasks. Its numerous web applications organize volunteers for community watch programs, for the pruning and watering of trees, and for many other tasks that save municipal funds.[95]

Such tools are of little use without lots of citizen volunteers. According to Code for America founder Jennifer Pahlka, real change—the kind that alters society—requires citizens to *willingly assume a level of responsibility for public services.*

This willing attitude distinguishes consumers from changemakers. Bill Drayton is the founder of Ashoka, an organization seeking to elevate the citizen sector to the same level as the business sector. Ashoka operates in seventy countries and does more than perhaps any other organization to support dynamic social entrepreneurs wanting to make change in the world. In the words of Drayton, who has popularized this term, once a citizen changemaker has "decided that the world must change in some important way, they simply find and build highways that lead inexorably to that result. Where others see barriers, they delight in finding solutions and in turning them into society's new and concrete patterns."[96]

Pahlka and the latest wave of social entrepreneurs offer living proof of that ethos. "We're not just consumers, in that we're not just consumers of government where we put in taxes and receive services," Pahlka says. "We're more than that, we're citizens. And we're not going to fix government until we fix citizenship."[97] In thirty-five countries evaluated by Johns Hopkins University and the United Nations, fully 20 percent of working-age citizens volunteer with the civil sector, and in some European nations such as the Netherlands, the volunteer rate is even higher.[98] The technical skills of these volunteers will determine the usefulness of crowdsourcing in the years ahead.

Sizing the Solution Economy

VOLUNTEERING

The economic value of volunteering globally was $1.3 trillion in 2011.

Companies increasingly recognize the value of skills-based volunteering as well: 40 percent of American companies and even more in Australia have a volunteer paid-time-off policy, meaning they can use some work time to do volunteer work.[99] These companies increasingly reward top performers with an opportunity to deploy their expertise toward community organizations. From developing a nonprofit's social-impact metrics to expanding the reach of a proven approach, skills-based pro bono work builds off the core strengths of a consultancy (for example, Deloitte), while offering the best and brightest a coveted chance to channel their talents toward societal needs they are passionate about. For Deloitte, top US performers will contribute a forecasted $170 million in pro bono hours between 2009 and 2015. In the United States as a whole, one hundred companies have committed $1.7 billion and 11.5 million hours in pro bono services as part of the A Billion + Change campaign, and the organizers plan to engage three hundred more companies.[100] We have seen how a new social ethos in organizations and a new empowerment among citizens is rewriting the rules around social problem solving. In the next chapter, we'll describe how new technologies have enabled the rapid growth of the wavemakers and their ability to quickly scale social innovations.

THE WAVEMAKERS:
IN A NUTSHELL

THE BIG IDEA

A new set of nongovernmental contributors—wavemakers—is bringing unprecedented resources, versatility, and creativity to societal needs. Many contributors focus on solution economy connection points to achieve the greatest change possible.

MEET THE WAVEMAKERS

- **Investors:** individuals and organizations that seek specific social returns by pledging large sums of money to a cause

- **Conveners:** individuals and organizations that assemble an array of leaders to address big societal concerns, cultivating solutions that transcend geography and individual reach

- **Multirational multinationals:** businesses that measure performance by social impact in addition to shareholder value

- **Innovators:**
  - Social enterprises: organizations that tackle marginalized needs, reinvesting earned income to further a social mission
  - Market innovators: profitable companies that develop innovative, market-based business models to solve social problems

- **Steady suppliers:** established organizations that deliver services on behalf of government

- **Citizen changemakers:** individuals who independently or collaboratively contribute to public benefit and who are often empowered by disruptive technologies

GROWTH TRAJECTORY

- Philanthropy has doubled in assets between the late 1990s to 2000s.

- Two hundred surveyed US companies collectively gave more than $15.5 billion in 2010.

- Socially responsible and environmental investment accounted for 11 percent of all US assets under management in 2012, a 22 percent increase from 2010.

- In 1990, just seventy CSR reports were published. Today, 80 percent of *Fortune* 500 companies produce CSR reports.

IMPACT

- Aggregate market value improves by $10 billion for companies that issue CSR reports.

- Companies that seek to address the best interests of *all* stakeholders rather than just shareholders outperform the S&P 500 by a significant margin.

SURPRISING NUMBERS

- The world's four billion people at the base of the pyramid collectively represent $5 trillion in purchasing power.

- Business process outsourcing—or microwork—to individuals at the base of the pyramid will employ 780,000 economically disadvantaged people and reach $20 billion in sales by 2015.

- The civil society sector amounts to 5 percent of GDP annually across thirty-five countries—an amount equal to the world's seventh-largest economy.

- Western private philanthropy to the developing world now surpasses the monetary contributions of Western governments.[101]

QUESTION FOR THOUGHT

Who are the wavemakers you can collaborate with to create public value?

TWO

Disruptive Technologies

Creating the ability to mobilize massive resources

Despite endless public service announcements and community campaigns, American recycling rates remain stubbornly low. For more than a decade, the overall solid-waste recycling rate has hovered at around a third, a far cry from Denmark's 69 percent, for instance, or the zero-waste future dreamed of by many environmentalists.[1]

In a number of cities, however, recycling rates have *not* stagnated; they've soared. Recycling jumped from 2 percent of waste to 65 percent in a matter of months in Wilmington, Delaware. In parts of Philadelphia, recycling rates skyrocketed from a dismal 7 percent to 90 percent in months.[2]

What was the difference? These cities had one thing in common: a partnership with an organization called Recyclebank. This innovative social enterprise has turned recycling into a game: by recycling, households can earn points that can be redeemed for real prizes, such as vacations and discounts on products from hundreds of companies. The number of points earned by each household is calculated by radio-frequency identification device (RFID) sensors on recycling bins. The sensors record how much waste each household recycles. The more you recycle, the more points you get. In just a few short years,

Recyclebank has gone from an interesting idea to a company operating in hundreds of cities, with a membership of three million households.

Recyclebank was launched in the early 2000s by Ron Gonen and Patrick Fitzgerald, two grad students in their twenties. Neither man had any experience in the recycling arena. What they *did* have was boatloads of passion for the environment—and business savvy. Their audacious idea? To transform the entire recycling industry.

"As I started looking at the recycling industry, I saw massive inefficiencies," explains Gonen. "Cities were sending tons of garbage far away and paying for transportation to landfills that were very expensive, costing taxpayers hundreds of millions of dollars. Anywhere there is such inefficiency, there is an opportunity."[3]

As they evaluated the current US recycling system, they concluded that one problem was unfair pricing: "The problem with waste in the US is that it's not priced properly. We pay for our garbage use as much as our neighbors do, even if they throw out much more than us. For waste, *we pay for a share of what everyone throws away.* In that type of system, people can't easily take personal responsibility for what they use."[4]

It quickly became apparent, however, that reconfiguring the waste disposal system to charge households for their volume of waste would involve considerable logistical and political hurdles. The Recyclebank model instead sidesteps punitive measures altogether in favor of an incentive-based solution. It was a classic case of carrot versus stick—except that Recyclebank bet on the carrot.

To reward individuals for recycling, the pair developed the innovative idea of installing cheap, versatile RFID chips on plastic recycling bins. During waste pickups, the hauling trucks would weigh the filled bins, scan the RFID code, and credit the household's account accordingly (a sort of information-age upgrade to the old container-deposit laws that rewarded consumers for returning used bottles and cans).[5] Points earned could be redeemed through an online exchange for rewards, similar to frequent-flier miles.

It was a compelling business model, but one centering on a then-nonexistent product, the RFID-equipped plastic bin. Explaining the model left most bin manufacturers uninterested. The two-person team—with limited funds, no experience in recycling, and no immediate market—was met with "noble idea, no way you'll pull it off" time and again.

Undeterred, the two finally connected with Cascade Engineering, a $250 million firm well respected for its environmentally sustainable business practices. Cascade CEO Fred Keller was immediately interested in the Recyclebank concept. On a handshake, he agreed to supply the new company with RFID-equipped recycling bins, providing the lifeline the anxious entrepreneurs desperately needed. Gonen acknowledges that "without Fred and Cascade, the venture wouldn't have launched."

With the all-important recycling bins accounted for, Recyclebank's next hurdle was building a network of key partners. Gonen and Fitzgerald needed buy-in from waste management companies and municipalities, as well as the companies that would offer "prizes" on the Recyclebank exchange. Fortunately, many companies quickly recognized the opportunity to reach environmentally conscious consumers and demonstrate their commitment to recycling. In a matter of months, the exchange added deals and discounts from large vendors such as Coca-Cola, Whole Foods Market, and Macy's, as well as green offerings from local vendors.[6] As the network grew, waste hauling company Blue Mountain Recycling decided to take a chance on a partnership with Recyclebank.[7]

Once the various business partners committed, the incentive scheme jumped from a catchy concept to an executable reality. "The Recyclebank ecosystem consists of a network of brands," explains CEO Jonathan Hsu. "While they offer different products and services, their shared interest collaborating around sustainability produces a network effect that drives others to join." In this model, he explains, "Recyclebank offers the currency that stitches them together. More partnerships mean a stronger currency that invites participation."[8] Similar models fuel the ridesharing services described in the previous chapter.

The lineup of partners made the model an easier sell as Gonen began to approach cities. Even still, numerous municipalities Gonen approached with the untested idea backed away, clearly doubtful that such a radically different approach would work. In 2004, Recyclebank succeeded in capturing the interest of Philadelphia public administrators willing to test the new model.[9] In the city's first pilot, twelve hundred residents of Chestnut Hill received RFID-equipped bins, an unusual addition to a neighborhood known for cobblestone streets and old colonial homes.

Adoption of the large recycling bins was just the beginning of the test, however. Would residents actually go online, check how much they recycled, and redeem the points accrued? Soon enough, rows of bright blue bins appeared in the street on recycling day. This change, and the gradual increase in web traffic to the Recyclebank exchange, pointed toward progress. In a matter of months, the neighborhood's recycling rate tripled, from 30 to 90 percent.[10] The model was working.

The experiment was repeated across town in West Oak Lane, a lower- to middle-class area with a recycling rate that had been hovering at just 7 percent. Although adoption was slower initially, a full 90 percent of households were regularly recycling within months of the start of the program.

The successful pilots inspired other neighborhoods and cities to try Recyclebank. Some, such as Wilmington, Delaware, faced looming limits to their landfill space and viewed Recyclebank as a potential answer. Wilmington mayor James Baker sought out Recyclebank in 2006 to help the city reduce waste to a neighboring landfill that was nearing capacity. "An additional landfill would have been costly, and wouldn't solve the problem, so we worked with what we already had," says John Rago, Wilmington's director of communications and policy development.[11]

As with earlier pilots, it didn't take long for recycling rates to jump with the introduction of Recyclebank. Soon, more than a third of Wilmington's waste was diverted from the landfill. The avoided landfill fees meant that Recyclebank was paying for itself, and the deals offered by 140 Wilmington retailers on the Recyclebank exchange were bringing in new business.[12] Most importantly, the deals offered enough incentive to keep citizens committed to recycling, saving each household an estimated $130 annually.

Other cities that have adopted Recyclebank's model report significant savings. In Hollywood, Florida, increased recycling rates produced $500,000 in savings on waste disposal fees and more than $250,000 in recycling revenue within the first year of implementation.

In less than a decade, Recyclebank's active network of participants grew to more than three hundred communities in the United States and the United Kingdom.[13] The company has established new partnerships with waste haulers, most notably a national partnership with Waste Management Inc., which serves twenty million households. Investors swarmed to Recyclebank's model, with funding from major venture capitalists, including Al Gore's company, Generation Investment Management, and Kleiner Perkins.

Recyclebank took an existing technology and applied it in a manner that, with modest costs, prompts large numbers of people to voluntarily alter their behavior in socially beneficial ways. The technology makes tangible what had previously been invisible. It raises consciousness in its purest form. That sounds very 1970s, doesn't it? Yet the proof is in the results; far more trash is recycled without overbearing enforcement mechanisms.

Technologically enabled awareness has other potentially transformative applications. The environmental impact of an individual's mobility choices are invisible. Your choice to walk, bike, or drive a car has different environmental impacts, but they are unseen, unquantified, and seemingly unquantifiable. Most economists have traditionally approached such a problem by trying to figure out how to get individual decision makers to internally weigh the costs and benefits of their decisions. For example, an economist would try to increase the use of mass transit by altering the cost structures. London's congestion pricing scheme that charges people for driving into the city has increased public transportation usage and reduced traffic by forty thousand cars per day.[14]

Such a program, however, is politically difficult to implement and involves significant investment in technology and public transit. But start thinking like Recyclebank, and new opportunities emerge not only to use technology to alter prices but also to make tangible the effects of people's choices. Recyclebank has done just this, moving beyond trash and capitalizing on the real innovation underlying the company—its business model. The company has partnered with the UK government's Transport for London to persuade the city's residents to pursue travel options other than driving and public transport. To do so, Recyclebank developed a GPS-enabled app that tracks distance traveled by foot and bike, calories burned, and emissions avoided. The application thereby quantifies the benefits of a Londoner's choice of travel. And by providing data that can easily be shared through social media like Facebook and Twitter, one person's noble, environmentally conscious choices are shared with others. Think of it as a humble boast or an encouraging enticement. Either way, it changes behavior for the better.

Supply Shock

A few years ago, the notion that a different kind of recycling bin could transform hundreds of communities' habits would have seemed far-fetched. Imagine trying to explain to someone who had never heard of Facebook or Amazon.com how sensors, a social network, and an online marketplace of deals and discounts could lead millions of people to make more environmentally friendly decisions. Recyclebank didn't invent the online exchange or RFID tags; it didn't pioneer point-rewards systems or social networking. But it developed a model, building from each innovation to power its own rapid growth—and continuing to disrupt the market it occupies.

Emerging technologies enable innovators to apply new approaches to an incredibly diverse range of challenges, at radically lower costs than previously possible. Mobile phones, social media, cloud computing, and data analytics have each triggered profound ripples in the solution economy. These powerful tools, particularly when combined in unprecedented ways, are enabling a host of new business models for everything from catching criminals to sharing vital health information—or a ride across town.

Economists sometimes call this phenomenon a *positive supply shock:* technological advances drop the price of a good or service, thereby boosting output and consumption. The market opens up as more people can afford to supply and consume the good or service.

Recent supply shocks have transformed entire industries. Stock trading was once conducted entirely by hardened pros who worked with sharp elbows on a chaotic trading floor. The abrupt arrival of online trading, however, sent a hush across trading floors as the action moved online. Suddenly, anyone with an internet connection and a brokerage account could place a trade, and daily stock trading volumes skyrocketed. Charles Schwab introduced online trading to clients in 1992; by 2002, 80 percent of its trades were being placed online.[15] Transaction costs shrank, information about stocks and companies became more widely accessible, and soon the market was flooded with new participants. In fact, between 2000 and 2008, the New York Stock Exchange (NYSE) volumes tripled in this period of major growth for the online-trading community.[16]

The power of technology to disrupt the finance sector may not be surprising, but what about the world of antiques and collectibles? Finding a rare antique or a discontinued piece of china used to involve foraging through shops, yard sales, and church bazaars. Prices were unpredictable and set largely at random. eBay utterly transformed this model. Anyone can offer a baseball card or an old vase for sale with a few simple keystrokes, and the seller can have a good idea of the likely sales price by looking at results for similar items. Today, millions of people use eBay each day. Long-term observers note that prices in some collecting categories have risen in the eBay era, while others have crashed; the markets have quite simply become much more efficient, informed by a massive influx of new participants.

In finance as with antiques, technology disrupted the existing market, making it more accessible to a much wider population. With the number of online searches quadrupling in 2011 alone, and the value of payments transmitted via mobile phone predicted to quadruple between 2010 and 2014, the pool of participants is skyrocketing.[17]

The solution economy is also being shaped by the low marginal cost of offering and using new online services. Barriers such as cost and the high thresholds of technical expertise are falling. As a consequence of these lower barriers to participation, small organizations (and even individuals) can exert power previously limited to governments and large corporations.

In the solution economy, moreover, those who design services are often the same persons benefiting from them. For instance, an individual who builds an app to help fix infrastructure problems in his or her neighborhood, such as the app FixMyStreet, which allows UK residents to report potholes and burned-out streetlamps, also benefits as a resident. A driver who shares her car with other passengers via a ridesharing site is helping to reduce traffic congestion—and her own gasoline budget.

Citizen-generated supply shocks offer incredible value to government. They can provide public services at a fraction of previous costs and benefit far more citizens than can traditional public services. The beauty of apps like FixMyStreet and SeeClickFix is that the citizen's service request shows up on a map so that other citizens can support existing campaigns and don't waste time duplicating reports. Meanwhile, government benefits from discovering problems that would otherwise have required an army of local government workers to unearth. However, the apps also increase the expectation that government will follow through on *its* side of the bargain:

responsiveness to the issues that citizens identify. With the benefits of transparency comes the expectation of action; the clock starts when the citizen hits "send." If government and citizens can learn to work together toward better, faster service, these kind of distributed, light-weight solutions that don't require massive capital investments will replace the industrial-age structures still dominant today. Such positive market disruption occurs when entrepreneurs merge the right technologies with a viable business model (discussed in more depth in chapter 3), unleashing untapped societal potential to solve societal problems.

Mobile Technologies: The Great Equalizer

If you have a smartphone and a strong signal, you can access a world's worth of knowledge with the tap of a button or screen. But the mobile revolution's impact won't be judged by connectivity alone; how this resource is *put to work* is the disruptive factor. Therein lies opportunity for all varieties of organizations—tech companies, entrepreneurs, and governments among them. Innovators in all these arenas are exploiting powerful consumer technologies for a wide array of uses, from simplifying monetary transfers to the physical transfer of people through transportation apps.

This is particularly true in Africa, now the second-largest cellphone market in the world, with 649 million subscribers at the end of 2011. The numbers are impressive, but the creative ways in which cell phones are being used are even more remarkable. In countries such as Kenya and Uganda, mobile phones fill gaps in essential services from banking to farm advice and ad hoc health insurance.[18]

Until recently, banking in rural Africa generally entailed hiding money or walking great distances to a city. The M-Pesa (mobile *pesa* [Swahili for "money"]) transfer service employed by telecom provider Safaricom changed that for millions in Kenya. Through M-Pesa transfers, people can easily deposit, send, and withdraw money using their cell phones. Suddenly, the ability to purchase goods, pay bills, make person-to-person transfers, and send remittances became far simpler transactions. Today, about 70 percent of households in Kenya have at least one M-Pesa user.[19] "It's made our lives easier because we don't have to travel long distances to give our relatives and friends money," says livestock herder Emmanuel Sironga.[20]

But mobile money opportunities extend beyond saving shoe leather. William Jack of Georgetown University and Tavneet Suri of MIT's Sloan School of Management suggest that mobile money systems can play a significant role in reducing risk and protecting people from adverse events. Savings accounts and painless person-to-person transfers make mobile money an attractive solution for assisting the uninsured and promoting public health. One health-care provider offers expectant mothers a prepaid savings account, allowing M-Pesa-equipped moms to drop money into the account at any time, including delivery day. Kilimo Salama, a crop insurance product offered by the Sygenta Foundation for Sustainable Agriculture, lets M-Pesa users pay crop insurance premiums and receive payouts, demonstrating one of a growing number of independently provided services that integrates with M-Pesa.[21]

Of course, cell phones can transmit words as well as numbers. Through text messaging, mobile networks are also being used to spread vital information about farming and health care to isolated rural areas in India and Africa—areas particularly vulnerable to the effects of drought and disease.[22]

Cell-phone networks, while far more prolific than computers, are still unavailable to many of the world's poorest. The Grameen Foundation, however, is helping bridge this digital divide by leasing smartphones to farming communities in the Ugandan countryside. The foundation pays "community knowledge workers" via mobile money to share with their communities important information such as weather reports, crop prices, planting advice, and disease diagnostics. They also collect farming information and relay it to agricultural organizations and food programs. To date, Grameen has trained five hundred knowledge workers in thirty-two Ugandan districts, reaching a hundred thousand people.[23]

It may be no exaggeration to say that mobile devices already have had a greater impact on parts of Africa than decades of foreign aid. "Foreign aid changes people's lives temporarily and that's it, when it's gone it's gone," explains Michael Joseph, the former CEO of Safaricom. "People in Kenya tend to be quite industrious. The mobile phone has been almost perfect for that because it allows people now to create jobs for themselves."[24]

Citizens equipped with mobile phones can even act as makeshift reporters. The Satellite Sentinel Project hopes that a community of video journalists will help shed light on the conflict in the Sudan. The George Clooney–supported watchdog organization aims to increase accountability by enlisting the public to monitor and report on human rights abuses.[25] The project's tagline says it all: "The world is watching because you are watching." The takeaway is simple: help others by letting them help themselves. All you need to do is provide them an enabler, like a smartphone, and a platform to amplify their impact.

Handheld-inspired disruption isn't limited to Africa, of course. In Singapore, schools are experimenting with a program called Learning on the Move, which uses mobile devices to orient students on field trips or "learning trails." Students travel through wetland reserves and national parks, scanning barcodes along the trail to pull up location-specific information on their phones. At certain checkpoints, teachers can administer geography and science tests to see how students are doing and pinpoint their knowledge gaps. The aim is ubiquitous learning: learning anywhere at any time.

Across the Pacific, San Francisco residents use mobile technologies to tackle big problems, from air pollution to traffic. San Francisco public transit's NextBus offers commuters on-the-minute estimates of when their rides are coming. Now, instead of standing in the rain for a late bus, commuters can linger in the coffee shop for a few minutes. Dozens of transit systems around the world now offer similar services to track the transportation grid, from high-speed rail in China to ferry schedules in the Virgin Islands.

Of course, the car is the world's most ubiquitous form of transportation. Each day, nearly a billion people commute by car. Mobile tech has made real strides in simplifying life for drivers, too. Take the constant and often maddening search for parking in a crowded city. Swerving, double-parking, and U-turning their way into a spot, drivers seeking parking places generate as much as 30 percent of downtown traffic congestion. A UCLA researcher found that drivers within a fifteen-block district in Los Angeles drove an estimated 950,000 miles a year just looking for a parking space.[26] The average American wastes 3.5 to 14 minutes a day looking for parking, or up to 85 hours a year. With more than 210 million licensed drivers in the country, this amounts to 17.8 billion hours lost annually.

To clean up the streets and the air, the San Francisco Municipal Transportation Agency (SFMTA) offers drivers an app that provides real-time updates on parking availability and rates. Sensors installed in seven thousand metered spaces and 12,250 slots in SFMTA-managed garages communicate wirelessly to iPhones, Android devices, and SFpark.org, showing which blocks have spaces available and which are filled, saving drivers time and the stress of cruising around on the hunt. While a significant timesaver for the smartphone-equipped driver, the app does little for those without smartphones. Another development is SFpark.org's regular adjustments of parking prices according to the availability of spaces in a given area, spreading out demand by raising prices in heavily congested areas and lowering them in others.[27] We estimate that if every city in the United States adopted the SFpark.org model, it would be worth about $391 billion in time savings to the economy.[28] Because the data is being offered publicly, new third-party applications are springing up and applying the technology in creative ways. After the launch of the SFpark.org program, SFMTA released a spinoff service, PayByPhone, which allows smartphone users to pay for their parking spots remotely through the app; users of normal cell phones can pay via text message.[29]

Mobile technology's biggest impact may be how personal health monitoring revolutionizes health care. Between health apps, light-weight medical devices, online communities, and rapid advances in health analytics, individuals of modest means can now calibrate their bodies to a level of detail that a decade ago, professional athletes would have envied. By one projection, health-care providers could save up to $5.8 billion by 2014 by using widely available mobile health technologies. Another study found that for every dollar spent on wellness programs, medical costs fall by about $3.27 and absenteeism costs fall by about $2.73. The market is responding quickly, with mobile health services slated to reach $4.6 billion by 2014.[30]

When anyone with a phone can use mobile technology in new ways to address his or her most immediate needs, sharing the new solutions with a global audience, the reach of the technology far exceeds even the most forward-reaching expectations of its original engineers.

Social Media: Powering Collaborative Problem Solving

The radical expansion of social media has penetrated even the most far-flung regions of the world, now reaching over 80 percent of the world population. Growth has been most rapid in developing regions, where a quarter of all time spent online in Latin America, the Middle East, and Africa is dedicated to social networking. This communications pathway has proven valuable to all players in the solution economy.[31]

Sending a tweet, for instance, may seem trivial compared with attending a sit-in, but tweets can sometimes achieve the same goals by spreading awareness. Social media played a pivotal role in the United States during the controversy concerning the Stop Online Piracy Act. Over the course of the public debate, 3.9 million related tweets were sent out.[32] This display of civil unrest played a major role in pushing the legislation off the table.

Each day brings new evidence of the power of social media to create citizen changemakers. In India, more than half a million people signed a petition on Avaaz.org in thirty-six hours to clean up government corruption. Less than a week later, India's government provided written agreement with the movement's demands, approving an anti-corruption law to be drafted by the people rather than politicians.[33] In this way, social media is helping to organize and aggregate the efforts of many and build them into substantial initiatives.

Jeremy Heimans, who cofounded Avaaz.org, self-identifies as a "movement entrepreneur" and works to mobilize citizen energy toward targeted social outcomes. Heimans now runs Purpose, a New York City–based social enterprise that brings campaign-building savvy to wavemaker organizations of all shapes and sizes. When Heimans runs up against skepticism about the strength of "slacktivists" who merely "Like" a cause, he notes how Purpose campaigns have a way of persuading participants to do more. Plus, like much else in social media, movements can evolve fast. When gay activists in Iraq faced life-threatening opposition in 2012, a campaign raised the funds necessary to airlift the activists out of the country within twenty-four hours, a quicker timeline than most charities could manage, Heimans points out.[34]

Surprising new uses for social media seem to come in nearly inexhaustible supply as the number of connected citizens and organizations climbs. In Virginia, for instance, the CIA's Open Source Center combs through an ever-expanding catalogue of tweets, Facebook messages, and chat logs from Pakistan, Egypt, and China. These analysts, dubbed "vengeful librarians" by other agents, digest massive amounts of social media to gauge the social climate abroad.[35] Angry tweets are cross-referenced with local papers or blogs to paint a surprisingly accurate portrait of how a population is feeling at a given time. It's called *meme-tracking*. Though still in its infancy, this sort of sentiment and mood analysis has become a core activity in the defense and intelligence communities, supplementing and at times supplanting traditional surveys.

Governments and nonprofits alike are becoming more and more skilled in using social media to leverage citizen energies. In March 2012, the US Department of State and the US embassy in Prague sponsored a social media contest called the Tag Challenge. Teams from around the world organized an online effort to locate five fictitious jewel thieves in the United States and Europe.

On the day of the contest, mug shots of the thieves were posted on the Tag Challenge website, as teams spent the day tweeting, tracking, and eventually photographing the bandits in their cities. CrowdScanner, an MIT-affiliated team, won a $3,000 purse after locating three of the five fugitives in New York, Bratislava, and Washington, DC, using chained-recruitment strategies on Twitter and Facebook to nab the crooks and secure the win. According to the project organizer, Joshua deLara, "the project demonstrates the international reach of social media and its potential for cross-border cooperation—a team organized by individuals in the US, the UK, and the United Arab Emirates was able to locate an individual in Slovakia in under eight hours based only on a photograph."[36] Tag Challenge demonstrated the collaborative power of social networks—and showed law enforcement novel ways to track down terrorists and find missing people.

Even within a country's borders, social media invites citizens to engage directly with leaders of government agencies and corporations, most of whom were previously inaccessible without wading through numerous levels of bureaucracy. Suddenly views can be shared from all sides, enabling fast adjustments to policies or services, and a highly public form of accountability.

Big Data's Big Moment: From Anecdotes to Evidence

In October 2010, Chicago Police Department's new Predictive Analytics Group was analyzing 911 calls. It printed a report showing that a shooting was likely on a particular block on the South Side. Just minutes later, Brett Goldstein, director of the group, felt his Blackberry vibrate. The text reported a murder.

"I recognized the address," he says. "I'm looking at it, saying, 'Didn't I just send out a target?'" He checked the time stamps. The data had predicted the shooting three minutes before it happened.

"It was one of those really, really weird things," he says. "If you didn't look at the time stamps, you wouldn't believe it."[37]

A city's 911 calls are the kind of data it collects in enormous quantities. Yet, very few police departments examine these calls for larger patterns. Although the world is awash in such data, the organizations collecting it can rarely parse its meaning.

But some companies and governments, such as the city of Chicago, are learning how to turn data overload into opportunity, using powerful new methods of analysis. In the words of Clay Shirky, "there is no such thing as information overload, there's only filter failure."[38]

Analytics will prove transformative across the solution economy. The inability of organizations sitting on the largest troves of data to understand how to use it is driving the development of new business models focused on unlocking its full value. Data itself is a traded commodity capable of uses far beyond its original purpose of collection and, as we discuss in chapter 4, stands as a currency in its own right. For many organizations, the ability to pinpoint a potential source of problems and predict outcomes by analyzing big data is a game-changer. Nowhere is this truer than in law enforcement. Here data can save both lives and dollars.

Policing traditionally has been a reactive enterprise: see crime, stop it, punish. But recognizing destructive patterns in the data can help head off crime before it occurs.

In 2010 in Washington, DC, a shooter was firing at military buildings after hours. His targets seemed random: a marine recruiting station, a military museum, the Pentagon. Psychologist and data mining expert Colleen McCue studied the areas the shooter had chosen; she looked for patterns in the locations' socioeconomic demographics, levels of foliage cover, and access to highways. With help from the US Department of Homeland Security and powerful technology, she produced a map of likely targets, which flagged the shooter's next two appearances—the latter of which became the scene of his arrest.[39]

These analytics, useful for solving crimes, can help discourage it as well. Just as retailers track how store layouts affect buying habits, data-driven placement of police resources can alter crime habits. McCue, a leader in the field of police analytics, told *Popular Science,* "How do you move someone through a store? How do you position things on shelves? We're doing similar things. We're asking, 'How do bad guys move through communities? How can we position our policing assets to be unfavorable to crime?'"[40]

She first applied this theory in 2003. In Richmond, Virginia, random gunfire spiked every New Year's Eve. People celebrated by firing guns in the air, producing a rain of plummeting bullets. Rather than chasing shooters in response to 911 calls, Richmond police attempted to prevent the shootings altogether. Using crunched data from past New Year's Eves, they set up patrols in hot spots and aggressively confiscated weapons.[41]

"I was a nervous wreck that night," McCue told us. "If everything had gone sideways, I would have had a lot of explaining to do, given that I had encouraged them to move forward with fifty fewer officers." Richmond rang in 2004 with reports of random gunfire halved from the previous year, and gun confiscations up 245 percent. The city also saved $15,000 by not having to pay fifty additional officers.[42]

Two main challenges to the use of predictive analytics in policing hold true for analytics in general: how can patterns be recognized across complex, sometimes erratic data and translated into terms nonmathematicians can understand? In police work, McCue explains, "our data frequently are extremely poor quality (victims are frightened, witnesses get confused, and suspects lie) and often not available where and when we need it."

Data visualization helps. In the 1990s, the New York City Police Department found that tying complex data to maps of the city via a tracking program called CompStat significantly improved the police's ability to fight crime. Maps are a simple way to visualize data, and elegant solutions bear repeating. The city of Santa Cruz shows officers likely locations of "after-crimes"—a pattern of crimes that occurs in the wake of an initial crime—on digital maps. "If the end user cannot understand and/or use the analytic output, then it's useless," says McCue.

Of course, the benefit of big data extend far beyond crime enforcement. Twitter data has become a source for tracking disease outbreaks. Advances in analytics help more quickly pinpoint the source of a problem before it compounds, from tracking the triggers of asthma to the patterns of obesity. Or consider the field of education, where data analytics promises to disrupt learning—but not the way the class clown does.

Much of the positive disruption arises from the ability of analytics and technology to improve education by customizing offerings for each student. In the past, the school was the overarching education provider. In recent years, however, an ecosystem of private education firms that both supplement and compete with traditional education delivery is changing the rules. For example, the GMAT prep program Knewton quizzes students as they go, and it adjusts its difficulty level to reflect their pace. Knewton decides when the student is ready for the next lesson and tracks mastery of the concepts already encountered. Gone is the traditional review class, in which teaching is geared toward the average student's pace, leaving the slowest behind and the quickest unchallenged.

Online learning without embedded analytics has been likened to a car without wheels. Resources such as Knewton that are known for their educational content also offer built-in analytical tools to track progress, giving teachers a quick snapshot of where an individual or the overall class stands on a certain topic.[43]

The adaptive nature of these programs individualizes the student experience, helping the student move at a pace that allows him or her to fully understand the material. Thousands of teachers have combined such programs with classroom learning in an approach called *flipping the classroom,* in which lectures that introduce key concepts become the homework. Students watch the lectures online, and the material is then reinforced through teacher-led exercises in the classroom.[44]

These educational resources are still developing, but eventually should help communities squeeze more impact from each education dollar, so that student and teacher time is spent as effectively as possible.

In a world overflowing with data, significant advantage will come to those who can make the best use of it. Otherwise, data remains a useless collection of numbers and figures—a complex code without the essential cipher. Only through the filter of analytics does data become useful.

Cloud Computing: Redefining Scale

Scientists like to say that they are standing on the shoulders of giants. They recognize that their own research builds upon the foundational work of so many others before them. What if it were possible for technology to multiply the synergistic effect of putting many great minds to work on the same problem?

Scientific discovery relies on thousands of human-hours of thought and research. It took years of painstaking lab work, for instance, to determine that a protein called BRD4 is related to midline carcinoma. To develop that discovery into a cancer treatment could easily occupy a career.

One way to accelerate the process is to help the world's scientists share their findings more efficiently. This approach is evident in the Human Genome Project, which sequenced the human genome through a worldwide collaboration of public and private labs. As Michael Nielson writes in the *Wall Street Journal,* "When you read in the news that a certain gene is associated with a particular disease, you're almost certainly seeing a discovery made possible by the project's open-data policy."[45]

Such collaboration can be promoted through *cloud computing*, that is, the use of off-site hardware and software for data storage and other computing needs. Organizations can use the cloud to increase their computing capacity without the need for new infrastructure, personnel, or software. Cloud computing allows virtually anyone to swiftly upscale an operation or temporarily surge to additional capacity without the up-front capital costs associated with on-site data storage.

Cloud computing can be used to unearth relationships between genes, cancer, and treatments. Mapping thousands of patient genomes alongside patient data would take hundreds of years' worth of computing time—but if separate laboratories shared their results on the cloud, they could form a massive database much sooner. Statistical analysis of the genes could unearth important relationships.

Consider cancer research. As Jay Bradner notes, "So far in just the dawn of this revolution, we know that there are perhaps 40,000 unique mutations affecting more than 10,000 genes, and that 500 of these genes are bona-fide drivers, causes, of cancer."[46]

Bradner, a medical doctor at a small Harvard-sponsored cancer lab, has already used the cloud to disseminate a breakthrough in cancer treatment. After his lab created a molecule to target a specific cancer, the researchers then consulted "the collaborative network that we have access to in academia."[47] Bradner's team shared the molecule with at least seventy laboratories, swiftly achieving a decade's worth of research in many directions. The labs used the molecule to identify promising treatments in mice for leukemia, bone marrow cancer, and certain liver disorders.

The normal pace of discovery multiplied. In the cloud, public data has provided an international sandbox for scientists, allowing hundreds of minds to study the individual pieces of a complex problem. Such collaboration runs counter to the culture of many preeminent research institutions, where scientists sequester themselves until their breakthrough is published and they can claim full credit. The cloud-based model of rapid, collaborative research stands to completely turn the traditional model on its head.

Cloud computing affects the solution economy in three ways. First, as the example of cancer research demonstrates, cloud computing allows large numbers of people around the world to work with the same huge data sets in real time. And government, possessing more data than any other organization, could benefit greatly from this sort of mass collaboration.

Second, by making computing power vastly more affordable, the cloud can allow people to launch new initiatives and resources quickly for a fraction of the former price. High-end servers that once cost more than $1,300, for example, are now available through Amazon. com for just $0.02 per hour.[48] As costs continue to plummet, new business models can emerge that previously would have been cost-prohibitive. Thus, the rate of innovation accelerates, and the number of new entrants into the public services marketplace expands.

Finally, by radically reducing the costs of operating IT systems, cloud computing can eventually allow governments to reduce their spending on IT infrastructure, freeing up resources for services that directly help citizens. One caution: the lines can blur when it comes to who is responsible for protecting data housed in the cloud. For this reason, individuals making purchasing decisions should ask the savvy questions, particularly where databases containing personally identifiable information or confidential information are at stake.[49]

In developing nations, giving small organizations access to world-class technology via the cloud can profoundly affect public services. A social entrepreneur with an internet connection is no longer limited by his or her less developed environment, since the entrepreneur has access to the most sophisticated tools and information the world has to offer. A Google account is free, as are its collaborative tools such as documents, spreadsheets, and presentations. Other applications such as Weebly, for starting websites, and SlideRocket, to build presentations, are free as well. In Ethiopia, for instance, teachers use Microsoft's Azure Cloud service to "plan and download curriculums, keep track of academic records and securely transfer the student data to make it available throughout the education system."[50]

In sub-Saharan Africa, where many impoverished communities depend on mobile devices to access critical information and services, the Praekelt Foundation uses Amazon.com's cloud to cheaply upscale its mobile platform for people living with HIV and AIDS. The foundation's Young Africa Live (YAL) is a portal with continually updated stories, live chats, and essential information about HIV/AIDS, including medical facts and contacts for referral organizations to support patient users. Over thirty million South Africans a month access YAL's lifesaving content, courtesy of the cloud.[51]

For the Praekelt Foundation, moving its tools to Amazon.com's cloud in 2011 was a no-brainer. As Simon de Haan, chief engineer for Praekelt Foundation, says, "international bandwidth is very expensive in Africa, making local hosting impractical in many cases. For us, the benefit of using [Amazon.com's cloud] is that we can scale up as demand requires it."[52] Moreover, while its audience may be in Africa, the foundation's hosting centers are in Ireland, where network connectivity is stronger—yet another benefit of remote computing services.

But it's not just developing countries that harness the power of cloud computing. These rapid technological advances lower the barriers to entry for social entrepreneurs everywhere—people who can run entire businesses out of their basements.

Creatively used, the cloud will hasten change in new ways and reduce IT costs for public services and societal problem solvers.

Convergence: Bringing the Combined Power of Disruptive Technologies to Bear on a Problem

A great meal is usually the result of inspired cooking: an ordinary ingredient transformed by interacting with another. Great innovation often requires a similar combination of resources. When different technologies and problem solvers converge to tackle immense challenges, each variable reorients itself in terms of another. Coordination and great impact can follow.

For instance, social media can help recruit volunteers—and the data the volunteers bring with them. Add cloud computing to an online community, and you can crowdsource and query massive data sets, or share data across distance and discipline. Or consider this example of convergence: a personal genetics testing company starts out as a simple way for customers to learn about their genetic risks, but using the dynamic combination of big data, social media, and cloud computing, the company develops a model that could end up revolutionizing medical science.

Sergey Brin, the cofounder of Google, and his wife, Anne Wojcicki, the cofounder of 23andMe, are using the convergence method to accelerate scientific discovery, specifically in the search for cures for Parkinson's disease. By employing an array of technologies, recruiting patients as partners in research, and collaborating with research institutions and foundations, the couple has helped uncover some of the genetic causes of Parkinson's, at a fraction of the cost of traditional research.

Their story begins in 2008, when Brin first discovered—as a beta tester for his wife's personal genetics testing company—that he carried a rare mutation that put him at fifty-fifty odds of developing Parkinson's. Undeterred, Brin and his wife started tugging at a simple question that is central to the shortcomings of the medical research industry: how can patients better perform and support research about the diseases that affect them?

Medical research projects are typically financed by government and carried out by large institutions. For people who want to contribute to a particular field of research such as the Parkinson's-linked LRRK2 gene, this limits their options. They can participate in cumbersome studies at large government centers or donate to a research foundation and hope their cash finds the right research.

Today, 23andMe and its mix of disruptive technologies has changed all that. In 2009 Brin bankrolled the Parkinson's Disease Genetics Initiative at 23andMe, a collaboration between the Fox Foundation, the Parkinson's Institute, and the Cleveland Clinic, among others. The program invited anyone diagnosed with Parkinson's to donate DNA and fill out online surveys about his or her health and lifestyle. In return for participating, volunteers got free access to 23andMe's personal genetics services, including an online community where they could ask questions, talk about their symptoms, and share what treatments were working. Patients contributed directly to 23andMe's engine of discovery while directly benefiting from new findings.

Word spread through Parkinson's conferences and social media. The goal was to test ten thousand volunteers with Parkinson's disease. As of January 2013, the initiative has nearly reached this goal—by far the world's largest Parkinson's community for genetic research.[53] The internet-based approach to genetics research has made it possible to involve unprecedentedly large numbers of participants in research programs and to do it cheaper and easier than ever before.

It works like this: for a few hundred dollars and a tube of spit, 23andMe will look at a million genetic variants in customers' DNA to predict traits like what type of earwax they have (wet or dry), as well as their ancestry and risks of certain diseases. Customers can then use the company's website to access their genetic information (or genotypes) along with up-to-date research to better manage their health throughout their lives. But since the launch of the Parkinson's initiative, customers can also participate in several other 23andMe research initiatives.

If a user chooses to participate in a study, his or her genetics data and information from the online surveys enter a cloud-backed database. Researchers from 23andMe and participating organizations can then mine patients' DNA analysis against hundreds of other data points about environmental factors, disease progression, and family history. Emily Drabant, the research director at 23andMe, explains: "We know that there are many genes, so the idea is when you aggregate across many thousands of people you can start to see genes that have perhaps a small effect on risk for Parkinson's."[54]

The web-based approach makes it easier to find volunteers and radically cuts the cost of research. To gather more data, 23andMe acquired CureTogether, a social network of people with chronic conditions (or phenotypes). CureTogether allows its customers to share quantitative information on more than five hundred medical conditions and their experience with treatments. Like 23andMe, shared information is collected in a cloud-backed database, leveraging public experience to fast-track medical science.

Recently, Brin challenged the Fox Foundation to raise an additional $50 million by the end of 2012, promising to match donors dollar-for-dollar. Half of that will go into what others have called "the Manhattan Project" to devise drugs against LRRK2.[55]

In time, isolating interactions between genes to pinpoint genetic causes of diseases—an extremely difficult, time-consuming, and expensive task using conventional research methods—might become as easy as a Google search. Already, the data collected has led to the discovery of two new genetic associations with Parkinson's. Brin and the group of collaborating drug companies are standing by, ready to act on what the data reveals.

From finding potential volunteers through social media, to crowdsourcing patient data to the cloud, to foundations working with drug companies on the data from 23andMe, Brin and Wojcicki's approach revolves around convergence. In the next chapter, we'll take a closer look at some new business models that are applying the technologies profiled in this chapter to their full capacity.

DISRUPTIVE TECHNOLOGIES: IN A NUTSHELL

THE BIG IDEA

Disruptive technologies enable the mobilization of massive resources around big challenges. As technologies evolve and converge to form blended models of service delivery, we can expect to see a spike in societal problem solving, while costs plummet.

TECHNOLOGIES THAT DISRUPT

- **Mobile:** Millions of people use their mobile devices to access innovative, entertaining, and lifesaving services the world over. These mobile tools will revolutionize health care and education in the developing world.

- **Social:** Online communities of all stripes engage people, improving collaboration and crowdsourcing solutions—sometimes unwittingly—to solve big problems via social networks (e.g., the CIA's meme tracking).

- **Analytics:** People everywhere are mining data to address thorny problems. With increased storage in the cloud and the flow of data through social channels, data sets are increasing in size—and value.

- **Cloud computing:** Remote computing services allow mass collaboration around huge data sets, bringing affordable scale to computationally intensive problem solving. Cloud computing closes the digital divide by making collaboration across distance and discipline possible and cheap.

SURPRISING STATISTICS

- High-end servers that once cost more than $1,300 now are available as needed through Amazon.com for just $0.02 per hour.

- In India, more than a million people signed a petition to clean up government corruption on Avaaz.org in thirty-six hours.

- Smartphones are outselling computers four to one. Today, there are more mobile phones in Uganda than there are light bulbs.[56]

LEVERAGING DISRUPTIVE TECHNOLOGIES

- Using a combination of emerging technologies, Recyclebank made recycling fun and competitive and grew recycling by sevenfold in some jurisdictions.

- Safaricom's M-Pesa mobile money transfer service allows millions of Kenyans to easily deposit, send, and withdraw money using their cell phones.

- The personal genetics testing company 23andMe uses social media to recruit patient volunteers for its Parkinson's Disease Genetics Initiative. It has tested nine thousand participants—the largest Parkinson's research community in the world—keeping its data in a cloud-backed database to perform analysis with partnering research institutions.

- Khan Academy's distance learning software uses its powerful analytics engine to tailor students' problem sets much like a Genius playlist on iTunes.

QUESTIONS FOR THOUGHT

What new use for an existing technology was most striking to you? In what innovative ways could you deploy it in the organizations and communities you are a part of?

THREE

Business Models That Scale

Radical innovations in delivering public benefit

For many city dwellers, owning a car is a major hassle. You may use your car only occasionally, yet still have to fight for parking spaces and shell out a fortune for garage parking on top of your monthly car payments. As costly and inconvenient as owning a car is, it generally beats renting. Unless you live at an airport, you're going to have trouble finding a rental car agency in the city. Once you do, then you get to wait in line and pay upward of $50 a day. You only need a car for a couple of hours? Doesn't matter—it's still going to set you back $50.

In many cities, though, there's a way around this frustrating trade-off. Car-sharing services such as Zipcar and Car2Go allow urban residents to pick up a car within blocks of their homes and use it for less than $10 an hour. You can pick up a sports car for that special date one night and use a pickup truck the next day to take your new sofa home. It offers a more flexible, and a bit more expensive, alternative to the ridesharing discussed earlier. In cities where both are options, users may alternate between the two, depending on their needs for a given day.

Wave a card over the windshield to pop the locks, climb in, and you're ready to drive. As with Recyclebank, Zipcar's easy customer experience wouldn't be possible without numerous cutting-edge technologies: powerful microprocessors, RFID cards, sensors, GPS, wireless networks, and sophisticated databases.[1] Just unlocking the car requires sensors that detect the member's card and wireless networks that query the reservation system, check availability using GPS, and activate the user's reservation.[2] The pile of paperwork from a traditional car rental is replaced with a few electronic confirmations.

Drivers aren't the only ones excited about car-sharing services. "Zipsters" drive less than their car-owning counterparts; it's estimated that a single car-share vehicle can replace four to eight personal cars while serving twenty-five to fifty people.[3] The public benefits are clear: less traffic congestion, less money spent on transportation, and less pollution.

Willi Loose, a car-share expert in Germany, explains that for car owners, "the depreciation of a new vehicle is seen as unavoidable, leading to the attitude: 'since I've paid for the car, I should use it as much as possible.' The cost structure of Car Sharing is exactly the opposite . . . apart from a small monthly fee, almost all costs are directly related to car use."[4]

Furthermore, since users can match their vehicles to their task and tend to make reservations for short trips, fuel-efficient cars perform the majority of trips. A study of German car-share users found that 70 percent of all rides employed minis or small family cars. In Switzerland, car sharing reduced the average Swiss car-share participant's carbon dioxide output by 290 kilograms annually.

There is another public benefit: car sharing frees up precious space previously needed for parking. After a neighborhood in Freiburg, Germany, agreed to use car shares, it was able to build several playgrounds where parking lots used to be.[5]

Car shares aren't new. Robin Chase, cofounder of Zipcar, insists that she simply took the best ideas from existing programs and used technology to expand their appeal. The concept is catching on. Car sharing is growing in Europe, with programs such as European Car Sharing, which has fifty-six thousand members in more than

550 towns. Similar car-sharing services operate in more than 1,000 cities. Meanwhile, peer-to-peer car-sharing programs, such as GoLoco and Getaround.com, allow car owners to rent out their car when they won't need it. Even BMW and Mercedes have entered the market to create "premium" sharing arrangements. An entirely new industry has emerged to serve the masses migrating to cities.[6]

As with ride sharing, the market today for car-sharing programs is relatively small and currently confined largely to urban areas, but it's growing. When Avis, one of the largest car rental companies in the United States, announced its acquisition of Zipcar in early 2013, the announcement signaled a significant expansion and validation of the model.[7] Zipcar and now Avis appear to be onto something: an internal Zipcar study shows that most members of the millennial generation value access above ownership and are receptive to "collaborative consumption" programs as an alternative to the costs of car maintenance. Also, 55 percent of millennials "actively made an effort to drive less."[8] More and more, members of this cohort calculate social impacts in their consumer decisions. To succeed, companies are finding innovative ways to meet this demand.

Business Models for Change

Car sharing's broader significance to the solution economy is that it's an entirely new business model—one predicated on using technology to break trade-offs. The same goes for Recyclebank, M-Pesa's mobile banking in Africa, and the dozens of new online education approaches sprouting up around the world. These shifts today may still be relatively small in the big scheme of things, but they are growing . . . fast.

Peer into the future with us. Ten years from now in many big cities, regularly sharing a car or a ride with virtual strangers will be more commonplace—and easier—than owning a car yourself. Tens of thousands of communities will use a reward-points approach to dramatically boost recycling rates and reduce energy consumption. And cures for some very deadly diseases will have been discovered through massively crowdsourced, open innovation models like Sergey Brin's and Anne Wojcicki's audacious Parkinson's initiative.

The solution revolution removes old trade-offs, often producing dramatically better results for a lower cost. And unlike many of the advances people have grown accustomed to in the private sector, these innovations don't just meet consumer needs. They solve deep-seated societal problems.

We've previously introduced the growing and diverse army of wavemaking problem solvers and seen technology's role in driving the solution sector. This chapter explores the new business models and organization structures emerging from these shifts. Business models may even be too narrow a term, as these fundamentally different operating models enable new relationships between services and clients, between government and citizens, between manager and worker, and between neighbor and neighbor and stranger and stranger. Just as a computer's operating system provides the foundation for all the software, these new operating models enable a whole new set of social and economic relationships and knowledge-sharing protocols that break through existing limitations.

Consider the relationship between mobile technology and business models. A smartphone is at once a compass and GPS; a nutrition log and recipe-finder; a connection to work; a pathway to a fast answer; and, in the case of an addicting game, a brief respite from reality. The effectiveness of *how* technology is employed to meet a need—and how it stacks up against the competition—ultimately determines which adaptations of technology succeed. A good business model combines technical capabilities in a way that maximizes their usefulness while offering a deceptively simple user experience. The ability of a toddler to navigate an iPad touchscreen to play a favorite game, before he or she can even walk, is a testament to the device's simplicity. The fact that commuters on a train can use a smartphone to do everything from researching world energy prices to playing sudoku is a testament to the usefulness of this tool.

Similarly, when it comes to incorporating a social-impact agenda, the execution of the business model is everything. A car-sharing company may employ the most environmentally friendly fleet of cars in the industry, but if pickup locations aren't conveniently located, or hourly rates exceed full-day rentals, few will use the service.

Recognizing this, we will examine a few of the most disruptive and breakthrough approaches that directly challenge existing ways of doing business and that fuel new entrants in the public service marketplace. What does this mean in the context of business models? These models eliminate trade-offs, redefining the limits of what is possible at any given time.[9] Why can't we find thousands of different capabilities in a single, sleek mobile device? Or for car sharing, who says that choosing a certain mode of transportation means deciding between price and performance or between access and performance? You can live like you have a car—plan impromptu errands, get across town quickly, or take a day trip—without the cost and hassle of actually owning one.

Policy makers and citizens confront huge trade-offs every day. The most common is between the "price" we pay in taxes for a public sector good and the quality of its performance. In education, for instance, it is generally assumed that better performance requires more teachers, smaller class sizes, and better facilities. Under the traditional model of schooling, reducing the number of teachers and increasing class size typically harms performance.

Dozens of companies and nonprofits are actively trying to eliminate this trade-off via business models that leverage *online* learning, or a blended learning environment of digital learning and traditional instruction. How? By personalizing the learning experience according to individual student learning styles and pace and doing so without increasing the number of teachers. Organizations that may start with a common business model diverge with their own distinctive twists, perhaps targeting specific age groups, focusing on select subjects, or tailoring the features to disabled learners.

In India, wavemakers of all stripes are hard at work trying to break the trade-off between high-quality health care and low health care costs. The Narayana Hrudayalaya hospital chain does more cardiac bypass surgeries each year than just about any other hospital in the world. It has used its high volumes to improve quality and to drive down costs. The large number of patients allows individual doctors to focus on one or two specific types of surgeries. The price of cardiac bypass surgery is a fraction of what it costs in the United States: $2,000 compared with $100,000. Yet the quality does not suffer: the mortality rate is lower than that in the average American hospital. This specialization business model has similarly been successfully applied to dramatically lower costs for cataract surgery and maternity health in India (table 3-1).

TABLE 3-1

Lowering costs through business model innovation

Sector	Solution	Organization	Business model innovation used	Reduction in cost[a]
Health	Cardiac surgery	Narayana Hrudayalaya	No-frills service and specialization	60%
	Drinking water	Voltic	Franchise	95%
	Infant health monitoring	Pesinet, Mali	Mobile-enabled nonfinancial services	95%
	Pair of lenses	Aravind Eye Hospital	No-frills service and specialization	93%
	Doctor attending childbirth	Lifespring	No-frills service and specialization	72%
	Outpatient maternity care visit			80%
Education	Primary education	Gyan Shala	Franchise	88%
		Bridge International Academies	Franchise/no-frills service	88%

Source: Deloitte Research/Monitor Deloitte Analysis and Monitor Deloitte, "Promise and Progress: Market-Based Solutions to Poverty in Africa," May 2011.

a. Reduction in cost compared with the average cost of alternative commercial or governmental channels.

This chapter looks at several business models, or operating models, that disrupt current public service approaches, scale quickly and help enable the solution economy.

Franchises

As companies downshifted during the great recession, thrifty franchises like McDonald's revved up. From 2006 to 2011, McDonald's restaurants saw a 4 percent increase in sales (despite rising food prices) and notched an astounding fifty thousand new hires in April 2011 alone.[10] That was a fairly common tale for many living in the world's richest countries as families acclimated to a more modest lifestyle. However unglamorous they may seem in the West, lean franchises have played a transformative role in developing countries, offering a sturdy ladder out of poverty. Consider some of the no-frills solutions to the lack of options for quality education in the developing world.

In a move to combat poverty, Kenya passed its Free Primary Education initiative in 2003, universalizing access to free primary education. But increased enrollment did not translate to increased funding. As a result, schools became overcrowded, supplies were exhausted, and educational systems that were already broken deteriorated further.

As it turned out, "free" primary education in Kenya is not necessarily free, either. Many public schools levy desk, exam, and school maintenance fees. Research has shown that government-run primary education costs many parents in Nairobi more than $3 a month. And teacher truancy is high. When teachers do show up, they spend on average only 90 minutes of the entire day on instruction.

But for $5 a month—about one day's pay—impoverished families in Nairobi now have the option to send their kids to a high-quality commercial alternative, thanks to Bridge International Academies and its franchise-like network of ultra-low-cost, for-profit primary schools.[11] The company has been scaling fast since 2009: identifying land, building structures, and educating underprivileged children from the slums and remote villages. By 2013, with hundreds of academies, Bridge was already the largest chain of any kind.

The social enterprise was cooked up in 2007 by former technology entrepreneur Jay Kimmelman to bring affordable, quality education to poor families in the developing world.[12] Kimmelman had spent three years scouring the developing world looking for ways to create scalable public services. His whirlwind search came to an abrupt end at a schoolyard in Africa—while he was on his honeymoon with his cofounder-to-be, Shannon May.

"We realized that every time we drove up to a school the kids all seemed to be at recess," Kimmelman recalls. "Children were not learning because no one was teaching them. Most of the private schools were sole proprietors, so there was no consistency."[13]

That was the crack *and* the mortar in the education system: consistency.

As of May 2013, Bridge International Academies has grown to a network of eighty-three private schools spread across Kenya, serving roughly twenty-six thousand kids. Early studies show that Bridge's students are drastically outperforming their government-educated peers (by more than 100 percent on core reading skills)—proof that, like McDonald's, you don't have to pay more to get more. Minus the saturated fat, of course.[14]

Kimmelman's original vision was that a financially self-sustaining and scalable education model was key to breaking Africa's cycle of poverty. And to be scalable, the new schools had to be cheap. Bridge had to reengineer the entire value chain of primary education. The result was its unique, yet highly repeatable "school-in-a-box" model: a low-cost blueprint that can be used to create schools that allow local managers to operate on an extremely low-cost basis. The schools are designed to serve 1,500 students, but reach profitability once they enroll 200. By 2012, they averaged 313 kids per school.[15]

With the entire network hinging on delivering an effective school-in-a-box, the contents of the box were critical. Before launching, the founders developed all the tools, curriculum, processes, and even growth plans for school managers—everything needed to run an ultra-affordable, but high-quality school. The box includes everything from construction to curriculum, from testing to teacher training. Teachers receive identical training and even read scripted lessons.

Like many young companies upending the old order in business, Bridge uses computer power to do things faster and cheaper than an unplugged teacher can. The team built technical infrastructure to track success and pinpoint problems across widely dispersed schools. Smartphone applications as well as web-based data management and support tools offer valuable connectivity at low cost.[16] Parents even pay by cellphone via the M-Pesa mobile payment system, leaving the actual schools cashless and therefore less corruptible.[17]

"As a result of creating such a cost-effective model," Kimmelman explains, "we're able to raise sufficient capital, start schools, and have those schools be sustainable, commercially viable and continue to contribute to the overall growth of the organization."[18]

With a $1.8 million equity infusion from Omidyar Network, Bridge aims to expand into new sub-Saharan countries and to establish eighteen hundred schools by 2015—an average of about two a day. The effort will create jobs for fifteen thousand educational workers in local communities, representing another tonic to systemic poverty.[19] Their ultimate goal: teach 10 million children in the developing world.

Profitable schools are by definition sustainable, and the promise of wealth creation is the fuel that drives replication. Fifty years ago in the United States, coffee shops and burger joints were the quintessential mom-and-pop operations. Coffee and burgers aren't by nature necessarily scale enterprises. But franchises such as Starbucks and McDonald's developed a formula that proved profitable, and the profit-making capacity fueled the launch of tens of thousands of very similar stores. A Big Mac in Chicago tastes like a Big Mac in Boston, and if you walk into a Starbucks, you won't be able to tell if you are in Seattle or Miami. A Bridge International school in Nigeria will operate just like one in Senegal.

As with other franchise models, profits help fund additional schools in the network, and Bridge also has the flexibility to make cost-effective interventions where they are needed most.[20] Because Bridge's model is so much cheaper and more effective than traditional approaches in this part of the world, the student learning results-to-cost ratio is four to six times greater than that for the traditional public model.[21]

Kimmelman isn't the first entrepreneur to tackle societal problems with a franchising model tailored for the base of the pyramid, nor is he the first to do so using the classroom. In Ahmedabad, India, an NGO shares Bridge's results-to-cost ratio by using a similarly Spartan, if data- and worksheet-heavy, formula. Gyan Shala (Hindi for "a school for knowledge or wisdom") offers the poor an extremely cheap and effective private school option by renting single classrooms in slums and employing local women from the informal sector as teachers.

Cost savings and disruption occur at the pedagogical level. The organization leverages highly standardized elements like predesigned worksheets for students and step-by-step manuals for teachers to optimize results. However, unlike Bridge International Academies, there is also a strong adaptive component to the model, because the role of teacher is segmented into three parts. While one teacher focuses on day-to-day activities centered around the worksheets and manuals, another senior teacher rotates through classes, spending time with students weekly to focus on more complex content. The third, a "designer," responds to teacher feedback and student performance to adapt the curriculum from one week to the next. What teachers may lack in relative skill and experience, Gyan Shala can make up for with its strong back-end design and management team.

As with Kenyan schools, teacher truancy is staggeringly high in India's public schools. Gyan Shala has kept it down by making shifts short—three hours a day—and by hiring women who live within walking distance of their classroom. Moreover, hiring women from the informal sector immediately increases their status and their earning potential, which has helped keep teacher turnover much lower than their public school counterparts. The result: the state government was so taken with the model that families no longer need to pay Gyan Shala school fees; the government now covers 80 percent of the cost for the 350 slum locations, and grants cover the rest.[22] Although it remains to be seen if Bridge International and Gyan Shala will ever become the McDonald's of education, these nimble, franchise models have proven that they can compete in some of the most harrowing environments.

The fact that the majority of sub-Saharan Africa's half billion inhabitants reside in rural areas populated with only seventy-seven people per square kilometer lends itself to roving microfranchises capable of serving large geographic areas.[23] Also referred to as *direct-sales-agent models,* they too employ a business-in-a-bag concept whereby locals are trained to serve members of their communities and neighboring communities directly, bypassing shops and intermediaries.

LivingGoods, based in Uganda, equips female sales agents with a ready-made business for selling everything from malaria nets and clean-burning cook stoves to nutrient-rich fortified foods. Health-Keepers and Toyola Energy employ similar models for selling health products and cookstoves throughout Ghana.[24]

Once an organization has provided the essentials, it offers the entrepreneurs incentives to build their customer bases. To do so, the entrepreneurs often leverage their own existing relationships. Compensation is linked to sales, encouraging strong performance and the expansion of the model. The formula is not unlike the one the cosmetics behemoth Avon International uses to sell its wares across one hundred countries through 6.5 million agents.[25] Since the nineteenth century, when its founder started putting women to work as sales representatives, the company has been turning relationships into sales funnels and the financially dependent into enterprising businesswomen.

In the developing world, many organizations use Avon's microfranchise model for social ends. LivingGoods, for example, charges market rates for its detergent so that it can subsidize its door-to-door malaria and tuberculosis medicine. Though medicine is supposed to be free in Uganda's health-care system, stocks in community clinics are often empty, forcing patients to trek to the nearest pharmacy. Through LivingGoods, tuberculosis and malaria medicine cost $0.75—less than one-tenth of what it would cost in a drugstore. That's without the door-to-door service. "Cheaper than free," as LivingGoods' founder likes to say.[26]

The direct-sales-agent model may not be the anytime, anywhere service that Westerners expect. It may instead be limited to the windows of time when a sales agent is visiting, but for remote inhabitants, the model brings valuable resources where they are otherwise lacking. And as long as there are eager entrepreneurs and customers interested in the products, there is room for expansion.

Platforms

In the past, marines who wanted air support had to first know their own coordinates. Under fire, a marine had to pinpoint the position among landmarks on a map and then shout them over a radio to a helicopter pilot. The helicopter crew then often had to flip through reams of paper maps to find the correct target.[27] A mistake would leave comrades unprotected—and could cost civilian lives.

But when Marine Light Attack Helicopter Squadron 369 provided close air combat support to ground units in Afghanistan in the summer of 2010, its crew chief consulted an iPad instead of the traditional sixty to eighty pounds of paper maps.[28] The idea was the brainchild of army pilot Jim Carlson. The drawbacks of shouting map coordinates into a radio during a firefight are obvious, and what could be simpler than for ground units to use their iPads to convey their location and that of enemy forces to other support units?[29]

After they adopted iPads for the job, ideas for other uses sprouted. The army experimented with an app to auto-record a unit's past travels and suggest alternative routes in the future, reducing the risk of ambush.

To encourage such ground-up app development, in 2010 the US Army launched a program then called Apps for the Army, a pilot application-development competition for soldiers. About 140 teams participated, and twenty-five new apps made it through the certification process.[30] One app, the Command Post of the Future, displays bombings and firefights occurring nearby. Another translated a 400-page exercise manual into a searchable multimedia format.[31]

The US Department of Defense has allocated millions of dollars to create an app marketplace, a digital platform for downloading, discussing, and rating all manner of new army apps. The goal is to encourage soldiers to collaborate with developers and provide feedback for useful improvements. Soldiers provide direct feedback through beta testing or by posting comments, just as the Apple App Store and Amazon.com feature customer reviews. Soldiers can also use the site to request apps they need.

"The army marketplace will do more than sell existing apps. It'll help generate ideas for new ones," says Lt. Col. Gregory Motes, chief of the army's new Mobile Applications Branch. "Imagine that a soldier wants an app instructing how to call for artillery fire, and the app doesn't exist yet. The soldier would post a description of what she needs on a Marketplace forum, attracting discussion from fellow soldiers and potential designers."[32] Vendors then could bid on the right to design the app.

Such moves provide small businesses an unprecedented incentive to apply their creativity to military problems. Sniping, for example, has always been a mathematical task. Snipers must calculate wind speed, distance, altitude, temperature, and a number of other variables before they can take a shot.[33] With the right app, however, and an iPhone fastened to a rifle, snipers can calculate all these variables quickly, including the Coriolis effect from the earth's rotation.[34] Many sharpshooting apps, such as Bulletflight, are publicly available, making it much easier to place new technology in soldiers' hands.[35]

Of course, there are also dangers. The ease of bringing military-strength apps to soldiers may also mean nonmilitary individuals may get their hands on similar apps, presenting safety and security risks to citizens. In parallel, the low barrier to development also puts it within reach for militant and terrorist groups. What such groups lack in budget and scale they may seek to overcome through technological advantage.

Beyond the US Army's apps platform, it seems that every industry today relies upon some form of platform business model—many of them internet-based. Doctors quickly cross-check prescriptions to identify interactions between drugs, job-seekers exchange insights about various employers, and property values and other attributes of a given zip code are easily comparable. Successful platforms in a solution economy exhibit one or more of these three characteristics: (1) they invite participants to *collaborate and exchange* at little or no cost; (2) they encourage decentralized, user-generated content; and (3) they enable average citizens to contribute to problem solving.

Take the first point. Well-built platforms allow the collaboration of large groups of people who would never interact otherwise. Anthony Goldbloom, CEO of Kaggle, a platform that runs competitions built around analytics and predictive modeling, notes that "often a winning team will be made up of individuals who have witnessed each other's work in previous competitions and chose to partner up." That they live thousands of miles apart and range from economists to government employees to top hedge-fund traders makes no difference—diverse groups are more the norm than the exception.

Second, successful platforms are designed to make it easy—and often profitable—for users to create content. Take the iPhone. Millions of people have and still are developing innovative apps for iTunes. Users benefit from the abundance of offerings, while the platform provider benefits from the volume of transactions, often taking a cut—30 percent in Apple's case. With more than $5 billion in sales since it launched, the Apple App Store has been a lucrative operation.[36]

Platforms beyond Apple's garner user contributions that far exceed what any single business could ever create. The smartest entrepreneurs realize as much: of the start-ups that earned coveted positions in the incubator Y Combinator in Mountain View, California, in 2012, 13 percent rely on user-generated content.[37]

Third, useful platforms design the user content so that ordinary individuals can help solve problems. The individuals' contributions vary by the platform, from a professor's lecture posted to Udemy, to one-on-one tutoring supplied through Students of Fortune, to participation in a cancer treatment trial through MedTrust. Each platform harnesses the capabilities of private citizens to provide public value.

"Freemium"

Historically, giving away your product has seldom been a successful business model. Certainly, there have been exceptions, such as network television, which provided programs free of charge thanks to advertising. Other "free" products were offered only up to a point, or through cross-subsidy—shifting the cost of one product to another. Keep a $5,000 minimum balance, and you can have a "free" checking account. Buy a couch, get "free" delivery. Buy a $20,000 new car, and get "free" floor mats. This sort of phony free was harmless fluff of little consequence. In the world of commerce, truly free stuff was quite rare. A company that simply gave away its main product or service would have been asking for bankruptcy.

Not anymore. Thanks to disruptive technologies, an increasing number of wildly successful business models start with providing stuff for free. Organizations such as Craigslist and Wikipedia, famous for charging nothing for their services, have eliminated barriers to knowledge and provided vital services to millions. In doing so, they have knocked down (if not out) your grandparent's newspaper want-ads and encyclopedias. But how is "free" workable? And why is this business model such an important one in delivering public value?

Chris Anderson, author of *Free: The Future of a Radical Price*, contends that a new sort of *free* has emerged in the past fifteen years, a much more robust and impactful type of free. Thanks to technology, the cost of *creating* products and services is plummeting, while new disruptive technologies are creating whole new definitions of value.[38] As a result, free has become a real player in the solution economy.

In traditional TV and radio, commercials pay for "free" content, as evidenced by the likelihood that the phrase "Like a good neighbor . . ." conjures the rest of the jingle in your mind. The price of watching a football game is Viagra commercials. The internet has extended this notion, paying for eyeballs but also for information about users. Technology has helped extend the traditional advertising model since in addition to eyeballs, companies can sell information about you and your online behavior. Online search and social media companies don't just sell ads to you, they make money by selling information about you.

One new strategy made possible by ever-shrinking marginal costs is the "freemium model"—a play on *free* and *premium*—in which someone gives a product or service away and makes money by selling a premium or complementary product.[39] This model relies on a small percentage of users to cover the nominal expenses of the free majority. Skype, for instance, offers unlimited calls between computers, but calls to landlines and voicemail services come at a price. The model is gaining traction among companies such as Dropbox, which gives users five free gigabytes of online storage and then charges for additional storage space.

Offering free samples to consumers is an old tactic. What is new is the extent to which a company's *main service* can be free, thanks to the premium-paying minority. Also new is how these disruptive variations on the free theme have the potential to provide solutions to public problems.

Free can yield a wide array of public benefits. Socially minded hackers are building apps that map crime scenes, bike routes, and farmers markets, all from data that governments put on the web for free.[40] Open-source tools that equip citizens to create these types of contributions at no direct cost are multiplying rapidly. Forums for collaboration and codesign also abound, even bridging physical and virtual neighborhoods with services like Nextdoor, which brings local community coordination online.[41]

One of the most promising free trends involves initiatives such as the now famous Khan Academy, which grant unprecedented access to "the great equalizer" of education. When Salman Khan made a series of videos and posted them to YouTube in 2004 to help tutor his cousins, nieces, and nephews, he didn't know that his efforts would eventually affect entire educational systems. But soon after he uploaded the videos, total strangers began using them—and, as it happened, one of those strangers was Bill Gates, who used Khan's free, simple, and effective videos to tutor his own kids. With more than $15 million in funding, much of it from the Bill & Melinda Gates Foundation and Google, Khan Academy and its free online educational videos now are moving into classrooms and private homes across the world.

In just two years after receiving this funding, Khan Academy grew to serve about four million students *every month*. Students can choose from more than three thousand lessons that range from simple arithmetic to calculus, finance, and history. Each course is free and open to anyone with a web connection.

At last count, Khan's math program was being used in twenty-three schools, mostly in California. The Los Altos school district near San Francisco uses Khan software to "flip" its classrooms; students watch the Khan lectures at home so teachers can spend less class time on common lessons and more time working one on one with students on tough problems and concepts. And the Khan Academy approach works. Preliminary test scores show measurable improvements, especially among struggling students.[42]

Free is also transforming higher education. The UK government is giving free online access to the results of government-funded research for anyone who wants it. Nonprofit initiatives such as P2PU, Saylor.org, and University of the People cull open-courseware databases to offer online lectures and video presentations. In lieu of traditional university degrees, these free initiatives offer credentials their users can take directly to employers.[43]

Students may also use open courseware as a study resource to earn credentials such as chartered financial analyst (CFA) and actuarial science certifications. Charles Reynes, for instance, is a California science teacher who has won multiple state and national awards as an educator yet does not have a college degree in science. Instead, he mastered the science tests required to teach the subject by relying on open-courseware materials. Reynes acknowledges that the online content "was an invaluable study tool."[44]

MIT and Stanford are trailblazers on the new frontier of free, private education. MIT's OpenCourseWare (OCW) is available to the entire online world, offering nearly all course content from roughly twenty-one hundred classes and attracting more than 215 million users from around the globe, despite the lack of formal credit. Two-thirds of the persons who use OCW already hold degrees. About 9 percent of its users are educators, and 43 percent come from other universities, an indication that users may share the content with an even wider audience in their own classes.[45] It also indicates, as critics point out, that today at least, open courseware primarily enables educated individuals to become *more* educated, rather than improving graduation rates or reaching uneducated populations. This, however, is likely to change as more resources are devoted to achieving greater participation from those lacking degrees.

Recently, MIT took the additional step of tying a credential to its online offerings. In December 2011, the university introduced MITx, an online course offering an MIT-sanctioned certificate. By February, ninety thousand people had enrolled in its prototype course in circuits and electronics. The course and its credential are free. A small fee for the credential may be introduced in the future, but it will be a trivial cost compared with that of live courses at a college or university.[46] And in May 2012, MIT and Harvard University unveiled EdX, a joint initiative to expand free online course offerings to a global audience; the courses will provide "certificates of mastery."[47] Since introducing EdX, a growing list of top universities, such as UC Berkeley and Georgetown University, has jumped on board to offer free courses.

Stanford University has also put free courses online. The Stanford Engineering Everywhere (SEE) initiative allows students and educators to take online courses in computer science, artificial intelligence, linear systems, and other highly marketable skills such as iPhone application programming. Thanks to a Creative Commons license, all SEE materials are free to use, distribute, and adapt by anyone with an internet connection.[48]

A whopping 160,000 people signed up online for SEE's introductory artificial intelligence course. About 35,000 people turned in the first three weeks' worth of homework, making the course easily Stanford's largest class ever.

How do you make a Massive Open Online Course (MOOC) feel supportive? Faculty can't possibly respond to individual student needs when lessons are delivered on such a scale. Grading is also a challenge, especially for nontechnical subjects. In response, peer assessments and digital study halls, monitored by faculty, on platforms such as Reddit, Facebook, and Stack Overflow backfill the new ecosystem. The EdX platform is more integrated, with each lesson broken into a series of short videos and exercises and with comment boards for each section so that the participants can raise questions and engage in dialogue with classmates and teaching assistants.

The free platform ultimately benefits professors, forcing them to sharpen their pedagogical approach to make the online experience intelligible and engaging. "I can get away with things when I teach a lecture class that I can't online," says Sebastian Thrun, the first professor of SEE's hugely popular artificial intelligence class. "Now I'm thinking intensely about the student experience."[49]

SEE courses assign grades and a final class rank that includes online students. So far, the percentage of top performers in the online contingent is comparable to that of Stanford's high performers.[50] An astounding 248 students achieved perfect scores in Thrun's online course, compared with none in his in-person class. It's an encouraging revelation: there are many Stanford-caliber students outside the school's walls, and online programs will only find more of them as the programs' reach and breadth evolve globally. The SEE initiative is an important development in an era of tuition hikes and rising student debt—challenges pushing traditional higher education out of reach for many. Thrun considered it such an important development that in 2012, he cofounded a separate free online learning platform called Udacity, which offers various STEM (science, technology, engineering, and mathematics) courses for the masses.

Note the dramatic difference between the *new free* taking hold in higher education and the *old free* of public education. The new free expands access through technology and provides education that is geographically boundary-free. The old-school free approach is still locked into a brick-and-mortar model and jealously maintains a geographic monopoly. Traditional free education is expensive to taxpayers and often mediocre, while new free really is free and often of absolute premium standards. MIT and Stanford are a long way from Podunk University. The new free in education provides insight into how the new solution economy can solve public challenges in new ways that are impossible in the traditional paradigm.

To be sure, downsides also exist. What online courses bring in quality content they currently lack in face-to-face socialization opportunities that build critical soft skills and a sense of community. And while credentials are emerging, they are not yet at a point where a student can achieve the equivalent of a full university education, transcript and all, free of charge. But the cascading impacts of what individuals learn and can apply in their local communities certainly yields tangible benefit. Two Haitian social entrepreneurs, Jean-Ronel Noel and Alex Georges, for example, learned integrated circuit engineering from MIT's OpenCourseWare and subsequently used the knowledge to erect more than five hundred solar street lamps in Haiti's poorest communities.[51] "I was able to use the OpenCourseWare to learn the principles of integrated circuits," says Noel. "I found out that I could use an existing integrated circuit to make things more efficient, and I wanted an explanation about how it worked. I was able to learn this through the MIT OpenCourseWare."[52]

Moreover, as with any new software, there are kinks. How will you be rewarded for your effort? Where credit is offered, how do you curb cheating (an unfortunate reality of remote learning)? How can MOOCs help bridge the digital divide, serving demographics they have not yet reached in a meaningful way? Disruption does not guarantee quality. And learning curves for MOOCs that promise a high-quality education at high volume at no cost will be steep. But it's just the beginning, and MOOC 2.0 offerings are sure to come.

Initiatives such as MITx, EdX, and SEE are proving that a world-class education *can* potentially be delivered online without the crushing costs.[53] Extending education to a widening pool of participants sows future generations of changemakers and public-value innovators.

Citizen-Sourcing

Whereas free courseware expands the pool of future contributors, *citizen-sourcing* is proving all-important in plugging today's contributors into the solution economy. Popularized in books such as *The Wisdom of the Crowds, Crowdsourcing,* and *Wikinomics,* crowdsourcing harnesses the power of many self-interested, independent individuals to work on problems in a decentralized way.[54] The more that work can be broken up into small, manageable chunks, the more cost-effective it is to offload the tasks to the crowd. Sites like CrowdFlower, Cloud-Crowd, and Amazon Mechanical Turk offer crowdsourcing platforms that allow anyone with an internet connection to perform simple on-line tasks for payment. When paired with social media, and in particular with mobile phones, crowds of citizens, what we term citizen-sourcing, can perform everything from complex problem solving to crisis response.

Citizen-sourcing is especially effective in organizing "messy" information that can't be easily categorized. The Kibera slum in Nairobi, for instance, is one of the world's largest, with a population of up to one million people jostling for space in 550 acres. Kibera's residents live in informal villages, collections of slapdash shacks an arm's reach from one another. Garbage collects on the train tracks where children play. Pedestrians straddle drainage ditches and navigate gaps between the dried mud walls. Pathways shift position with the pulse of the slum's continual upheaval. Residents also have very limited access to sanitation. Every latrine serves at least fifty shacks. Young boys empty the latrines by bucket, into a nearby river.[55]

Because the area grew organically, Kiberans lack maps, a situation that increases the difficulty of finding scarce water resources. The lack of maps, moreover, makes it even harder to improve the slum. "Without access to a map," explains Erica Hagan, an American in Nairobi, "there is no way to plan for development and resource flows. Control of information, now more than ever before, determines who enters the conversation about policy-making and access to resources."[56]

To address these problems, Hagan and her business partner Mikel Maron assembled locals from each of the slum's villages to map Kibera. Using handheld GPS technology, they chose points of interest: water spigots, schools, toilets. OpenStreetMap.com, which provides free geographic data and mapping services, hosted the information. "Within three weeks, the mapping team had produced one of the densest maps ever made, labeling 'points of interest' throughout Kibera," says Hagan.[57] Local volunteers learned to use the technology, and some even registered their first email account.

Hagan and Maron hope that the map will help convince politicians to provide more services to the slum. For example, the map drew attention to a water line that bypassed the slum on its way to the suburbs without delivering any water to the slum, highlighting the resource imbalance and providing an opportunity to correct the issue. A similar crowdsourced mapping project is under way in neighboring Tanzania.[58]

Crowdsourced slum mapping helps these communities take ownership of their own future. Volunteers performed the work faster and more accurately than a massive, top-down project could have. And because of their personal stake in the result, the volunteers attended to details that hourly workers might ignore.

A world away from the slums of Africa, crowdsourcing is being used to tackle public works issues in dense urban areas. In cities like Boston, public works problems pop up like mushrooms after a rainfall. Potholes develop, graffiti appears, road kill must be removed. In October 2009, Boston city officials launched a simple yet elegant solution to this dilemma: a cell-phone application that allows the user to simply take a photograph of a problem and send it to the city. The application automatically collects GPS information and allows the city to generate a work order for a public works crew. It even sends citizens who report a problem a notification when the work order has been completed.[59] In this way, Boston uses the eyes and ears of thousands of its citizens to enhance its awareness of problems that need attention. The cell-phone application accounts for 20 percent of all service notifications the city receives.[60]

City officials Chris Osgood and Nigel Jacobs, the innovators behind Boston's Citizens Connect, call their approach urban *micro-volunteerism:* empowering citizens to make small commitments to the public good, with a huge aggregate impact. Like MIT's and Khan Academy's free education models, the Kiberan slum mapping and Boston public work apps are examples of previously impossible models of solving public problems virtually for free. With the trade-offs eliminated by technology, the entrepreneur has only to mold a working model that unleashes the power of free, applying that power to social problems.

Another example of micro-volunteering is Boston's Street Bump app. Bostonians need only download the app and activate it while they're driving. The app automatically detects bumps in the road and sends the data back to the city with GPS coordinates. The program can even distinguish and filter out bumps caused by manhole covers and speed bumps.[61]

Osgood has advice for organizations seeking citizen support for public services: "Find out problems that citizens are facing, then make [solutions] lightweight and low cost for the city and the citizens, so it's low risk. This dramatically increases buy-in."[62]

The crowd can be engaged to solve even bigger problems, across borders and oceans. Take translating the web, today mostly in English, into many different languages. How about doing it without any money? It may sound crazy, but Luis Von Ahn, the man behind this vision, is anything but. He's the Carnegie Mellon University computer scientist who helped invent CAPTCHA, the string of distorted text you're asked to translate when you fill out online forms. In the most recent version, reCAPTCHA, responses are actually used to help accurately digitize books for internet distribution—about 100 million words a day, the equivalent of about 2.5 million books annually. As of December 2011, about 750 million people, or more than 10 percent of the world's population, have aided this massive project simply by entering words through reCAPTCHA.

To translate the web, Ahn's newest project Duolingo will teach people a foreign language by giving them short translations to complete, based on their current language level. Every time one of these translations is completed successfully, a small part of the web gets translated into that language. By offering learners a free study system, Duolingo's approach cleverly solves the problem of motivation.

Ahn explains his approach to crowdsourcing on a mass scale through a historical analogy:

> *If you look at humanity's large-scale achievements, these really big things that humanity has gotten together and done historically—like, for example, building the pyramids of Egypt or the Panama Canal or putting a man on the moon— there is a curious fact about them, and it is that they were all done with about the same number of people. It's weird; they were all done with about 100,000 people. And the reason for that is because, before the internet, coordinating more than 100,000 people, let alone paying them, was essentially impossible. But now with the internet, I've just shown you a project where we've gotten 750 million people to help us digitize human knowledge. So the question that motivates my research is, if we can put a man on the moon with 100,000, what can we do with 100 million?[63]*

It doesn't get much bigger than digitizing human knowledge. Think of it. Technology and a clever business model allowing for the kind of large-scale coordination heretofore impossible in the annals of human history—without force and much of it for free. The next breakthrough will come from discovering which nonmonetary incentives can engage and retain 100 million active contributors. The upside is so monumental that many are working to unlock the answer.

Secrets to Successful Solution Economy Business Models

What can the successful business model innovators we profiled in this chapter show us about serving citizens in transformative ways?

For one thing, the innovators in the solution economy almost always begin with the goal of eradicating a chronic social problem. For Bridge International and Gyan Shala, it was the lack of a low-cost, effective educational option for Africa and India's poorest. For Recyclebank, it was low recycling rates. These change agents then delve into the structure of these enterprises so deeply that, as one social investor recently told us at a conference on the impact economy, "they can find pennies in the cracks in the sidewalk."

A second success factor is the ability to nimbly deploy and recombine technologies, refitting them to solve old problems in a new way. Zipcar and Khan Academy are utterly different in many respects, yet both rely on rigorous analytics to shape their services, whether the service is deciding on the most convenient parking place or which courses to recommend when a student completes algebra. Zipcar offers personalized customer support using real-time geospatial data; Khan Academy employs a game framework to coach users through a curriculum that leads to concept mastery. Both are known for high-quality, unusually affordable services, and both began with powerful preexisting technologies. Their founders' knowledge of which technologies to draw upon and how to combine them effectively differentiated each company from a multitude of competing offerings, paving the way for success.

Yet another thing successful innovators have in common is a business model that can scale. Not so long ago, it took decades for an organization to become large enough to serve hundreds of thousands of people. But in just a few years, MIT OpenCourseWare's reach extended into the *hundreds of millions.* Today, thanks to the internet and social, mobile, and cloud technologies, successful models can scale instantaneously—and can be designed from the outset with that intention. Bridge International's school-in-a-box model allows the social enterprise to build a new school every few days.

Lastly, an effective model is often quite versatile, serving wide-ranging social issues by operating from a variety of inputs, spanning educational content, health advice, open-source analytics software, and microloans, among myriad others. A good business model's versatility extends its value to prospective funders as well, offering ways to track and learn about an organization's performance.

In the next chapter, we'll show how the solution economy is being reshaped by a new definition of *currencies.* Wavemakers are extending the idea of currency far beyond the traditional government-issued currency to a transformative set of exchange enablers. These new nonmonetary currencies act as the fabric for the solution economy, enabling exchange and creating cohesion between the various players as they tackle a new challenge.

BUSINESS MODELS THAT SCALE: IN A NUTSHELL

THE BIG IDEA

Innovative business—or operating—models provide a base for the solution economy by enabling a whole new set of social and economic relationships and opportunities for knowledge sharing. Often using technology to break trade-offs, these models produce dramatically better results for a lower cost while solving deep-seated societal problems.

TYPES OF BUSINESS MODELS THAT SCALE

Some of the most effective business models pair new technology and approaches with tried-and-true business concepts:

- **Franchises:** In the solution economy, franchise models tackle societal problems with replicable businesses that are often tailored to work with underserved markets at the base of the pyramid.

- **Platforms:** These models convene a wide array of participants online, enabling the average citizen to contribute to problem solving. Content is decentralized and user-generated and can be accessed by users to improve or develop solutions.

- **Freemiums:** The freemium model enables an entrepreneur to offer a primary service or product for free by selling a premium or complementary product.

- **Citizen-sourcing:** This model allows citizens to perform small tasks—often online—that collectively contribute to public value. When paired with social media and mobile phones, citizens can contribute to everything from complex problem solving to crisis response.

SUCCESS CHARACTERISTICS

Improved social outcomes are pursued through innovative models that succeed at the following objectives:

- **Creatively apply or recombine technologies,** adapting them to tackle a chronic social problem in new ways.

- **Are built for scale,** with the potential to reach thousands, if not millions.

- **Bring transparency,** enabling funders to track and learn about the organization's performance.

INNOVATORS

- **Zipcar:** a car-sharing company that allows city dwellers to rent a car easily and quickly using cutting-edge technologies.

- **Apps for the Army:** a platform for downloading, discussing, and rating new US Army apps.

- **LivingGoods:** a social enterprise based in Uganda that provides ready-made businesses for selling everything from malaria nets and clean-burning cookstoves to nutrient-rich fortified foods.

- **Bridge International Academies:** a network of hundreds of private schools that serve roughly twenty-six thousand kids in Kenya. The franchise model costs parents only $5 a month, yet Bridge schools drastically outperform their government counterparts.

REALITY CHECK

Executing on a social-impact agenda requires just as strong and innovative a business model as does any for-profit endeavor. If anything, the large number of users expecting reliable service, even in adverse conditions and remote regions, pushes innovators to perform on a new level.

QUESTIONS FOR THOUGHT

Which business model discussed in this chapter are you most interested in experiencing firsthand? What other populations is the model well suited to serve, and what could it provide to them?

FOUR

The Currencies

How new impact currencies fuel the solution economy

World of Warcraft is one of the most massively successful video games of the last decade. The game has more than ten million players worldwide, a community larger than the entire population of Sweden.[1] Its devotees pour hundreds of hours into building stashes of online gold, virtual experience levels, and quest objects, spending real-world dollars to purchase high-level characters or *Warcraft* gold.

The global GDP of virtual games such as *World of Warcraft*, according to market trading estimates, is as high as $28 billion.[2] The third-party gaming services industry, providing microtasks such as gold farming, which employs an estimated hundred thousand workers providing player-for-hire services worldwide, generates about $3 billion in annual revenue, most of which stays in developing countries.[3]

Warcraft's economy, however, incorporates more than virtual goods and money. Characters can earn *reputation points* that vary for each in-game faction: for instance, if you slay a pirate from the Blackwater Raiders, your reputation among that group drops drastically, but you *gain* reputation among their rivals, the Bloodsail Buccaneers. An "honor system" currency rewards players for vanquishing one another, while certain currencies, such as a type of holy dust, are valuable only within certain factions.

In video games, virtual economies are built in an attempt to simulate the real economy. Often the games will draw from elements of real world behavior systems like reputation. A developer, for instance, does not earn *official* reputation points when he or she reinvigorates parts of a city, but the developer's reputation can gain a very real value. The developer can spend a painstakingly built reputation all at once in a drunk-driving accident, or lend his or her good reputation to an up-and-coming entrepreneur through an endorsement. And some currencies are valuable only to specific factions; you'll certainly find a higher value placed on carbon credits in some circles than in others.

These unofficial currencies circulate beneath people's daily interactions, even if a bottom-of-the-screen score and soundtrack don't track people's day-to-day triumphs and defeats. Even if less quantifiable, the rewards and consequences stemming from people's actions reinforce all sorts of positive and negative behavior. The gap between good intentions and quantified rewards, however, is closing from both ends.

Businesspeople such as Google's Sergey Brin, Whole Foods Market's John Mackey, and Virgin's Richard Branson place increasing value on *social returns* rather than mere profits. And new technologies are making it easier to identify and calculate such returns into tradable measures of value.

One company trying to think beyond the dollar is Zappos. When Amazon.com bought Zappos in 2009, Tony Hsieh, the company's quirky chief executive, decided to reinvest some of the $1.2 billion from the sale by moving Zappos to Las Vegas and improving the city itself. Vegas, he hoped, could become "the most community-focused large city in the world."[4]

The Downtown Project is Hsieh's $350 million experiment with a new business formula: fill a space with creative and motivated people, foster community, and thus ensure sustainable businesses and neighborhoods. Where better to gamble with an idea than Las Vegas?

Hsieh set aside a portion of the money for buying land, apartments, and offices in the city's dilapidated downtown area. Another portion will fund tech companies and small businesses that agree to move to the area. And $50 million will fund improved educational resources. Hsieh believes that if he can transform the Vegas urban core into an appealing place to live, it will boost his company's ability to attract and retain talent.

Hsieh scrutinizes the impact of each of these investments on his bottom line: community well-being. "Every factory in the world is doing everything they can to maximize ROI," says Hsieh. "We're doing everything to maximize ROC [return on community]."[5]

The wavemakers who value social return, like Hsieh, gauge success by the positive impacts they produce, impacts often measured in unorthodox units, such as children educated, prisoners reformed, or obesity rates reduced. By advancing how these units are measured, the wavemakers build the basis for quantifying and rewarding improvements, a concept best understood in the context of currencies. While it may be a while before Hsieh's "return on community" can be calculated in an agreed-upon fashion, it's valuable to recognize the forms these new currencies can take.

New Currencies for Public Value

When people discuss currencies, they tend to think of paper notes—American dollars, Japanese yen, or euros. Printed money, however, is only one form of currency. Throughout history, currencies have come in many novel forms. *World of Warcraft's* holy dust is only the latest in a long history of unconventional currencies, from the storied stone wheels of the Yap islanders to cowries, the mollusk shells that became a popular means of exchange in China more than three millennia ago.

Currencies have evolved over time from stones and seashells to the sophisticated currencies that enable today's global financial transactions. This evolution of the notion of currency continues today, as a number of new, alternative currencies grow in popularity.

Currency is how we create and exchange economic value through place and time. As in *World of Warcraft*, in the solution economy, value creation and exchange take place in new and different ways, and unsurprisingly, we're witnessing an explosion in the types of currencies in use—new currencies that can spur new ways of creating public value.

To understand the solution economy, we must rethink our conception of currencies. Currency can be anything that provides the various economic functions we currently associate with fiat money. It is anything that can serve as a medium of exchange, something that can be "cashed out" for goods and services or used to pay debt or to store value for future use.[6] As we will see in the examples that follow, new currencies are a key enabler of the solution economy, encouraging participation where existing monetary currencies fall short and incentivizing action where conventional commodities may be lacking.

Traditional, monetary contracts certainly have their place. But societal problem solvers are not being limited by these methods. Now more than ever, creative means of promoting public outcomes by attracting, targeting, and rewarding resources in creative ways form part of the solution design. Table 4-1 summarizes some characteristics of these "impact" currencies, and the following pages examine each of them.

Credits as Currency: Trading Public Goods

Alaska's Bristol Bay is one of the world's best salmon fisheries, the catchment for hundreds of pristine rivers and streams. It produces massive numbers of salmon (29.3 million in 2008); the area's salmon fishing alone creates an estimated direct economic impact of $324 million annually.[7] Blue mountains knife up from the ocean's edge, and fishermen operate bobbing craft perfumed by diesel and bait.

When a school of fish is sighted, boats jockey for space, crowding each other out, sometimes snagging nets in a rival's propeller—a difficult knot to cut loose in freezing waters. Much bad language and the occasional display of handguns have resulted.

TABLE 4-1

Essential characteristics of impact currencies

	Medium of exchange (easily traded for goods and services)	Store of value (capable of being saved and used for consumption in the future)	Unit of account (useful measuring stick)
Credits	• Credits and offsets are directly exchangeable for a fixed price per unit. • Points are redeemable for goods at a set exchange rate, e.g., 100 points = 1 gift earned.	• Credits generally are transferred through exchanges and can be redeemed any time.	• Individuals and institutions can easily compare their credits or offsets to their total consumption patterns (particularly energy consumption).
Social outcomes	• Organizations are willing to pay for specific social outcomes, and performance-based contracts require them to secure payment.	• Any inability to demonstrate strong social outcomes can diminish an organization's ability to secure impact investment (assuming there are competing organizations a funder can turn to).	• Multiple organizations seeking the same social objectives can be compared across standard criteria (e.g., GIIRS ratings).
Citizen capital	• Bartering and time banks offer ways to transfer capabilities and time among people.	• Time committed to a specific social purpose, if associated with a time bank or some form of register, may be redeemed for other goods or services.	• Hours volunteered and the measures of the reach of one's contributions (e.g., fed 200 people, taught 30 students) can be used to benchmark and compare various volunteer efforts.

(continued)

TABLE 4-1 (continued)

	Medium of exchange (easily traded for goods and services)	Store of value (capable of being saved and used for consumption in the future)	Unit of account (useful measuring stick)
Data	• Many partnerships entail data-sharing relationships. • By making data public, the government can generate better insights and solutions at less expense (competitions function similarly).	• Data appreciates in value when translated into meaningful information. • Data can be saved indefinitely, but data that grows stale diminishes in value unless it can be contrasted with more recent findings. • Individuals can subscribe to data streams, with legal protections for sharing certain data sets.	• Data can be measured easily by volume, accuracy, and other criteria.
Reputation	• The ability to transact relies on the parties' trust of one another; reputation may determine access to certain trading advantages and markets.	• Reputation is cumulative; appreciating or diminishing it will affect future prospects. • High ratings have enduring value and can attract other opportunities.	• Through ratings, reputation level can be compared across entities and may drive decisions of trading partners.

Bristol Bay is a classic *public good:* a finite resource everyone shares. In traditional economics, a market with limited supply encourages individuals to seize as much as possible. It's called the tragedy of the commons.[8] It's what depleted cod from the Grand Banks, the legendary Atlantic fishery, where resource managers now are struggling to bring the species back.[9]

Luckily, instead of fighting one another for salmon, Bristol Bay's fishermen can use the fish as a currency, in the form of individual, transferable quotas—a nonmaterial representation of a public good, in this case a food source. The fishermen thereby have some control in the event of any disruption to the supply of the underlying physical goods. This liberates the market from fears of hoarding and the tragedy of the commons, because everyone's fair take is negotiated before the boats even leave dock.

For any market to function well, of course, an independent party must manage the exchange and set rules. The Alaska Department of Fish and Game maintains Bristol Bay's elegant system: each year, after scientists estimate the number of fish the bay can yield sustainably, the department divides the season's catch into quotas. Each licensed crew receives a quota for tons of fish and can sell it to other fishermen, allowing some to hedge against bad luck while letting others buy enough quota permits to exploit a big haul.

This quota market is just one example of how the public sector can take a public good, which by definition fits awkwardly into market economics—how do you devise and trade a unit of wildlife sustainability?—and, with care and attention, create a viable market. Innovations such as data analytics and pay for success, which will be discussed in the next chapter, allow participants to trade contributions to the public welfare, applying market forces to the task of creating valuable if sometimes intangible public wealth. The idea, again, is to create *currencies* out of public value, or at least the behaviors we believe will further the goal.

In Alaska's case, Nobel Prize–winning economist Elinor Ostrom and her husband Vincent had a profound impact. Vincent advised the

Sizing the Currencies

CARBON CREDITS

The size of the global carbon credit market was estimated to be $176 billion in 2011.

drafting of Alaska's state constitution—particularly the passage saying that natural resources belong to the citizens, not the government.[10] He writes that goods need three qualities to survive in public trading: they must be *excludable* (not available to all), *qualifiable,* and *quantifiable.*[11] In other words, they must have qualities that can be measured, valued, and traded.

But trading quotas as a currency are not always straightforward. While carbon emissions trading, for example, is based on the same kind of quota trading as the Alaskan salmon quotas, the complexities involved are more challenging.

In the cap-and-trade system of carbon emission trading, environmental regulators allocate the right to use a resource (net carbon emissions) to industry participants. In any given year, for instance, regulators might allocate one thousand tons of carbon emissions to the power company GenCo, and GenCo would be required to buy additional emission credits on the open market if it exceeds its quota. This encourages GenCo to develop low-emission power sources, reducing the total amount of carbon in the atmosphere. Regulators may reduce total allocations over time, driving further carbon reductions. As with Alaskan salmon, the objective is to maintain a sustainable impact.

In the United States, this sort of cap-and-trade regime proved highly effective against emissions of sulfur dioxide, one of the main chemicals that causes acid rain.[12] The effort to limit carbon, however, has been much more problematic. Regulators have found it difficult to estimate exactly how much carbon is produced, and how much would be produced to allow for economic growth. And modern society has so many carbon sources that the sort of monitoring equipment used in acid-rain reduction would be administratively burdensome and cost-prohibitive.

In addition, there is no real agreement on just how much carbon the climate can sustain in a given year. There is only general agreement on carbon's effects over the next century or more. Carbon has proven difficult to definitively exclude, qualify, and quantify; it's a big problem with a maze of unknowns.

With data analytics, however, scientists can better gauge the impacts on the larger ecosystem. Consider the carbon emitted by the nation's electrical generation. Thousands of power plants generate electricity every day, fueled by hydrocarbons such as coal and natural gas and by alternative sources, including nuclear, hydroelectric, wind, and solar power. The grid delivers electricity from these plants to homes at nearly the speed of light, and once the electricity is on the grid, its source is physically impossible to trace. Tracking some carbon emissions from their point of consumption to their origin, then, is extremely challenging.

Increasingly, however, public and private organizations wish to share their carbon consumption information with their stakeholders. That's where analytics come in. To make this information easier to obtain and share, the US Environmental Protection Agency has created eGRID, an analytical tool that estimates just how much carbon is emitted in a section of the grid. eGRID forms the basis for generally accepted carbon accounting protocols.[13] Most organizations use eGRID to report their *Scope 2 emissions*—indirect emissions from power consumption. The ability to measure these effects makes it possible for companies to pay directly for their carbon footprints through renewable-energy certificates (RECs), often called offsets.

Whole Foods Market, for instance, offsets 106 percent of its carbon emissions through a combination of on-site power generation and RECs purchased from the third-party broker 3Degrees. Kohl's department stores, the city of Austin, HSBC North America, Carnegie

Mellon University, and many other organizations also offset 100 percent or more of their carbon emissions. A public good thus becomes private, available for use as a currency in a free market.[14]

While government has minted various types of environmental impact currencies—emissions permits, carbon offsets, and renewable-energy credits—market forces drive and determine their value, creating constraints and incentives that drive innovation.

Social Impact: Putting a Value on Solutions to Society's Problems

Within three short years of writing the code that would become eBay's DNA, Pierre Omidyar found himself standing on the trading floor of Goldman Sachs, watching the price for shares in his company triple. He now, really and truly, had more money than he knew what to do with. As with many successful entrepreneurs, it sparked thoughts of philanthropy.[15]

Rather than a traditional family trust or foundation, Omidyar chose an innovative approach to fuel social good: a hybrid limited liability corporation and 501(c3). This would allow Omidyar Network (ON) to invest in both nonprofits and for-profits, choosing the organizations that create the most significant social outcomes.[16] The foundation issues grants and loans, committing more than $442 million to date, and also runs equity deals as a venture capital firm would, depending on what makes the most sense for a specific fledgling enterprise. ON occupies a middle ground that welcomes constant collaboration with nonprofits, foundations, and blue-chip venture capital firms alike.

ON pursues social outcomes with *cascading* impacts that alter the underlying causes of problems. This is far more challenging than buying textbooks or medicine, which produce immediate but generally modest social returns. ON directs its investments to organizations that tackle complex, societal challenges in an unprecedented way, offering the potential to scale their innovations. How the organizations deliver on their goals is left to the ingenuity of individual social entrepreneurs.

"From our office in San Francisco," says Amy Klements, a vice president at Omidyar, "we can't identify the solutions that will be most impactful in an entrepreneur's community and others like his. The entrepreneur has often seen the challenges firsthand in their full complexity."[17]

ON can take its hands-off approach because it funds measurable outcomes rather than strategies. Measurable improvements, then, become a currency that these innovative organizations can offer to investors.

When ON was founded in 2004, much of the philanthropy community was unfamiliar with the notion of impact investing. Only a handful of organizations supplied critical, early-stage investments to social entrepreneurs. These included now widely known organizations such as Root Capital, Acumen, Skoll Foundation, Ashoka, and Echoing Green, one of the field's earliest pioneers.

"We don't have the financial return on investment to hang our hats on that a for-profit might have, culminating in a big exit, an IPO or acquisition," says Cheryl Dorsey, Echoing Green CEO.[18] So outcomes are the currency here, a yardstick by which an enterprise proves its effectiveness.

One of Omidyar's investments, d.light, has a unique approach to the health problems of developing nations, offering small, affordable solar lanterns.

"One in four families in the world lacks access to electric light," explains Omidyar. "The main alternative is kerosene, but many people can't afford it—and it is harmful to both health and the environment."[19]

The UK Health Protection Agency, for instance, says kerosene "may cause serious lung injury," while The World Bank reports that with poor ventilation, living with this kind of lighting is as bad for health as smoking two packs of cigarettes a day.[20] Kerosene is also a powerful accelerant, likely to start disastrous fires.

Sam Goldman, cofounder of d.light, recognized that the social impact of a cheap solar-powered lamp could be huge. Omidyar agreed and connected Goldman with development behemoth BRAC, which is based in Bangladesh and committed to a massive distribution of solar lanterns. By the end of 2015, d.light hopes its lanterns will have reached fifty million people worldwide. In this case, as with many others, ON was directly involved with significantly upping the impact of a social entrepreneur's innovative idea by initiating a valuable partnership, to the benefit of all involved.[21]

Social entrepreneurs develop solutions. But placing a value on solutions calls for an entirely new sort of accounting. The social enterprise KaBOOM!, for instance, which addresses "play deserts," where children lack access to safe play spaces, measures its impact in the number of playgrounds it builds—nineteen hundred by 2010.[22] Similarly, proponents of a bond project in Birmingham, England, weighed the costs and benefits of providing access to physical activity sessions for 1.1 million city citizens through an initiative called BeActive. They concluded that health-care savings, improvements in quality of life, and productivity gains associated with the program would exceed its costs by £445.2 million.[23]

Outcome measurement also helps organizations push themselves. Increasingly, organizations are investing in monitoring and evaluation schemes to ensure that their efforts attain the desired impact. For Jigar Shah, founder of the solar energy start-up Sun Edison, the important quantity is one gigaton: the amount of annual reduction in carbon emissions needed to stabilize climate change.[24]

Something about this figure clicked with Shah. "Someone had finally made a measure of what it took to make a difference . . . [I]t was either, you are growing this fast and you're getting to that end point, or you're not," he says. "If you're not, you're failing. If you are, you're succeeding."[25]

Shah joined Richard Branson's Carbon War Room, where the benchmark is to attract enough investment in renewable energy to reduce emissions by at least five billion tons of carbon dioxide annually.[26] The effort literally translates emissions benchmarks into investment dollars. Shah's ultimate goal is a *trillion dollars* in annual renewable-energy investment, up from the $260 billion invested in the sector in 2012.[27]

Throughout the solution economy, wavemakers such as Shah are setting real-world objectives to track their progress. To satisfy them, an entirely new branch of consulting has emerged that specializes in measuring *social return on investment* (SROI). Just as shareholders rely on risk ratings and metrics to determine whether returns justify owning a specific stock, SROI investors want unbiased third parties to help them identify promising areas for investment. Since its 2010 debut, the Global Impact Investment Rating System (GIIRS) has rated hundreds of companies and funds and now routinely evaluates more than $4 billion in assets annually.[28] (Disclosure: Deloitte is a founding partner of GIIRS.)

Citizen Capital: Converting Citizen Efforts from a Resource to a Currency

Jason Roberts, one of the founders of the Better Block project, believes he has a new template for municipal improvements. Without help from the government, Roberts and citizens across the nation are digitally organizing and building better blocks, turning lines of abandoned storefronts into pedestrian-friendly corridors where small businesses and community life can flourish.

Better Block started with a little impatience and a lot of raw energy. After experiencing the buzzing plazas and boulevards in Europe, Roberts, an IT consultant living in the Oak Cliff neighborhood of Dallas, returned home to contemplate a different kind of urban space. Many storefronts were abandoned, and cars rather than people dominated the streets.[29]

Instead of petitioning city officials and waiting for help, Roberts started his own initiative—swift and conspicuously unsanctioned community action. He began by looking for vacant buildings to fix up. A little research found old, cost-prohibitive ordinances and zoning rules, such as a ban on awnings and $1,000 fees for outdoor café seating. After identifying a series of these restrictive rules, Roberts and a group of other community activists picked a weekend to break all of them.

They assembled neighbors, artists, and potential business owners to reclaim the public space on a block and to pilot new storefront concepts, setting up shops and art galleries in abandoned buildings, bringing in outdoor seating and painting bike lanes on the streets. Then they posted on building windows all the rules they were breaking. Using social media, they got the neighborhood buzzing and invited city staff and council members to attend the block party. Attendees were startled to learn that most of the improvements made were illegal.

Many of the arcane rules changed. One of the pop-up businesses, an art studio, set up shop permanently. Other entrepreneurs snapped up vacant storefronts.[30]

"It helps the city demonstrate how they can make a difference quickly," Roberts said after a Better Block project in San Antonio. "Sometimes these ideas and concepts we put out here are abstract to folks until you actually build the connection. They can touch it; they can feel it; they can experience it."[31]

Robert's efforts show the potential of ordinary people. They possess untapped stores of creativity, energy, and enthusiasm. They can bypass government and NGOs entirely, directly helping each other and their communities.

Of course, there are only so many individuals willing to dedicate their Saturday mornings to volunteering for public benefit. For the rest, incentive schemes can offer a personal benefit in exchange for their efforts.

Recyclebank's point system led populations previously uninspired by recycling campaigns to make the extra effort. As discussed earlier, crowdsourcing models often engage citizens with point systems and badges that yield rewards, as do competitions, discussed later in the book. In Manor, Texas, residents earn "innobucks" when they submit or comment on community-improving ideas. The innobucks can then be redeemed for local rewards such as dinner with the mayor.[32]

Incentive schemes can transform citizens' time into a tradable commodity and another important category of impact currency. *Time banks* are a powerful example, allowing idled workers to trade their own efforts directly with others. Time banks allow people to volunteer their skills—tutoring English, say, or fixing a sink—in exchange for time-dollars. An hour's worth of time-dollars can be redeemed for an hour of another member's time. There are more than three hundred time banks in the United States and the United Kingdom, with memberships in the thousands. An additional hundred thousand members are enrolled in thirty-four other countries.[33]

The internet eliminates a number of constraints to human collaboration—such as the requirement that collaborators reside on the same continent. The US State Department, for example, for two centuries has housed civil servants in remote locations at a considerable price. Through its Virtual Student Foreign Service (VSFS) program, however, interns do the work once reserved for salaried career workers—work for which creative students may be better suited than desk-bound diplomats. Instead of an official foreign or domestic office, the intern's place of work is a college library, a coffee shop, or wherever else the student likes to go online. By diverting work from State Department employees, the VSFS program's 177 projects could save sixty-eight thousand work-hours, or more than $1.7 million in salaries, annually.[34]

Citizen action is powerful. In countries where volunteerism is culturally encouraged, such as the United States and New Zealand, 40 percent of the population reports volunteering time to some cause at least once a month.[35] The overall impact is significant: including volunteer time in employment figures for the nonprofit sector boosts its size by 10 percent in Western Europe and 3 percent in Latin America.[36] Volunteers contributed a whopping $63 billion worth of work annually to the thirty-six developing and developed countries surveyed by Johns Hopkins University, on par with the global sporting goods industry.[37]

Many factors can stimulate volunteer manpower. One is the use of open data. The Better Block project releases all of its project plans and strategies for other cities to adopt. Free information allows volunteerism to go viral and evolve swiftly, adapting from each iteration's mistakes and successes.

The US Agency for International Development (USAID) used a similar model when confronted with inconsistencies in its loan information for developing nations. The agency decided to crowdsource the task of cleansing its data. It contacted volunteers with Standby Task Force, a group that standardizes and collects data for aid agencies during disasters, and GIS Corps, a volunteer group of professionals who work with geographic information systems (GIS). Each volunteer manipulated data from which personal information had been stripped. USAID offered a narrow set of tasks, keeping the work process clear and efficient. In twenty-six hours, about 150 volunteers processed more than ten thousand records to create a simple dataset. USAID had budgeted sixty hours for the task.

"The records that were given to volunteers were records that we could not automate," says Shadrock Roberts of USAID. "This means that they contained some of the most difficult, confusing, and partial geocoded data of the whole set."[38]

With the clean data, USAID built an interface that entrepreneurs from developing countries could use to find nearby loan opportunities. Americans could also use the interface, to see the impact of their aid. And the volunteers, perhaps for the first time in their lives, felt it was truly *their* government. With USAID's invitation, they had created a force, a currency with real economic value, offering the chance to improve the lives of others. They tapped into technology to amplify their voices and volunteered their time to create a social impact. As one member of the crowd put it, "I haven't felt like this since the soup kitchens and food drives I used to do in college. I love this."[39] Looking ahead, the success of citizen capital rests in the ability of wavemakers to motivate even the talented individuals who are not the typical volunteering kind—who are not the typical soup-kitchen helper—to contribute their skills to public-value-boosting projects.

Datapalooza: When Information Pays

It's early Thursday morning. On stage is Todd Park, then chief technology officer for the US Department of Health and Human Services (HHS). Park is exuberant. "The goal is to catalyze the development of an ecosystem," he says, "an ecosystem that leverages data to improve health."[40]

Eleven universities are hosting viewing parties: yes, college students are gathering—college students, awake in the morning—to watch a bureaucrat speak.[41] People worldwide are streaming the video live. "America is giving you billions and billions of dollars of data for free," says Park. He means government data, like the kind that launched a $90 billion global positioning system (GPS) industry.[42] Data is the new top dollar. As he closes, the audience launches into a standing ovation.

Welcome to Health Datapalooza, a celebration of organized information. Having recently released troves of data, HHS is using the event to debut some of the best web and smartphone apps driven by open government data.[43]

One app, designed by Silicon Valley–based Palantir, matches patients to clinical trials. Another from the University of Rochester overlays Centers for Disease Control and Prevention data on the incidence of disease and related tweets on a map to track the spread of illness. A similar solution traces the path of a recent salmonella outbreak. Maya Designs, winner of a "code-a-thon," used the US Department of Agriculture (USDA) Food Environment Atlas to highlight sources of cheap vegetables in America's *food deserts*, areas lacking supermarkets or large grocery stores.[44]

Each program, if successful, promises to save or improve lives. Health-care data could add billions annually to the nation's economy, says Park, and he wants to attract more innovators to use it. As founder of successful start-ups Athenahealth and Castlight Health, he knows an opportunity when he sees one. Similar Datapalooza events have focused on energy and environmental innovation, demonstrating the potential value of free government data in those sectors as well.[45]

A generation ago, mounds of government data sat in file cabinets, tucked away from all but a few government officials. At best, governments produced prepackaged statistical reports—and charged user fees for special data runs.

Not all government data is digitized yet, but a growing movement seeks to change that. Just look at what happened in the 1980s, when the government released GIS data. The release fueled an industry that now includes over thirty million monthly Google Maps users, as well as a GPS market that has grown by 26 percent annually in recent years.[46] GIS data has transformed daily life for many citizens, simplifying travel and saving the time they used to spend muddling through glove compartments for maps. And GIS can be joined with complementary and cross-sector data to groundbreaking effect.

When a 2010 earthquake wreaked havoc in Haiti, for instance, response teams needed maps. Soon, the default tool for search-and-rescue teams was an open, crowdsourced application developed by the NGOs Ushahidi and Humanitarian Open Street Map. More than six hundred volunteers traced roads and encampments from aerial images into a computer program. They mapped data from The World Bank, Yahoo!, and Japan's space agency. In support, the US military released P3 and GlobalHawk imagery.[47]

Search-and-rescue groups could read the resulting maps from handheld GPS units. In the evolving disaster area, the map's crowdsourced markers identified resources such as refugee camps and cholera response centers. Multiple nations, NGOs, volunteers, and ordinary Haitian citizens came together in an unprecedented way, sharing information to save lives.

Take another example, the evacuation of parts of New York City during Hurricane Irene in 2011. New Yorkers flooded New York City's website seeking evacuation maps, browning out its servers. Luckily, the city had been sharing that information for more than a year. The *New York Times,* Google, and other organizations built evacuation maps from the city data—beautiful, interactive, and cross-referenced maps—in essence, doing the city's job with the city's help. "As long as the right information is getting to citizens, that's all that matters," says Rachel Stern, New York City's chief digital officer.[48]

Enterprising citizens can build real-world solutions out of data. Data from sources as disparate as crime records, reports of power outages, and personal accounts of corruption all tell a story to those who can translate it. The possible uses for government data far exceed what even the best government agencies can devise on their own. Making such data public taps the power of vast networks of capable groups and individuals.

Since the arrival of the internet, organizations such as the Sunlight Foundation and Transparency International have pushed governments to provide data online. At least sixteen national governments have major open-data initiatives. More than a million government datasets are now available worldwide, compared with just a couple of dozen a few years ago. From Australia to Kenya, from Denmark to Canada, open-data projects are under way at all levels of government.[49]

Norway, for instance, has created a searchable forum for data called the Open Data Hotel, which allows any person to upload any data to an exchange accessible to anyone with a computer.[50] The World Bank has released more than two thousand economic and societal indicators. Extensive open-data initiatives by the United Nations and OECD followed. These open-data efforts are becoming so widespread, countries that refuse to share their data arouse immediate suspicion.

To really see transparency in decision making, though, we need to hop across the equator. New Zealand updated its Police Act by posting the bill as an online wiki, inviting citizens to edit the law as they saw fit. Government employees monitored the edits for ideas before presenting them to parliament. The exercise showed that data exchange is multidirectional: governments share data with entrepreneurs and citizens, but citizens can share it back, improving government responsiveness.[51]

Of course, the power of massive data isn't available to everyone. The messier the data—the more multifaceted and larger the footprint—the bigger the data divide between power users and the average citizen.

This became particularly apparent during the Bhoomi project in the southern Indian state of Karnataka, which started an ambitious, groundbreaking initiative to digitize twenty million land titles. Masses of information became available, but the population that could actually use it was limited to a wealthy, opportunistic subset that could afford lawyers to challenge land titles and contest gaps in records of property ownership. The concept backfired, calling attention to the need for careful forethought before the release of government data.[52]

To make government data more widely available in the United States, on his first day in office President Barack Obama signed the Memorandum on Transparency and Open Government. The memorandum ordered federal agencies to make their mountains of data available to the public through open application programming interfaces (APIs).[53] An open API stores government data in a format that any programmer can use and develop, paving the way for dynamic enterprises that organize public data for social good. "A new generation doesn't see government as a problem of ossified institutions, but as a problem of collective action," says Jennifer Pahlka, founder of an organization called Code for America.[54]

Pahlka calls her organization a "Peace Corps for geeks." It hires midcareer software developers and embeds them with city governments, where they use their creative skills in partnerships with city managers.

Most Code for America applicants took drastic salary cuts to participate. The popularity of the program (362 applicants for the first twenty spots) proves that geeks *will* sacrifice cash for communities—if they believe they'll make an impact.[56] It's how Park ended up at HHS. It's an element of start-up culture that governments can adopt: win the best talent, not with salaries but with creative opportunity and openness to new approaches. It may not be an easy shift for change-averse agencies, but the growing host of success stories offers compelling motivations for a culture adjustment.

"This suggests how government could work better," says Pahlka. "Not more like a private company, not more like a tech company, but more like the internet itself. That means permissionless, open, and generative."[55]

One Code for America fellow in Boston noticed that homeowners shoveled snow from their sidewalks but left fire hydrants buried. This led to Boston's Adopt-a-Hydrant app, which allows citizens to commit to clearing snow from a fire hydrant, to keep it clear for fire department access. Because Code for America's programs are open source, other cities have adapted the app; Honolulu uses it to have citizens commit to checking batteries on its tsunami warning system, Seattle to clear storm drains, and Chicago to organize volunteer snow shoveling. At least five other cities are investigating uses for the app.

These shared algorithms are a kind of currency themselves, because they save municipalities the cost of coding from scratch. They also hand citizens responsibility for their communities. "It's not hard

Sizing the Currencies

OPEN DATA

In the United Kingdom, the value of public sector information was estimated to be £1.6 billion for producers and direct users of data in 2012.

to do things together," says Pahlka. "You just have to architect the systems the right way."[57]

Citizen coding began with city-hosted hack-a-thons to produce fixes for local government. Code for America represents its institutionalization on a nationwide scale. Governments are realizing that given the right data, citizens can produce valuable resources.

After all, as Pahlka puts it, "every point doesn't have to go back to the center, to government. If government can instead serve to increase peer-to-peer—people helping each other—then we can have more innovative services and services that can scale."

This is the power of open data, a vital twenty-first-century currency. And when government unlocks its databanks, shared information drives collective and sometimes *massive* action.

Reputation: Banking on Your Brand

Throughout history, individuals have banked on their reputations to advance their positions in society. For centuries, a connection with the right family was the best way to ensure a reputation and the influence accompanying it. The wealthy but lower-class tradesman seeking marriage with a daughter from a high-born but impoverished family was commonplace in nineteenth-century British novels—and real life.

The emergence of formal, written contracts for loans and other simple transactions is a relatively new phenomenon. In many areas of the developing world, reputation is still the only thing that counts in business. And even with all the legal trappings of a modern economy, reputation continues to be a powerful currency.[58]

Reputations can be built in many ways. In the developed world, it might be through signifiers: a prestigious college degree, a job with a top firm, a house in an affluent neighborhood. But today, for the millions who don't live in that world, reputation can be built—and used—in novel and inventive ways.

The proliferation of microloans and mobile banking, for instance, is helping many of the world's poorest build and trade on a good reputation. Consider Kiva Zip, an experimental initiative run by Kiva, one of the world's largest and most innovative microlending platforms. Standard Kiva loans involve a microfinance institution that acts as an intermediary. Through the Kiva Zip program, however, investors can offer zero-interest loans directly to an individual on the basis of the recommendation of a "trustee," an on-the-ground partner selected and trained by Kiva.[59]

The trustee's endorsement is fully transparent and posted for review by any potential investor. Perhaps a university dean endorses a top design student, or an association leader verifies an entrepreneur's capabilities. Others may comment on the posting, which can help or hurt the fledgling enterprise, as with reviews posted on Skillshare, Yelp, or Etsy. Programs such as these facilitate the exchange of reputation for real dollars.

Kiva president, Premal Shah, is optimistic that Kiva Zip can offer a viable alternative to conventional credit scores, extending resources to those previously considered unbankable: "Microfinance is meant for the edges of the banking world. Kiva Zip is on the edges of Kiva."[60]

Some economists argue that reputation is less a currency than a form of social capital, because the standings of both trading partners intertwine. If a Kiva Zip trustee vouches for someone who defaults, both reputations suffer. A reputation's value thus fluctuates with performance.

But the losses are not in equal terms: while the borrower's loss may be predominantly financial, the reputational hit may be larger for the endorser. Indeed, the loss of credibility may be as great a blow as any financial loss. This risk explains the conservative stance of many large institutions, which often avoid involvement in riskier ventures, to the detriment of innovative approaches.

Fortunately, these risks can be shared. Just as multiple banks may underwrite an initial public stock offering for both financial and reputational reasons, public-private partnerships and crowdfunding reduce the risk of financial and reputational failure for individual sponsors.

New technology, moreover, is making it easier to quantify reputation. While any single individual's endorsement may carry little weight, popular sentiment in the aggregate, whether through Yelp ratings of local businesses or user reviews on Amazon.com, offers powerful architecture that can support a business better than the most carefully conceived marketing campaign.

To test that structure, the field of *sentiment analysis* has exploded with the emergence of social media. Millions of consumers now voice their views on companies, positive or negative, and in turn influence others. Negative reviews that appear via a common Google search or a wave of caustic tweets can have devastating effects on an organization's reputation. Ratings extend the reach of an individual's opinion beyond a circle of friends to anyone with a computer. And consumers increasingly realize that *each purchase is a vote.*

Successful branding efforts now speak less to actual products and more to core traits that the company—and its consumers—want to embody. Starbucks knows that it's selling comfort as well as coffee. Starbucks CEO Howard Schultz says that customers want "the romance of the coffee experience, the feeling of warmth and community people get in Starbucks stores."[61] Nike's Phil Knight famously argued that Nike's goal was to "enhance people's lives through sports and fitness," not just to produce shoes.[62] Companies that translate lofty aspirations into an elevated consumer experience can benefit from higher premiums and stronger brand loyalty.

For consumers, a product can be an expression of self and a reflection of values, from yuppies toting biodegradable diapers to kombucha-swilling hipsters in thrift-store threads. Purchases are published on Facebook walls and hash-tagged on Instagram, and support for causes is carefully curated across a person's public persona. A parallel exchange shadows each transaction. Transactions that once exchanged money for status symbols now trade in a new status entirely: social value. Companies such as American Apparel (which offers American-made, sweatshop-free clothing) and Origins capitalize on their customers' desire to maximize social good alongside private utility.

New Currencies in Action: A Solution to Developing-World Waste Management

Selling investors on a radically new approach to waste disposal, one that serves impoverished regions where garbage heaps are common, is no easy feat. It's a messy business, rife with health and environmental risks. Obtaining the necessary resources to transform waste disposal, then, requires the utmost resourcefulness. The currencies of reputation, social outcomes, and credit trading can become partial substitutes for capital, creating a basis for relationships and transactions that launch the new model.

No one knows this better than social entrepreneur Parag Gupta, who is using every variety of currency at his disposal to turn India's trash into a social treasure, improving public health and the economy in the process. While working with top social entrepreneurs at the Schwab Foundation and the World Economic Forum, Gupta noticed something conspicuously missing from most social enterprises: scale. The deep-rooted challenges they address affect millions, yet most enterprises served only a handful of communities. Aside from microfinance, few solutions were being replicated across countries. Gupta began seeking to combine a common social issue with a business model designed from the outset to be scalable. Extensive due diligence pointed to one big issue facing the least developed countries: trash.

"When one looked at solid waste management as a whole, it was a tremendous issue that had to be dealt with, both in terms of the health and environmental issues locally but also with regards to climate change," says Gupta.[63]

Gupta chose to test his innovative business model, Waste Ventures, in India, where governments and contractors collect only half of the forty million tons of garbage its cities produce each year. The rest falls to an informal economy of 1.5 million rag pickers, who collect and sift the trash and sell anything remotely reusable, down to reasonably fresh bits of food.[64] A 2010 estimate indicated that 15 million people around the world depended on waste picking for their livelihoods.[65]

Waste picking provides some income to those who desperately need it and subsidizes cities that pay nothing for the service. But it's a brutal way to make a living. Pickers spend their days sorting through garbage in massive landfills that reek of methane. The workers make about $1.50 a day, barely enough for food and water. Many youths forget their empty stomachs and empty lives by inhaling shoe polish or turpentine. Their parents have life expectancies of forty-five. Often, the pickers' only direct interaction with government takes the form of brutal police beatings. And despite the cruel efficiency of the system, much of India's trash still doesn't get cleaned up.[66]

As Gupta researched waste management organizations, in collaboration with the Wharton and Harvard business schools, he was surprised to see hardly any focus on end-to-end solutions for waste removal. Some organizations had scaled composting, others recycling, and most focused on the human rights of the pickers, but few did more than one thing really well. Organizational nearsightedness was keeping profits low and prospects for scaling even lower. Gupta started Waste Ventures to change that.

Social Outcomes as Start-Up Capital

Waste Ventures used start-up capital from foundations, social-impact investors, and the Swedish International Development Agency to help pickers form waste management corporations that, with the right training, can use technology and best practices to harvest as much value as possible from trash. Rather than scrambling over dangerous garbage heaps, pickers collect refuse daily from households in a practice that improves both safety and the ability to compost and recycle. This model allows Waste Ventures to deliver social improvements in the picker's livelihoods and health, the environment, and the municipal sanitation system all at once.

The enterprise holds itself accountable to, and measures progress against, specific targets: triple a waste picker's daily earnings, cut waste accumulation by 80 percent, and reduce greenhouse gases that would otherwise be released. Tracking these social outcomes is essential because, says Gupta, "it's linked to our financial well-being as a business."[67] Such measures of success point to a sector-wide shift toward safe, inclusive, and profitable waste management. For many impact investors, that progress is well worth the investment.

Reputational Advantage

By Gupta's own account, he could not shape this sector-wide shift on his own. Breaking into unfamiliar territory as a brand-new social enterprise would have been significantly more challenging without the extensive network Gupta had established long before founding Waste Ventures. His reputation offered a currency of its own, opening doors to new partnerships, mentors, and experts in the field.

In India, it quickly became apparent that acting in isolation would be the quickest path to failure. Instead, Waste Ventures built corporations based on existing groups of pickers, often formed by local NGOs. These NGOs also proved to be critical allies in engaging communities and keeping a trained eye out for corruption, a rampant problem in India.[68] For Gupta, the time invested in understanding the local environment and building critical relationships is inherently productive. It builds trust and paves the way for future agreements essential to scaling.

Credits for the Environment and the Bottom Line

The Waste Ventures approach offers more-immediate dividends as well. Pooling compost made pickers eligible for carbon credits, opening new income streams. Now, besides selling recyclables, waste-picker corporations can offer composted biofertilizer and carbon credits.[69] When combined with the $1 monthly fees charged to households for daily trash collection, Waste Ventures' corporations are four times more profitable than alternative methods for waste collection in the region.[70]

The environmental effects are also dramatically better, reducing methane gas—a greenhouse gas twenty-three times more harmful than carbon dioxide—which otherwise festers in towering trash heaps. Worker life expectancy, as forecasted according to sick days and reported disease incidence, continues to improve, as does workers' pay, which has already doubled and is on target to triple.[71]

Beyond Measuring Expenditures

Throughout this chapter, we have shown how the solution economy engenders new ways to measure public value. Public data can be harvested and shaped into products that create real value. The time and talent that citizens bring to public challenges offer tangible benefits that can be measured and even traded. Social entrepreneurs are addressing stubborn problems sustainably and are building enterprises that create tangible value at the bottom of the pyramid. Even the biggest corporations have discovered the advantage of reputation that comes from public acts of goodwill. Benefits once vaguely viewed as valuable now carry increasingly quantifiable, shareable worth.

In this multidimensional environment, government is no longer the sole issuer of currency. Dollars, euros, and yen may dominate global capital markets, but a growing number of exchanges, to be discussed in chapter 5, spur wider adoption of these new currencies, encouraging citizens to transact in the resources at their disposal. A greater diversity of contributions means that more needs are met than whatever money—and big funders like government—alone can supply.

THE CURRENCIES: IN A NUTSHELL

THE BIG IDEA

To understand the solution economy, we need to entirely rethink currencies. Value creation and exchange are taking place in new ways. We are witnessing an explosion in the types of currencies in use—intangibles such as social outcomes or government data—as new approaches to measurement and exchange evolve. A growing host of wavemakers now deploys these vital inputs toward a wide array of productive uses, collaborating to help this new currency appreciate in value.

NEW CURRENCIES

- **Credits:** Investors can buy and trade credits, store wealth in credit form, and include the value of credits while tabulating net worth.

- **Social impact:** Sometimes the most important results of an endeavor are the hardest to measure: education improved or sickness avoided, for example. The more we quantify and reward value, the more resources we can attract and exchange toward solving a problem.

- **Citizen capital:** Citizen time can be transformed from a massive and growing public resource into a tradable commodity via mechanisms like time banks, microtasking, and game-based incentive structures.

- **Data:** In the right hands, data can produce billions of dollars in value. Governments are a prime source.

- **Reputation:** The value of reputation encourages corporations to contribute to public causes, because they know a brand translates into dollars. Meanwhile, social entrepreneurs can trade on their reputation to obtain needed resources.

THE NUMBERS

- Carbon credits trade in a $176 billion market.

- The Global Impact Investment Rating System routinely evaluates more than $4 billion in assets.

- Globally, people provide more than $1.3 trillion in volunteer services.

- More than one million government data sets have been opened up to the public in recent years.

SAMPLE TRADES IN IMPACT CURRENCIES

- Richard Branson's Carbon War Room invests dollars in renewable energy and yields reduced carbon emissions.

- The US government released GIS data, investing in an alternative currency that yielded a $70 billion GPS market.
- More than a hundred thousand ordinary people trade volunteer hours via time banks in thirty-four countries.
- Alaska's transferable fishing quotas allow fishermen to trade shares of a public good, much like carbon offsets.

NOTABLE "MINTS" OF NEW CURRENCIES

- Omidyar Network invests in outcomes—outcomes that it expects the entities it funds to produce.
- The US government is opening troves of data to those who can use it to produce public value.
- Code for America produces open code for trade, most of which helps harness and organize citizen volunteers.
- Kiva Zip allows informal reputation to replace a credit score, letting investors accept reputation as loan collateral.

CHALLENGES

As markets for these currencies evolve, participants must beware of currency manipulation. The early days of carbon credits were notorious for abuse.

QUESTIONS FOR THOUGHT

Had you ever considered the time of volunteers or the reputation of those you admire a form of currency? How might these currencies be leveraged and exchanged to build partnerships that bring value to your organization and the public?

FIVE

Public-Value Exchanges

New platforms that match capital to social need

Which of the following best assesses a student's critical-thinking skills and command of knowledge of a given subject?

a. A multiple-choice test

b. An essay

Everybody knows that option B is the correct answer. So why are high school students often asked to write just three essays per semester? Because of the high cost of grading them. When professional graders score essay portions of standardized tests, the price tag runs from $2 to $3 per essay.[1] Multiplied by millions of students, that's a hefty tab. Thus teachers make do with the less meaningful yardstick of multiple-choice tests because they're easier to grade.

Multiple-choice tests are a scalable form of assessment. Fill in the ovals with your number two pencil, and a computer can grade your test. But what if a computer could grade your essay just as well as your teacher could?

In spring 2012, the William and Flora Hewlett Foundation sponsored a $100,000 competition to find algorithms to replicate the scoring of human graders. It partnered with Kaggle to tap a global community of data scientists. Kaggle is a web-based exchange—a statistical/analytics platform that runs predictive-modeling competitions.

This competition began with scoring data. Kaggle provided the entrants with thousands of hand-scored essays from schools across the country. Competitors had three months to build a software engine to "read" and grade the essays, and the program best able to match the scores given by human experts would win the purse—and the bragging rights.

Ten years ago, nothing like Kaggle existed. The idea of a permanent virtual gathering of geeks pitting algorithms against one another to solve real-world problems was the stuff of cyberpunk. Today, it's a reality and a key part of the solution economy.

Kaggle is the brainchild of Anthony Goldbloom, who was a young Australian civil servant in 2007 when he entered an essay competition and won a three-month internship at *The Economist.* While working there, he became fascinated with big data and data mining. He had dealt with data analytics while working for the treasury in Australia, but thought little of it; at the time data analytics was just a way to predict abstract factors such as unemployment. At *The Economist,* however, he began to see its game-changing potential.

To Goldbloom, the potential of data analytics seemed nearly unlimited. But he noticed two things limiting its growth. First, even sophisticated companies found it difficult to assess the actual capabilities of data scientists, because their capabilities often had little to do with their grades or courses completed. Second, data scientists often lacked the data they needed to refine their techniques and test them against real-world outcomes.

After returning to Australia, Goldbloom taught himself to write code and launched Kaggle, kick-starting a global exchange of algorithms. Kaggle organizes competitions according to specific data problems, with the most accurate predictive model winning.

By the time Kaggle hosted its essay-scoring competition in 2012, the platform had grown to a user base of more than seventeen thousand data scientists from fields such as computer science, statistics, econometrics, math, and physics.[2] Competitions had already yielded improvements to various tasks, including the forecasting of travel times on Sydney highways and the creation of a genetic blueprint that predicted the progression of the HIV virus. One of Kaggle's most fascinating innovations was the competition itself, an enticement for thousands of data specialists worldwide to work on a single problem.

"If you're a lone traffic forecaster, you might try a few things and then stop," explains Goldbloom. "But the cut and thrust of a competition pushes data scientists to do better than they otherwise would."[3] Goldbloom also notes that entrants, hailing from unrelated disciplines, benefit from a lack of preconceptions. You don't have to figure out whether the geeky guy or gal trying something new is a little nutty or a genius; the results of the competition will tell you that.

One Kaggle competition sponsored by US, UK, and EU space agencies involved new algorithms to measure the way dark matter causes distortions in images of galaxies. Within a week of the competition's launch, a glaciologist from Cambridge University, Martin O'Leary, outstripped ten years of astronomical research by applying techniques used to map glaciers from satellite images to construct an algorithm that could map dark matter in space. Other competitors, including a pair of UC–Irvine astronomers who edged out O'Leary in the final stretch, eventually improved on his algorithm. Nevertheless, in deference to O'Leary's breakthrough, the White House announced that "the study of glaciers on Earth has now deepened our understanding of the cosmos."[4] The price tag for this truly astronomical breakthrough: $3,000.[5]

"One great thing about competitions is that [you] don't need to justify any experience in a specific field to enter," says Xavier Conort, an actuary based in Singapore. Conort improved credit scoring by accurately predicting individuals most at risk of financial distress two years before they file for bankruptcy. "Only my final result matters, so it's a great platform to learn new things."[6]

Kaggle's model attracts solvers with simple but effective game mechanics such as its global ranking system and real-time leaderboard. "It's hard to resist entering a competition when I see people I know at the top of a leaderboard," says Conort.

The key to Kaggle's success is the real-world factor. "I liked the problem because it's an interesting dataset, and a problem which comes down to a lot more than just number-crunching," says O'Leary, explaining why a glaciologist would enter a contest to score essays.[7]

Competition prompts collaboration. Wildly disparate groups are spurred to cross disciplinary boundaries, generating new insights. In any given competition, you might have quant gurus working with business experts, Russian physicists solving problems for the National Aeronautics and Space Administration (NASA), or a glaciologist like O'Leary studying syntax. Kaggle's exchange accelerates this sort of cross-fertilization, giving contest hosts inexpensive access to thousands of professionals and potentially saving months or years of R&D.

Sometimes the stakes can be relatively high. In the Heritage Health Prize, for instance, an HMO is offering a $3 million prize for an algorithm to help health-care providers reach patients before emergencies occur. Contestants use historical insurance claims data to identify patients destined for the hospital; the prize money will compensate for the intellectual property rights of the winning model. In this case, a $3 million investment could help capture some of the $30 billion wasted annually on unnecessary hospital admissions—and save thousands of lives.[8]

In the Hewlett Foundation's essay scoring battle, the $100,000 investment brought in many times that amount in resources applied to the problem, producing an astonishingly accurate algorithm that can closely predict the scores of a skilled human grader. Martin O'Leary placed sixth working solo—again, very close but just short. The prize instead went to a team including a data analyst for the National Weather Service, a British particle physicist, and a graduate student from Germany, none of whom had a background in education.

This exchange didn't involve a buyer and seller. It represents a new recipe: an algorithm exchange and virtual community that draw on new currencies such as data and reputation, with results that are a testament to the power of crowdsourcing.

New Models of Exchange

Kaggle's ability to engage data scientists across the globe demonstrates the powerful pull of two currencies discussed in chapter 4: data and reputation. Many companies and governments are awash in a sea of data. Contestants, by contrast, are *hungry* for data, and Kaggle offers them the real-world data sets they need to hone their edge. Through Kaggle, for-profit companies, nonprofits, and governments can outsource their data analysis, while contestants enjoy a free forum in which to build skills, exchange ideas, and test their products. In combination, they present an ideal example of an innovative twenty-first-century exchange.

As with Code for America (discussed previously), which persuades midcareer developers to accept lower salaries in return for creative license and citizen stripes, motivations extend beyond money. The thrill of the challenge, the ability to make a real difference in the world, and the bragging rights—not to mention job prospects—that come with success can be a bigger payoff than the prize money.

Unsurprisingly, new models of exchange are critical to the solution economy. They hold the secret to attracting capital of all types and from all sources and applying it effectively to societal problems at whatever scale is needed.

Advancements in web technologies allow people to connect with unprecedented ease. Today, a fifth of American relationships and 17 percent of marriages can be attributed to matchmaking sites such as eHarmony and Match.com.[9] A history buff in Montreal can bid on eBay for a piece of the Berlin Wall that's collecting dust in a garage in Munich. An investment banker in New York can use Catchafire, an eHarmony of sorts, matching skilled professionals with nonprofits, to find a volunteer opportunity with a nonprofit that needs help with market research.

Wikipedia, eBay, Facebook, and other platforms create communities of users and deep pools of shared information. Positive reactions from other users motivate further interaction, a key ingredient both for scaling virtual communities and for building the critical mass that keeps an exchange interesting. Savvy organizations recognize how people's social and transactional needs converge through online exchanges, and seek to cultivate both. As John Hagel and John Seely Brown explain, when participants in virtual communities connect and develop relationships, they can also create value for their hosts, a practice called "co-creation."[10] The LEGO Group, for instance, increasingly relies on its online fan base not only for ideas for new products but also for help with their design. Kaggle does the same through Kaggle Prospect, which lets organizations solicit ideas for producing value from their data from a community of experts. By encouraging people to share knowledge, networks such as Facebook and Twitter build trust among strangers, further nurturing a propensity for sharing.

"We're moving from passive consumers, to creators, to highly enabled collaborators," says author Rachel Botsman, who coined the term *collaborative consumption.*[11] Botsman points to the rapid evolution of the car market. As we noted earlier, in just ten years exchange models have altered the necessity for car ownership, yielding car-sharing platforms such as Zipcar, ridesharing platforms, and the newest exchange model, peer-to-peer car rental.

Exchanges provide mechanisms for the use of new, nonmonetary currencies. Catchafire trades intangibles such as expertise, while carbon exchanges trade specific environmental impacts and peer-to-peer systems trade reputation. Services such as Couchsurfing—which allows people to open their homes to travelers for free, through a platform based on their profile and reviews—are becoming as natural to many as booking a bed and breakfast. It turns out a lot of folks are happy to have strangers crash at their house, provided the visitors are the nice and hip and interesting sorts of people who have garnered good reviews on Couchsurfing. As one surfer told us, "Couchsurfing is the perfect marriage between technology and trust." The platform is self-sustaining—the more people who join the network and provide peer-to-peer feedback, the greater the site's impact and international reach.

In general, exchanges connect people with a need (for a ride, a place to crash, a problem solved, etc.) with someone who can meet that need and is willing to do so, for fun, profit, or sheer altruism. New models of exchange are finding innovative ways to move money and resources to the projects and individuals who need it most—and can generate the best outcomes (figure 5-1).

Many exchanges connect borrowers with nontraditional lenders. Crowdfunding a business may soon become as common as a loan from the bank. Supporters of crowdfunding exchanges such as Kickstarter invest to get early rewards and to show their appreciation of the project's intrinsic value. As of January 2013, more than eighty-three thousand projects had been launched on Kickstarter, with a success rate of

FIGURE 5-1

Public-value exchanges

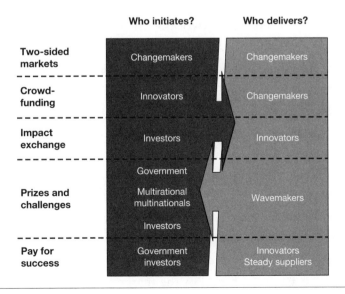

nearly 44 percent. These projects raised more than $464 million.[12] And the donations pass through another exchange, Amazon Payments.

In simple cases such as ridesharing and volunteerism, public-value exchanges can open vast new markets of citizen capital (time, talent, and tangible assets) that can be shared and traded to meet public needs while avoiding demands on the state. These new social exchanges have found their way into the commercial sector as well. The Johannesburg Stock Exchange, for example, runs the first socially responsible investment index in an emerging market, recognizing companies that meet environmental and social criteria.

From fixing neighborhood parks to addressing global infant mortality, new methods of pooling resources and directing investments to social issues are rapidly expanding.

Two-Sided Markets

For centuries, most businesses operated under some variation of the old manufacturing model: they built a product and sold it to a wholesaler, which sold it to a retailer, which in turn sold it to a consumer. Each transaction was a negotiation between a buyer and seller.

Recently, however, economists have begun noticing the emergence of *two-sided* markets and networks.[13] In these markets, an exchange connects two parties—as an Xbox connects avid gamers with game designers, Craigslist connects landlords with renters, and Airbnb connects beds with travelers.

Unlike a traditional sales transaction, the two-sided market links the creator and consumer directly and protects both. It attracts participants by providing protections and standardizing transactions, reducing the cost of structuring a deal each time.[14]

eBay, for instance, unites sellers and buyers. To ensure a minimum standard of service, eBay lets buyers rate users. To ease shopping, it offers an internal search function. Both of these attributes, quality and search, improve with a large user base: the more participants, the more valuable they are to each side of the market. A high volume of sellers increases your likelihood of finding that 1992 Eric Lindros rookie card, and more user ratings let you know which seller to trust. And if you realize it's a fake after it arrives? You have recourse through eBay customer support.

Successful two-sided markets tend to subsidize one side, giving the market a money side and a subsidy side. Search engines, for example, charge advertisers but not searchers.

With faster internet service and the ubiquity of mobile devices, two-sided networks are thriving. Ridesharing services, described earlier, epitomize these networks. Lyft, for example, offers a phone-based platform that enables users to geolocate nearby registered drivers and ask for, well, a lift. The company provides the platform; drivers and passengers share the cost of commuting. Drivers receive funds to offset their fuel cost and often gain access to high-speed high-occupancy-vehicle lanes. Passengers get safe, reliable transportation without the hassles of full car ownership. And the company that connects them gets a cut of the revenue.

"This shift in power to the consumer and citizens is not temporary or the product of faddish technology," writes Simon Mainwaring in his recent book *We First.* "It is clearly one of the most fundamental and enduring characteristics of the modern digital world, and it will influence how capitalism moves forward."[15]

Transportation is just one area in which two-sided markets can address a broader societal issue. Another is retraining people in an era of exponential technology change, in which skills quickly become obsolete. To address one of society's biggest challenges, governments spend huge amounts of money on retraining, but the results are unclear at best. In the United States, the General Accounting Office evaluated forty-seven job training programs, whose combined cost was $18 billion annually. The office noted that "only five programs have had an impact study completed since 2004 to assess whether outcomes resulted from the program and not some other cause."[16]

Job training schemes in Great Britain face similar criticism. According to the National Audit Office, the British government's new training programs are "underpinned by assumptions about likely performance, but there is a significant risk that they are over-optimistic."[17]

Two-sided networks pose a different solution: perhaps citizens could retrain *each other*. In the same way that ridesharing platforms connect drivers to passengers who need a ride, two-sided markets could connect those who can teach a skill to those who need it. Indeed, numerous start-ups are building exchanges for citizens who want to trade on their expertise.

Several peer-to-peer learning companies, including Skillshare, School of Everything, and TeachersPayTeachers, understand that the best person to teach a lesson is often someone who has just mastered it. SkillKindle, a Delhi-based start-up, marries the virtual world with in-person instruction.[18] SkillKindle classes, both in-person and via the internet, range from traditional academic subjects such as English as a second language to more contemporary pursuits such as writing code.

Avi Flombaum, a former chief technology officer of a small tech start-up in New York City, quit his day job to become a full-time Skillshare teacher, making $100,000 teaching in 2012.[19] His success illustrates the rising demand for tech talent and a new mechanism for delivering it. A programmer by trade, Flombaum notes that Skillshare offers a lot of tech-inspired classes precisely because the market demands them.[20]

Flombaum is proof that services such as Skillshare can fill a critical knowledge gap. "You cannot learn 'How To Start A Blog' in college," he says. "Anything that's tech, the education industry has really fallen behind on providing to people, so it just makes sense that Skillshare offers that."[21]

Of course, there are limits to these two-sided exchanges. Peer-to-peer training may train citizens but may fail to link unemployed workers with future careers. And today, it lacks the networking capabilities of traditional welfare-to-work training or apprenticeship programs.

These exchanges, however, are quickly growing in sophistication. Udacity, the online, open-source university cited in chapter 3, offers pupils the sort of career services once exclusive to physical institutions. It even offers an option to pass enrolled students' résumés to one of its twenty partner companies. While Udacity is not exactly a peer-to-peer platform, many of its features resemble those of Skillshare and SkillKindle, and it's not hard to imagine similar career services being offered to peer-to-peer participants in the near future. Platforms that specialize in high-demand skills are understandably ahead of the game, with recruiters pushing for early access to top talent. Students who take one of General Assembly's online and in-person tech courses can get reimbursed for the tuition costs if they join one of the partner companies.[22]

The public sector must think carefully about how it regulates this space, or risk citizen backlash. Already, regulators have been struggling to define how to manage new participants in two-sided economies such as Airbnb and Uber. The learning space, and job retraining in particular, is certain to face significant government scrutiny. Minnesota briefly prohibited colleges from offering unaccredited programs such as Coursera without first registering with a regulatory body. This prohibition lasted a day, before widespread citizen complaints about the outlawing of free online education forced the state to rescind the ruling.[23] While the regulatory instinct often is to provide safety nets for citizens in an informal economy, such reactions can hinder the success of potent two-sided marketplaces.

Crowdfunding

Let's say you read about a sustainable aquaculture farm that is bringing much-needed revenue and nutrition to a poor rural region. Previously, you've had little opportunity to invest, and you probably wouldn't feel comfortable sending money to someone five thousand miles away. But the microlending platform Kiva allows anyone with internet access and a little capital to fund ventures around the world. To date, more than 1.3 million Kiva users have shared nearly $400 million in loans for efforts in sixty-nine countries.[24]

Kiva does not itself manage or even prioritize among projects. It leaves those matters to the market it has created and then provides quality assurance. Field partners on the ground screen borrowers, whose loan history and records of repayment appear on the platform, providing transparency to lenders.

A diversified base of borrowers and small loan amounts make Kiva more comfortable serving regions that would unnerve more traditional establishments. Kiva president, Premal Shah, has noted that in postconflict zones such as Sierra Leone, high repayment rates on Kiva loans offer a "demonstration effect" to other organizations, showing that the region is more stable than previously thought.

Entrepreneurs without a prayer of finding nearby funders outside the local loan shark gravitate to platforms such as Kiva to raise capital directly from networks of supporters. This practice of crowdfunding connects social entrepreneurs to the potentially enormous impact of socially conscious citizens.

Crowdfunders have a more personal stake than do traditional investors, usually being motivated as much by social impacts as by economic returns—a clear demonstration of a new type of currency in action. As a consequence, these lenders often double as customers, beta-testers, focus groups, and informal marketers. Most crowdfunding begins with a "friend phase," drawing funding from people the entrepreneurs know and then strengthening these relationships.[25]

More Than Me, for example, began as an enterprise to employ and educate Liberian women after fourteen years of civil war.[26] The organization needed start-up capital. Founder Katie Meyler decided to pass on grant writing, in favor of making a direct appeal to her social network.

"I don't have the first clue how to raise money from big-time investors, but I know hundreds of people who believe in us," she explains.[27] Volunteers donated experience and time. One even drafted the organization's business plan. Instead of a single powerful benefactor, Meyler used a network of engaged benefactors and one powerful idea. Its network of supporters is More Than Me's strongest currency and the foundation of this model's success.[28]

A third party in crowdfunding is government, which sets the regulatory constraints. The 2012 Jumpstart Our Business Startups (JOBS) Act, for example, simplifies the US requirements for crowdfunding and standardizes rules nationwide. Under JOBS, cash-hungry ventures can solicit the public for early-stage equity financing, a previously illegal activity. The law also increases the number of shareholders that can invest in a company before triggering SEC reporting requirements. Under this provision, start-ups enjoy greater flexibility and more time to perfect their operations before entering public markets.

Crowdfunding sites cater to lenders' individual interests. Sellaband lets supporters buy a stake in a new music album, motivating them to promote it. Emphas.is crowdfunds photojournalistic investigations, freeing journalists from editorial restraints. Crowdrise, a philanthropic platform, makes it easy to tap social networks to sponsor a charity run or, in times of crisis, to channel money toward a community in need. ResearchGate lets scientists crowdfund research projects.

Michael Norman, cofounder of WeFunder, sees crowdfunding as an ideal way to fill the lag between fast-evolving citizen demands and steady government resources, noting that crowdfunding is perfect for "social enterprise models that have a very good chance of reaching sustainability and being a good business, but are never going to create that kind of home run that a VC needs to justify an investment." Because they focus on important social problems, "those companies also really access the excitement of the crowd."[29]

What's more, support networks are transferable. A blogger can transfer his or her network to a crowdfunded project simply by posting a link. Stephen Colbert calls the transfer of his educated fan base to a cause "the Colbert Bump." The Yellow Ribbon Fund received $350,000 after a few Colbert-led efforts to focus his network's attention on the charity, which helps wounded American soldiers. How is this different from traditional celebrity endorsements? The key is speed and scale. The *Chicago Tribune* estimates that Colbert's viewers raised $3.5 million for various causes between 2005 and 2011.[30]

At least fifty-six countries have crowdfunding exchanges.[31] Brazil's Catarse.me is crowdfunding an employment project for a slum in Rio de Janeiro. The Idea.me platform, which functions much like Kickstarter in Latin America, has just expanded from Argentina and Chile to Mexico.

The number of crowdfunding exchanges worldwide by 2013 was 536. That's a fivefold increase from 2007, representing significant volume: the industry raised $1.5 billion in 2011, funding more than a million initiatives. This total is likely to hit $3 billion in 2013.[32] And these numbers don't include NGO campaigns that also tap the philanthropic power of the crowd. Governments have also begun to get in the game with Philadelphia and other cities launching crowdfunding platforms to fund local projects like tree planting and park restoration.

But some of the early investors have witnessed enough to be wary, pointing to Kickstarter projects that in concept sound cool but take longer than expected to yield a final product, or perhaps never get off the ground. One study found that fully 75 percent of technology and design projects on the platform didn't finish on time.[33] Kickstarter doesn't take this criticism lightly. To prevent investors from defecting, Kickstarter requires project creators to refund investors in the event of a nonperforming project.

The next innovations may combine crowdfunding with other forms of crowdsourcing such as crowd voting and crowd labor. In Washington, DC, Popularise invites locals to vote on new uses for dilapidated buildings, allowing developers and site planners to learn what nearby residents prefer. "Popularise is the 21st-century version of a community meeting," explains founder Ben Miller.[34]

The ideas behind Popularise may herald a paradigm shift in the intersection between crowdsourcing and crowdfunding. Popularise paved the way for Fundrise, a start-up that allows individuals not only to vote on, but also to take an equity stake in, real estate developments.[35] "By tying together the crowdsourcing of public spaces with the crowdfunding of ideas, we become owners in new ways," says Peter Corbett of iStrategy Labs.[36]

Impact Exchanges: Connecting Investor to Enterprise

We've seen how crowdfunding exchanges help regular people invest in good causes. But the $1.5 billion raised through crowdfunding in 2011 is only a blip next to global equity markets, which even in a weak economic year stood at $45.7 *trillion*.[37] Social investment, however, represents a growing portion of those equities.

Social investment opportunities are flourishing. Investors find it increasingly easy to use their funds to earn returns *and* reward socially conscious, publicly traded businesses, which account for 10 percent of all managed assets. The number of funds that exclude industries or companies because of social concerns has risen from only fifty-five globally, worth $12 billion in 1995, to more than seven hundred mutual funds spanning $1 trillion in investments in 2012.[38]

Greater corporate transparency is one reason that investors can easily choose socially conscious businesses. The rise of stock exchanges that require social and environmental standards for listed companies is another. For instance, both the Johannesburg Stock Exchange in South Africa and BM&FBOVESPA in Brazil have pressured listed companies to improve their standards of responsible governance and sustainability. Those scoring highly on the Brazilian exchange even secure a spot on the Novo Mercado, an elite listing board.[39] The public sector is also influencing the investment landscape through social-impact bonds (SIBs), a new form of funding social outcomes that we discuss later in the chapter.

While these are positive developments, even funds labeled "socially responsible" vary in the scale of the social impacts they deliver. There is a significant difference, after all, between simply avoiding companies that do harm and funding enterprises that spark positive transformation.

Fortunately, several socially and financially blended investment products have emerged. At one end of the spectrum, a crowdfunding exchange offers the grassroots intimacy of investing directly, although with less certainty that the entrepreneur will actually meet the social objective *and* repay the loan. At the other end of the spectrum are socially responsible investment funds. These provide more financial certainty but exclude smaller entities and offer limited visibility for the investor into any social benefits an investment produces.[40] In between these extremes are impact investments that fund social enterprises; these deliver more-direct social improvements, but may offer more modest financial returns.

Gauging social returns is no easy feat. For the most part, financial ratios and credit ratings traditionally employed to select investments lack equivalents in the social-impact arena. Social metrics often vary; a microfinance enterprise may cite microfinance operating efficiency and communities served, while an NGO distributing water filters measures potable water produced and a solar company estimates reductions in greenhouse gas emissions.[41] Evaluating social returns is still largely a human rather than an algorithmic exercise.

Singapore-based Impact Investment Exchange Asia (IIX) raised $70 million in its first year by individually matching investors to social enterprises. The UK think tank Nesta considers informed financial planners "gatekeepers, influencing the deployment [into impact investment] of a significant proportion of the UK's wealthy retail investors' funds under management."[42] Planners can help investors navigate the challenging, personal questions an exchange alone cannot solve: does this investment fit my asset allocation model? Is it philanthropic? What is my risk exposure with this combination of investments? These questions can be uniquely difficult to answer in the context of impact investment, where the lines between social and financial returns are deliberately blurred.

Impact investing also differs in time horizon. Resolving societal problems requires patience, but a couple saving for a child's college tuition needs liquidity. For such investors, IIX plans to develop a liquid market for social-impact securities with an online exchange for debt and equity in social enterprises.

Fortunately, many drawn to impact investment realize the complexity of the underlying challenges and are comfortable with a longer time horizon as long as they receive routine updates. When exchanges require such information, investors can compare social impacts across enterprises more easily.

Regular investor updates, similar to quarterly earnings reports required for a listing on the New York Stock Exchange, are another key advantage of centralized exchanges. Valuing the independent evaluation and consistent reporting these exchanges provide, investors use these features to compare options.[43]

Mission Markets, a new stock-exchange system offering shares worth more than $336 million in double- and triple-bottom-line companies, requires businesses to carry one of a few approved third-party assessments, ratings, or certifications.[44] Standards such as the Global Impact Investment Rating System and B corp certification have emerged to meet this need.

As global impact investment grows, emerging options are helping eliminate the old trade-off between effective social involvement and competitive financial returns. The RSF Social Investment Fund (offered by RSF Social Finance), for example, allows a middle-income mother to invest in the small manufacturer of her child's biodegradable diapers—and earn healthy returns while doing so. While some impact investors are ready to accept below-market returns, the RSF Social Investment Fund has actually outpaced the S&P 500 for the past decade. It is just one of two hundred impact investment funds worth a combined $50 billion operating today.[45]

Even with these advances, the current market vastly underfunds early-stage social investment. Our Monitor Deloitte colleagues call this the "pioneer gap."[46] Monitor's research in Africa found that only six of eighty-four funds investing in the continent offered early-stage capital.[47] New ideas serving marginalized populations strike many investors as too uncertain.

On the other hand, for brave investors like Gloria Nelund, a former executive at Deutsche Bank, this pioneer gap is a call to action. "I interviewed probably 30 funds that at least peripherally called themselves social-impact funds or social-focused funds," she told us. "In those interviews, every single one of them said their biggest challenge was attracting capital. That is when I knew how my background and experience could help scale the impact investing industry."[48] Nelund left investment banking to create TriLinc Global and its $1.5 billion Global Impact Fund.[49]

Trilinc's Global Impact Fund serves the "main street," a surprisingly novel move in an industry that offers few investment options for middle-class impact investors seeking competitive returns. Nelund is struck by the irony: "As we [in the industry] talk about issues impacting 'the missing middle' we are actually creating a missing middle, by only letting the elite participate in this new asset class."[50] By contrast, the minimum investment in Trilinc's fund is $2,000, allowing a much broader swathe of investors to contribute toward social enterprises in developing countries—enterprises carefully chosen to support the fund's targeted 7 percent annual returns. In a weak financial market, that's enough to make even those unacquainted with impact investing take notice.

"Changing behavior begins with creating products that look, act, feel, and are even distributed like traditional investment products," Nelund explains. "We want to be a catalyst to help the industry grow."

With social-impact exchanges rapidly maturing and new funds such as TriLinc gaining momentum, participation in the solution economy is growing dramatically. J.P. Morgan anticipates the social-impact investment market to reach between $400 billion and $1 trillion by 2020.[51]

Another way anyone from regular citizens to world-class scientists can participate in the solution economy is by entering the growing number of competitions geared to solving big problems.

Prizes for Public Value

On April 20, 2010, a blast rocked the *Deepwater Horizon* drilling rig in the Gulf of Mexico. Flames engulfed the collapsing platform as rescuers evacuated more than one hundred oil workers. A plume of oil billowed into the ocean.

The *Deepwater Horizon* oil spill pumped 2.5 million gallons of oil per day into the Gulf of Mexico, ultimately costing the region's fishing industry billions of dollars. Such accidents are an increasing concern given the rise of deepwater drilling; at least thirty-five platforms in the gulf produce oil from a thousand feet below the ocean's surface. Clearly, improved oil recovery technology is an urgent need.

The Wendy Schmidt Oil Cleanup X Challenge was intended to inspire R&D into oil spill cleanup.[52] The challenge specifically aimed to double the industry's best oil recovery rate to 2,500 gallons per minute and to improve the efficiency of oil collection by 70 percent—exceedingly ambitious goals.

The challenge lured three hundred and fifty teams, of which two actually met the demanding criteria. The winner, Elastec/American Marine of Carmi, Illinois, designed a system that dipped rows of grooved, rotating disks into the water perpendicularly, lifting goopy oil at the start of the rotation and scraping it off before it returned to the water. The invention, resembling a floating combine harvester, collected 4,670 gallons per minute, almost quadrupling the industry's former best effort.

Outsized results such as these highlight the utility of contests. Prizes and challenges convene the brightest minds from multiple fields and can elicit collaboration in unique ways.

Incentives for public-value-producing innovations range from the Ensign Group's $150,000 Eprize, for innovations in nursing-home care, to awards of $10 million or more from the X PRIZE Foundation.[53] The organizers set a challenge, offer a prize, and then stand back as a horde of smart, ambitious people vie to produce the best solution.

Challenges are important for the solution economy; they unite problems with problem solvers, filling holes in business models that cater mostly to traditional buyer-seller relationships. As journalist Tina Rosenberg observes, prize programs engage problem solvers often neglected by traditional initiatives such as university research programs. And unlike patents, prizes can spur and reward innovations that don't promise an immediate payback in the marketplace.[54]

Prize programs also offer a cost-effective alternative to traditional government procurements. They eliminate trade-offs in a way that typifies the solution economy: traditional procurement funds approaches, whereas prizes reward results. And while the procurement system favors players with traditional credentials and proven track records, competitions accept anyone, thereby multiplying the number and diversity of brains tackling the problem.[55]

Furthermore, contests promote the comingling of ideas in a way that isolated, closed-door R&D efforts can't. In open contests, ideas can build on one another, as with the astronomers who perfected a glaciologist's model of dark-matter detection for Kaggle. It's a competition, but it often nurtures collaboration.

Not all problems lend themselves to challenges, but those that do can reap impressive results. Even the losing proposals can advance an industry. The $10 million Ansari X Prize spurred twenty-six teams from seven nations to invest more than $100 million in space flight, investments that may accelerate development in technologies ranging from rocket fuel to seat belts. Such a tenfold return on investment is not uncommon for prize challenges.[56]

The US government now uses prizes extensively. Challenge.gov, launched in September 2010, provides an online platform that federal agencies can use to create competitions. Within its first two years, Challenge.gov posted 212 challenges from forty-eight federal agencies and awarded more than $34 million in prize money.[57]

The principles of good competition design are fairly universal. Luciano Kay of the Georgia Institute of Technology's School of Public Policy says a successful prize program will involve a challenge that is exciting and ambitious, yet achievable. Not every problem lends itself to a challenge. The sponsor should define the problem simply enough to declare a winner without controversy, yet leave room for numerous creative approaches.[58] As NASA's Jenn Gustetic puts it, many challenges seek unspecified solutions to specific problems.[59]

Joe Parrish and Jason Cruzar from NASA have overseen dozens of challenges. Like Kay, they say that the objectives of the contest should be "simple enough to explain in one breath." In their experience, if a goal is broadly applicable, where participants stand to gain additional value out of their competing concept, commercial enterprises want in since the enterprises will retain the intellectual property.[60] Contests structured like NASA's offer opportunities beyond the prize itself—a chance for the winners to take their innovations and run with them.

As the *Wall Street Journal* reports, critics "dismiss the newest trend in prize-giving as a form of advertising that masquerades as public service—and a clever ploy to attract top research talent at a discount."[61] But sometimes, publicity is exactly what a public service needs, as when the US Veterans Administration increased access to its

QUALITIES OF A GOOD PRIZE CHALLENGE

- Is open to anyone
- Is amenable to cross-disciplinary approaches
- Is challenging
- Has simple objectives, multiple potential solutions
- Has broad market potential
- Enables losers to emerge with valuable developments
- Often encourages open-source iterations
- Has potential to attract angel investors

NASA'S OPEN INNOVATION CHALLENGE MODEL

NASA's Open Innovation initiative releases challenge statements, via Inno-Centive and other platforms, to solicit solutions from as many disciplines as possible.[a]

NASA developed Open Innovation in response to budget cutbacks. When 45 percent of the Constellation program's budget was cut in 2005, Jeffrey Davis, director of the Space Life Sciences Directorate at Johnson Space Center (JSC), recognized that JSC's goals couldn't be reached "just doing 45 percent less. We need to approach this whole program in a new way."[b]

NASA's first three challenges, issued in late 2009, drew 1,217 initial responses from sixty-five countries. The administration ultimately selected and evaluated 128 entries. The challenges asked contestants to learn how to keep food fresh for as long as three years; to design a zero-gravity resistance mechanism for exercise in space; and to devise a way to forecast solar activity so that NASA could schedule launches to minimize exposure to harmful radiation. NASA's challenges have generated a variety of breakthroughs. The Green Flag Challenge, for instance, sought to attain superior aircraft fuel efficiency by beating the industry standard of 20 passenger-miles per gallon. The winner attained a remarkable 406 passenger-miles per gallon. The top four entrants spent $5 million collectively designing their super-fuel-efficient aircraft.

Joe Parrish, a deputy manager in NASA's Jet Propulsion Laboratory, estimates that NASA received more than $3 in research and development benefits for each dollar it spent on the prize. "The Green Flag Challenge was one of our smallest expenditures yet one of our biggest achievements," Parrish says.

a. Sander Olson, "X-Prize Director Describes Incentive Prizes in an Interview with Sander Olson," *Next Big Future,* June 3, 2011, http://nextbigfuture.com/2011/06/x-prize-director -describes-incentive.html.

b. Andrea Meyer, "Frugal Innovation at NASA," *Working Knowledge,* August 1, 2011, http:// workingknowledge.com/blog/?p=1522.

Blue Button health-care service with a contest specifically designed to raise awareness about it.

Clearly, prizes for a few superlative inventors cannot sustain an entire scientific community. X Prize's Erika Wagner says, "Prizes aren't good for stimulating basic science, and we need to have a strong science infrastructure in this country."[62] But by creating a forum that links problems with potential problem solvers, challenges provide a powerful vehicle to unite talent worldwide in fruitful collaborations.

Pay for Success

From the outside, Doncaster Prison, about an hour's train ride from London, looks like any other—it's big, imposing, and drab. Step inside, however, and it resembles a mixture of job training facility and community center. Bright signs cover the walls with warm and fuzzy proclamations such as "People are our business." A "Night at the Musicals" poster and sign-up sheets to watch the play *Oliver* adorn multiple walls painted in bright shades of blue and yellow. For those aspiring to the stage, there's a chance to work at Second Shot Productions, a social enterprise housed within the prison walls and specializing in theater, television, filmmaking, and graphic design.

The production company, along with several other organizations, is housed within the prison's resettlement wing, where prisoners spend their final three months before being released back into the free world. The wing is designed to replicate the outside community within the prison walls. Case managers coordinate intensive job training, job readiness, and reintegration services, all directed toward preventing inmates from returning to prison. This is a huge departure from most prison systems, which leave released inmates largely on their own to deal with the shock of reintegration into society.

Operated by privately owned Serco Group, Doncaster Prison is part of a pathbreaking experiment to reduce recidivism by aligning provider payments with outcomes, with the ultimate goal of reducing the prison population without spurring an increase in crime. Ten percent of Serco's payments from the government are contingent on reducing recidivism by at least 5 percent. If Serco fails to achieve the target, the company is out a cool £2.5 million. It's a bold experiment, to say the least.

"Delivering public services is not cheap," explains Sean Mason, assistant prison director at Doncaster. "Getting it wrong is now quite expensive."[63]

The Doncaster Prison project is part of a much larger initiative. The UK government is engaged in an ambitious experiment to shift funding across a range of public programs—everything from welfare to work to youth services to offender rehabilitation—to focus on real-world results.

Naturally, exchanges are springing up around this concept. *Pay-for-success* (alternately called *payment for results*) exchanges connect buyers of social outcomes—typically governments, foundations, international development institutions, and corporate philanthropists—to solution providers, allowing buyers to shift from traditional contracts and grants to rewarding specific outcomes. As with prizes and challenges, this approach attracts new providers, new approaches, and radically new business models.

"Currently, the boundaries in which public service providers can innovate are quite narrow," says Tom Gash of the UK Institute for Government. "Payment by results enables new business models to emerge."[64] In this way, pay for success represents an important stage in the creation of functioning markets for social outcomes.

A pay-for-success system transcends departmental territoriality and allows providers to scrap experiments swiftly if they prove ineffective. Fast failures along the way can even be advantageous if they lead to improved results before the clock times out. Pay for success is not just an innovation; it's an innovation *multiplier* that creates incentives for creative solutions.

Pay for success is not a new concept. Previously, however, it was beset by countless challenges: the need for objective measures, the time needed to achieve results, the correlation of an organization's specific role to the overall result, and so on. In a dozen ongoing pilots, the United Kingdom is systematically trying to overcome each of these challenges.

Take metrics. Governments traditionally spend money reactively, not preventatively. Crime prevention is much trickier than punishment. Consider Doncaster again. Negative pressures from fellow criminals must be overcome with positive support, from personalized vocational training to the maintenance of constructive relationships beyond prison walls.

To adjust prison programs and conditions by legislative decree can produce knots of red tape, and some experiments may prove ineffective. With pay-for-success schemes, government can allow providers (nonprofits, contractors, and social entrepreneurs) to master the details and shoulder the risks. The United Kingdom is rewarding contractors on specific metrics, such as the requirement that Serco reduce recidivism by 5 percent. Conditional payment offers a compelling stimulus for Serco to align its goals with government.

Creating such metrics presents one of the biggest challenges facing pay-for-success exchanges. The exchanges must avoid creating perverse incentives and must avoid tactics such as cream-skimming, that is, serving the best applicants while neglecting less promising candidates. Contracts must set achievable goals that account for nationwide trends such as economic recession.

"You have to write contracts so that you're not paying for stuff that would have happened anyway," says Antonia Romero of the UK Ministry of Justice.[65] This is why payouts at Peterborough Prison, another UK experiment in pay for success, are measured against recidivism rates at similar prisons.[66]

Public service providers have long hesitated to pursue potentially effective projects such as early intervention in child development because the providers can't be assured of long-term funding, regardless of results. Nonprofits want to grow, says Sir Ronald Cohen, a British venture capitalist who has long advocated funding for social entrepreneurs, but "the volatility in funding makes it impossible."[67]

In the current landscape, "the majority of nonprofits [in the United States] bring in less than $500,000 annually," explains Yao Huang, founder of The Hatchery, a New York City–based organization that cultivates social entrepreneurs.[68] There are 1.8 million nonprofits out there. Should all of them, judging by performance, exist? No! There's unnecessary overlap, and the ones that demonstrate strong effectiveness should attract the funding.

Social-impact bonds (SIBs), mentioned earlier, represent an attempt to ameliorate the problems of volatile funding, lack of accountability for results, and an overcrowded field of nonprofits. This new financial instrument allows individual investors to buy shares in a project that has a clear and quantifiable social objective, such as reducing a school district's dropout rate by a targeted margin. If the target is met, investors recoup their full investment; a missed target means some money is lost, while an exceeded target earns an attractive return.[69] Thus the SIB guarantees long-term financing while spreading the risk between the three parties: government (which pays for the outcome), investors (which are willing to fund the outcome), and providers (which deliver the outcome).

Those who have witnessed the success of payment by results are among the most enthusiastic about SIBs. In 1996, Minnesota passed a pay-for-success model, one of the earliest of its kind, to help the state's unemployed return to work. The funded nonprofit, RISE!, produced an estimated 624 percent return in economic value to the state.[70] Now Minnesota is piloting a $10 million Human Capital Performance Bond in the hope of repeating this success with a larger pool of capital. To accomplish this, the state is enlisting philanthropists, high-net-worth individuals, and foundations to help with up-front investment and risk.[71]

Where there is an opportunity to turn a profit, social programs attract new investors. Goldman Sachs, for instance, has committed

$9.6 million for a New York City program intended to reduce jail recidivism by 10 percent. If the program reaches the 10 percent target, Goldman Sachs will be repaid in full. If the recidivism rate declines by less than 10 percent, the investor will not be repaid; if the rate declines by more than 10 percent, Goldman Sachs can make a profit of up to $2.1 million, or 22 percent on its investment.[72]

These are risks and returns that Goldman Sachs, and a growing number of banks, are willing to accept, particularly given the public benefit. In this way, SIBs align incentives around outcomes that benefit both society and investors. Government pays only for programs that work, and it can evaluate effectiveness according to the metrics it prioritizes.

Payment by results also provides entrepreneurs, private companies, nonprofits, and social enterprises with a strong incentive to team up, creating a shared, vested interest in meeting the objective. A diverse cast of contributors can produce new, innovative approaches.

Antonia Romero, of the UK Ministry of Justice, expects pay-for-success schemes to spur more innovations such as Doncaster Prison's "daddy day care" program, which allows fathers to see their children. "Keeping the family unit together is a key driver in reducing recidivism," she says. "Things that might be considered to be soft stuff actually work in reducing reoffending. The great thing about alternative providers is they often have more freedom to do things like that."[73]

UK-based Ingeus is using results-based funding from the government to spur its employees to find jobs for welfare recipients. "The milestones for which you get paid, and what you actually get paid for, are more challenging than any predecessor program," says Dean James, Ingeus CEO.[74] Instead of receiving a fee for processing a client, Ingeus receives its biggest fees when a client retains a job for six months. This approach is sometimes called "black box," meaning that Ingeus and other providers face little interference and have a tremendous amount of flexibility in how to achieve the prescribed outcomes.

BIG SOCIETY CAPITAL: THE MARKET MAKER

Traditionally, venture capital firms have provided two assets to the firms in which they invest: capital and savvy advice. Fledgling firms with a good idea would receive an infusion of cash and some great guidance, which helps the young businesses take off. Once they invest in a company, venture capitalists take an active role in helping it to succeed.

But where can a "start-up" social enterprise look for such a boost? Traditional venture capitalists often can't make enough of a return. As a result, a social-mission corporation with a good idea often fails to make as much impact as it could.

That is changing in the solution economy, however. "Our mission is to develop the market for social outcomes," explains Nick O'Donohoe, director of Big Society Capital (BSC), a privately run, £600 million social-investment fund that claims to be "the first ever social investment market builder."[a] O'Donohoe is a former J.P. Morgan investment banker recruited by the UK government to lead this groundbreaking institution.

Privately run and answering to a board, BSC is funded from fifteen-year-old dormant bank accounts that revert to the government if unclaimed. BSC's charter is to radically enlarge the social investment landscape by making affordable financing and advice available to social enterprises and charities.

The fund makes three major types of investments through financial intermediaries: SIBs, funds that invest in social enterprises, and direct investments in intermediary companies that support the market infrastructure. For instance, one SIB supported by BSC committed £4.5 million to the UK Department of Work and Pensions to tackle youth unemployment in Liverpool. The program, Triodos Bank's New Horizons, aims to improve the behavior and job prospects of thirty-nine hundred young Liverpudlians over three years through one-on-one coaching and other behavioral interventions.[b]

"If they can demonstrate they can address unemployment for 4,000 kids in Liverpool, they can then take that model to three to four other cities," O'Donohoe says. "That's how they achieve scale." If New Horizons succeeds, BSC adds another market-building investment to its portfolio, while society benefits as vulnerable young people receive a better shot at becoming productive citizens.

BSC also acts as a wholesaler for the social investment market. Instead of investing directly in social ventures such as urban renewal programs or shelters, BSC invests in funds and intermediaries that support these frontline social ventures. These intermediary organizations, called social investment finance intermediaries, include social banks, nonbank social investors, and support providers. As a group, they represent a new financial market, connecting social-impact investors with organizations in need of funding.[c] Eventually, O'Donohoe hopes BSC can help UK organizations coalesce broadly around agreed-upon social outcomes.

In the United Kingdom and throughout the world, pay for performance is still expanding. "In five years," O'Donohoe says, "there will be more people involved in delivering outcomes, more investors and more intermediaries. Our goal is nothing less than a sea change in how social outcomes are funded and delivered."

a. British Prime Minister's Office, "Prime Minister Unveils Big Society Capital," April 4, 2012, www.number10.gov.uk/news/prime-minsiter-unveils-big-society-capital/.

b. Andrew Holt, "£4.5m DWP Social Impact Bond for Merseyside," *Charity Times*, January 23, 2012, www.charitytimes.com/ct/4.5m_DWP_Social_Impact_Bond_for_Mersey side.php.

c. "Our Vision and Mission," Big Society Capital, accessed February 6, 2013, www .bigsocietycapital.com/our-vision-and-mission/.

"It's forced us to really think about what a fundamental shift in welfare-to-work would look like," James says. The approach encourages radically different approaches. For example, job counselors could supplement their work by connecting clients to online peer-to-peer groups that could share learning, advice, and references.

Pay-for-success models are spreading globally. President Obama pledged $100 million to pay-for-success schemes in his 2012 budget. Instiglio, based in the Harvard Innovation Lab, is consulting with developing nations on using SIBs to improve school attendance, access to potable water, and financial literacy. The UK organization Social Finance Limited has received funding from the Omidyar Network to develop SIBs in Ireland, Scotland, Australia, Canada, and Israel.[75]

Thus, an entirely new solution economy infrastructure is emerging, involving both monetary and nonmonetary currencies that engender new ways of keeping score. New markets and new exchanges enable intangibles (such as reputation) to trade alongside tangibles, yielding a bottom line that brings profits *and* social impact.

PUBLIC-VALUE EXCHANGES: IN A NUTSHELL

THE BIG IDEA

The impact currencies of the solution economy are now being traded across a variety of novel exchanges. Enabled by web technologies, these exchanges drive public value by connecting capital of all types to societal problems and to those who wish to solve them.

TYPES OF EXCHANGES

- **Two-sided markets** link buyers and sellers directly, with one side of the market typically subsidizing the other.

- **Crowdfunding platforms** raise capital directly from networks of supporters, connecting social entrepreneurs with socially conscious citizens.

- **Impact exchanges** invest via both traditional and specialized equity markets to reward socially conscious businesses while they earn returns.

- **Prizes and challenges** convene the brightest minds from multiple fields, uniting problems with problem solvers.

- **Pay-for-success** arrangements connect the buyers of social outcomes—governments, foundations, philanthropists, etc.—with solution providers, enabling a shift from traditional contracting and grants to rewarding specific outcomes.

GROWTH TRAJECTORY

- The number of crowdfunding exchanges rose to 537 worldwide by the end of 2012.

- The number of funds that exclude industries or companies because of social concerns has risen from fifty-five funds globally in 1995 to more than seven hundred in 2012.

- Funds labeled socially responsible investments account for 10 percent of all managed assets.

- J.P. Morgan anticipates social-impact investments to be a $1 trillion market by 2020.

EXCHANGE ACCELERATORS

- Peer-to-peer platforms have dramatically reduced the transaction costs of collaboration and encourage people to share knowledge.

- Third-party assessments, ratings, or certifications of social enterprises and funds—such as the Global Impact Investment Rating System and B corp certification—empower impact exchanges by providing investors with independent evaluations.

- The innovative use of metrics enables pay-for-success exchanges, with goals based on historical data and payments based on data-supported outcomes.
- Social-impact bonds spread the risk of investing in social projects.
- Social investment finance intermediaries connect social-impact investors with social sector organizations in need of funding.

EXCHANGE INNOVATORS

- **Kaggle:** This platform organizes competitions for data problems, in which the hosts post a data set, and the most accurate predictive model wins.
- **Kiva:** One of the largest microlenders anywhere, the organization enables anyone with internet access to fund ventures around the world.
- **Skillshare, School of Everything**, and **TeachersPayTeachers** use peer-to-peer exchanges to teach and train people over the internet.
- **Mission Markets:** This new stock exchange offers shares worth more than $336 million in double- and triple-bottom-line companies.
- **TriLinc Global:** The firm's $1.25 billion Global Impact Fund connects "main street" retail investors to social entrepreneurs.
- **Challenge.gov:** US federal agencies can use this online platform for prizes and challenges.
- **Big Society Capital (BSC):** This UK government-sponsored, privately run social investment fund provides affordable financing and advice to social enterprises.

QUESTIONS FOR THOUGHT

Which of these varieties of exchange have you observed in action? What type of organization operated the exchange, and did it meet the desired goal? In light of the examples shared here, is there anything you would change about the exchange?

SIX

The Ecosystems

Converging around big, hairy, audacious problems

In traditional business thinking, a company discovers an unmet demand and brings a solution to market. But what if there were no demand? And no market? And your potential customers were literally dirt poor? Traditional thinking would tell you to give up.

In the solution economy, the winning approach is to capitalize on your role in a broader ecosystem. If a problem exists, the answer is to create an environment in which the solution can organically, sustainably, *profitably* be brought to bear—even if there is no market demand in the traditional sense. Sound impossible? Well, that's exactly what Unilever did in India to address a critical public sanitation problem. How the company did it demonstrates the role that ecosystems play in the solution revolution.

Sometimes the best solution is as simple as a bar of soap. Diarrhea kills 1.5 million children a year worldwide, making it the second-most common cause of death for children under five. Yet the remedy has been known for centuries: basic sanitation practices such as hand washing cut the risk of contracting the disease in half. The usefulness of soap in this regard was understood as far back as in ancient Babylon.[1]

Remarkably, though, perhaps a billion of the world's poorest inhabitants do without this most basic of essentials. For many, soap doesn't fit their budget (about 1.2 billion people earn less than $1 a day), and many others are unaware of soap's sanitizing properties and critical role in hygiene.[2]

These consumers occupy what business strategists C. K. Prahalad and Stuart L. Hart call the bottom, or base, of the global economic pyramid.[3] As discussed earlier, conventional businesses historically neglected the needs of those at the base of the pyramid, unless the companies were selling supplies to humanitarian relief organizations. It was considered impossible to serve remote, impoverished regions without taking a sharp financial loss. In many cases, the basic market features wealthier societies take for granted—grocery stores, pharmacies, and other retail outlets for hygiene products—simply don't exist. In addition, the special needs of this consumer population had never been researched by the marketing department.

Into this market void stepped HUL, Unilever's subsidiary in India (hereafter known simply as Unilever). Over the years, Unilever has become one of the most sophisticated companies in the world in selling to the poor, employing a host of strategies in many countries to reach this very hard-to-reach market segment. In the case of providing soap in India's rural villages, Unilever recognized a blue-ocean opportunity, that is, an opportunity to serve a huge, untapped market. In 2000, the company revamped its business strategy to accommodate this opportunity. To reach the potential market of more than 600 million low-income Indians, Unilever would have to create an entire ecosystem. Because its product would address a serious public health issue, it was able to partner with NGOs, banks, and schools to create a market for cleaning products in rural India—while lifting women from poverty with microloans and jobs, improving public health and sanitation, and enhancing public health awareness through educational campaigns—all while turning a profit.

Unilever's initiative began small, in the rural hinterlands of India, by tapping into organic networks of local female entrepreneurs.

The company worked with microlending institutions to open lines of credit for these women. Once a woman could obtain a microloan to buy Unilever soaps, she could provide this essential resource to her entire village. She would typically charge a 7 percent markup, which allowed her to pay off the loan and draw a steady income. "When my husband left me I had nothing but my daughters," said Rojamma, one of the new entrepreneurs. "Now everyone knows me. I am someone."[4]

Unilever's program equipped women like Rojamma with a job, met a basic sanitation need, and gave Unilever access to a remote region it couldn't affordably reach otherwise. What began with seventeen women expanded within a decade to forty-five thousand saleswomen, who in turn reached more than three million households. Similar programs are flourishing for Unilever in Sri Lanka, Bangladesh, and some African nations.[5]

Prahalad and Hart contend that multinational corporations "must build an organizational infrastructure to address opportunity at the bottom of the pyramid." Unilever put this insight into practice. In addition to a specially tailored, nontraditional sales force, Unilever also created a new specially tailored soap brand, Wheel. To protect the environment, the company made Wheel with a lower oil content, because the poor often wash in rivers. In addition, Wheel is sold in small quantities at very low prices, because customers cannot afford to buy more than a few days' worth at a time. Unilever "decentralized the production, marketing, and distribution of the product to leverage the abundant labor pool in rural India," explain Prahalad and Hart.[6]

To market the products, Unilever's Lifebuoy brand sponsored Swasthya Chetna (Health Awakening), at the time the world's largest private hygiene education program.[7] In 2008, a Unilever-backed NGO sponsored the first of a now annual Global Hand Washing Day in more than a hundred countries and coordinated with more than fifty organizations in nineteen countries for the event.[8] Schoolchildren learned soap jingles and made hand-washing pledges. Many continue to do so every morning of the school year.

The Swasthya Chetna program began with a goal of educating 20 percent of India's population—200 million Indians—to wash their hands after going to the bathroom. About 150 outreach teams speaking seven dialects spent two years travelling to eighteen thousand villages, where the team members shared lessons, posters, and literature on sanitation. To emphasize the message, they revisited each village, applauding good hygiene practices and offering additional instruction as needed.

Their visits often included dramatic performances, hand-washing demonstrations, and the introduction of the concept of germs. Children rubbed their hands with powder, which simulated dirt and germs, and the kids then washed it off using plain water. But under a black light, their hands still showed traces of the powder, which glowed under the light. They then repeated the experiment, this time washing with soap. The glow was now gone, dispelling the myth that clean-*looking* hands are clean hands. The Swasthya Chetna marketing campaign cost Unilever only $2.7 million.

Unilever's research partners in the academic and scientific community tested the effectiveness of these campaigns, even planting sensors inside bars of soap to see how often control groups washed. They also tested the effectiveness of hand washing itself, finding a 48 percent reduction in diarrhea cases and a 46 percent reduction in eye infections among participants.[9]

About six thousand children worldwide—most of them under the age of five—die from diarrhea each day. Unilever is well aware that its work helps to reduce this suffering.[10] Even so, says Unilever's Harpreet-Singh Tibb, the effort is still a business undertaking.

"Swasthya Chetna is not about philanthropy," he says. "It's a marketing program with social benefits. We recognize that the health of our business is totally interconnected with the health of the communities we serve."[11] The business challenge was immense. Unilever had to sell soap to people who didn't know they needed it, who couldn't afford it, and who had nowhere to buy it. To succeed, Unilever had to change its business model drastically to adjust to local customs and market challenges and to engage with a multitude of nontraditional partners. It succeeded by thinking beyond the simple seller-buyer paradigm and creating an entire ecosystem that enabled supply and encouraged demand. NGOs contributed their cultural expertise to the program design and gave Unilever's efforts legitimacy. Scientists researched the effectiveness of public health campaigns. Banks and NGOs provided the microloans. Local village entrepreneurs became the sales and marketing engine. Government agencies introduced Unilever's programs to schools and sponsored public health messages. In return, Unilever delivered engaging health instruction at a scale the government wouldn't have provided otherwise, and the firm left a lasting example that could be used to hone future public education campaigns.

In building this solution-economy ecosystem, Unilever also planted the seeds for future wavemakers. "It is not only my own prosperity that means so much to me," says Feroza, an entrepreneur from Joyeeta, Unilever's sister project in Bangladesh. "People get inspiration from me. They say, 'If Feroza can do it, why not me?' I'm more than a representative of Unilever; I'm an ambassador of life, hope and dreams."[12]

From Silos and Sectors to Ecosystems

In the solution economy, various factors combine to create a new problem-solving environment. New organizational models, new currencies, new applications of technology, and a new generation of wavemakers are attacking some of society's toughest challenges. It's an economy built on more than money, where the old definitions around commerce, profit, nonprofit versus for-profit, and public value are being challenged regularly. Breaking through the traditional ways of thinking allows for the development of solution ecosystems.

Wavemakers begin by seeing a problem (such as preventable deaths from poor sanitation) and ask, "What would it look like to really make a difference? What can I do to get there?" They form relationships to work together effectively, regardless of their specific sectors, silos, and roles. Why shouldn't a multi-billion-dollar company take the lead in educating rural Indians about sanitation?

The rigid silos of traditional industry, government—and even many foundations—run directly against the disruptive thinking of the solution economy. Rather than navigating fragmented hierarchies to advance an agenda, social entrepreneurs and organization "intrapreneurs" begin with the problem itself. Why can't an inventor better known for robotic limbs and souped-up scooters create a device that purifies water, as Dean Kamen did (see chapter 1), and enlist a company like Coca-Cola to distribute it throughout developing countries?

A core issue or objective, such as fighting malaria or revolutionizing higher education, becomes the center of an ecosystem. As connected citizens share their concerns about, and interest in, the topic (in a conversation now made easier with the advent of social media and the internet), market demand grows and enterprising contributors converge to meet the gap in the market.

In biology, ecosystems represent a community of living organisms interacting as a system. Likewise in solution ecosystems, partner organizations gain when one organization evolves its distinct role to complement the other's contributions. (Both public schools and Unilever had a shared interest in getting kids to wash their hands, but the traditional roles of these two players would never link them up.) Together, various groups can move toward their goal much more productively than if each group pursued it separately. These dynamics are replicated across the ecosystem. The larger the mixture of players, the more opportunities for partnerships that serve all parties.[13]

Consider d.light, the scrappy start-up focused on a huge, largely unknown problem: access to lighting in the home. The company targets the one in four people globally who live without electricity. Although d.light had some innovative designs that caught the interest of the Omidyar Network, enormous distribution challenges stood between the promising design and the billions of people who needed it.

The individuals most in need were scattered across remote regions at the base of the pyramid.

To address this concern, the Omidyar Network drew on its tight network of international development organizations. At an Omidyar Network party, the CEO of d.light was introduced to a representative of BRAC, the largest, most mature service provider in Bangladesh. Ten days later, the two companies were meeting in Dakar, negotiating a pilot project to bring d.light's products to five BRAC communities.

"BRAC has unparalleled distribution, so the impact on volume was incredible," says Susan Phillips of the Omidyar Network. "BRAC is in 110 countries. The potential for collaboration within the network can be staggering."[14] Today, d.light has reached ten million people in more than thirty countries.[15]

Some ecosystems benefit from a backbone organization that serves as a central organizer, a source of accountability, and a convener. In some ecosystems, this role is played by a "connector" company and its platform. In the business world, this is best illustrated by platforms such as eBay or Amazon.com, which create simple market conditions and a user culture that facilitates interactions between buyers, sellers, and package shippers. In the social sector, the connector role is taking shape through clever public-private partnerships where there is often an integrator pulling the ecosystem together. As will be discussed later in this chapter, the role has been pioneered by large academic institutions like MIT and Harvard in the online education market and by Ashoka in the affordable housing ecosystem.

Another example is what the Global Alliance for Vaccines and Immunizations (GAVI) has done to increase access to immunizations in the world's poorest countries. In 2000, a plethora of new technologies and medicines was coming out or already available for children in the West, but other regions—where the medical innovations were needed most—were relative deserts. The discrepancy was a textbook market failure. Not until the World Health Organization, UNICEF, academics, pharmaceutical companies, and funders converged at the World Economic Forum in Davos was the need addressed and ground broken on a solution space. GAVI is that space, and its achievements are the sum of its partners. Like a field-specific version of Davos, GAVI brings together under one roof the vaccine industry and various NGOs, donor countries, and developing countries to reshape the vaccine market. By pooling demand from developing countries for vaccines and matching it with reliable, long-term financing, GAVI delivers massive impact—370 million additional children have been immunized, preventing 5.5 million future deaths with its support—without any of its own boots on the ground.[16] It simply connects existing major players.

Many of the market innovators operating in developing countries must *create* an ecosystem to serve previously unmet needs. Take Husk Power Systems, whose mission is to electrify the poorest villages in India by building radically affordable, thirty-kilowatt power plants. Husk's biggest challenge is not necessarily building power plants cheap enough to serve a population whose annual salary is less than $200, but the lack of low-cost suppliers to build the plants and maintain the systems in these areas. This meant that Husk also has to invest in metering, a sales force, electrical engineers, training, and education.

"Why is it so hard for many of these entrepreneurs?" asks Sasha Dichter of Acumen, one of Husk's investors. "It's because they are literally creating markets. There often is no market. No ecosystem to draw from. They're building it from scratch."[17]

Much like the unique, converging causes of a problem, the resulting problem-solving ecosystem emerges and expands through its own distinct process. Certain versatile elements are adapted, technologies are leveraged, and currencies gain new context. Existing exchanges and business models may find fresh relevance in the budding ecosystem, and participants, often playing nontraditional roles, contribute to the flow of both resources and ideas, allowing new self-sustaining solution markets to thrive. In the examples that follow, we will show how the foundational elements of the solution economy discussed from chapters 1 through 5 can be traced across ecosystems.

Revolutionizing Education: An Innovation Ecosystem

Disruptive innovations force entire industries to adapt or become obsolete. Netflix adapted to the digital revolution; Blockbuster didn't. IBM adapted; Wang didn't. Apple thrived in the era of digital images; Kodak disappeared. UPS and FedEx have boomed along with online shopping, while many postal services, with their monopolies on mail, struggle. Indeed, the very insulation provided by monopoly status, traditionally viewed as a boon, has been a challenge to public institutions that must adapt to changing ecosystems.

Nowhere is this more the case than in education. While many public schools are still locked in a student-teacher, brick-and-mortar mind-set, new participants in the education marketplace are exhibiting all the characteristics of an emerging ecosystem. A horde of new entrants is scratching at the margins, finding niches and refining the offerings (figure 6-1). Some rise to prominence, and others die out, their best ideas swiped and incorporated into stronger competitors. Far-reaching shifts in the education ecosystem are radically changing higher education, private schools, online learning, adult learning, and indeed the very idea of what it means to be a teacher, a student, or a school.

For students of all ages, education already has evolved significantly. Now anyone with an internet connection can learn, with top-quality lessons available 24/7. Whether it's taking a refresher on linear algebra through Khan Academy; mastering the basics of computer programming with CodeAcademy; or pursuing actual course credit from online, for-profit institutions such as StraighterLine or the University of Phoenix, millions now draw from a rich array of educational resources. Academic Earth, Udemy, Coursera, and more than 250 other institutions now offer open courseware, granting free access to acclaimed university courses. The resources now available in the educational ecosystem allow teachers and students to personalize education and connect in unprecedented ways.

FIGURE 6-1

Expanding education ecosystem

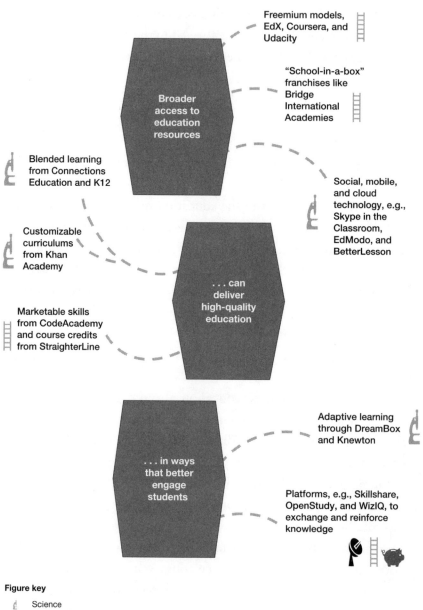

Freemium models, EdX, Coursera, and Udacity

"School-in-a-box" franchises like Bridge International Academies

Broader access to education resources

Blended learning from Connections Education and K12

Social, mobile, and cloud technology, e.g., Skype in the Classroom, EdModo, and BetterLesson

Customizable curriculums from Khan Academy

. . . can deliver high-quality education

Marketable skills from CodeAcademy and course credits from StraighterLine

Adaptive learning through DreamBox and Knewton

. . . in ways that better engage students

Platforms, e.g., Skillshare, OpenStudy, and WizIQ, to exchange and reinforce knowledge

Figure key

- Science
- Advancement
- Communication
- Savings

Consider an internet-equipped sixteen-year-old. Perhaps her own high school doesn't offer a macroeconomics course she wants to take. She can study from home in a virtual school for credit during her off hours. Or she can take a free macroeconomics course from EdX, joining 100 million others who have taken courses from MIT, Harvard, and a growing number of other elite universities online. At the end of the year, if she takes an AP macroeconomics exam and scores well, she can place out of the course in college or place into a more advanced economics seminar.

The impact on online learning is magnified when multiple tools are used in combination. Since the macroeconomics exam is sure to have problem sets, our sixteen-year-old would-be economist can gain an advantage if she practices the problems on the website DreamBox, which adapts to her responses by altering the level of difficulty and the type of hints given. And just because no one in her school is taking the class doesn't mean it has to be a solitary activity. She can find study groups and peer-to-peer support via platforms such as Students of Fortune and WizIQ, since after all, the best person to teach you something is often someone who just learned it. And best of all, it doesn't matter whether this sixteen-year-old lives in an Upper West Side apartment, an urban slum in Lahore, or a hut in the Himalayas. Internet access now means educational access—for students of all ages.

Educators call the fast-growing combination of online and classroom resources *blended learning.* The 2011 Sloan Survey of Online Learning concluded that more than 6 million students took at least one web-based class in the fall 2010 semester, an increase of 560,000 from the year before.[18] Tom Vander Ark, CEO of Open Education Solutions, predicts that at least two-thirds of US students will do most of their learning online by 2020.

While some teachers in traditional schools may be fearful of what blended learning means for them, many recognize that these new tools can radically increase the quality of education a teacher can deliver and that many of these new resources are designed specifically for teachers. The distribution of class grades, cleanly displayed on a graph, can indicate if an exam may have been too challenging or too easy, for example. Teachers can swap tips and lesson plans on sites such as BetterLesson or TeachersPayTeachers. And as explained in chapter 2, some tech-savvy teachers so embrace blended learning that they teach with a flipped-classroom mentality.

What if a teacher is concerned that part of a student's paper seems uncharacteristic of his or her writing style? A teacher can run the essay through a software program like Turnitin or SafeAssign that picks up evidence of plagiarism; such software is an essential tool in an era of near-unlimited online information. Instead of scrawling "See me after class" in red ink on returned work, teachers can contact students and parents through platforms such as Edmodo. As these examples show, educational support is being developed for teachers as well as students.

Rapid technological advances in education are shaking up the system. For instance, brick-and-mortar schools often struggle to present math and science coursework effectively. Educators have long recognized that children learn in a variety of styles, particularly in these subjects. Unfortunately, one bad experience in grade school may lead to lasting resistance to these topics, creating a permanent disadvantage in a job market in which science and math majors are in high demand. Today, however, the education ecosystem offers numerous educational options to find the right fit for each student, personalizing the experience. Checkpoints built into certain online courses indicate how the material is being absorbed in real time or what needs to be explained differently. In this way, a student progresses on a personalized learning path, at a pace that maximizes content mastery and retention.

As demonstrated in chapter 5, adults too can gain a competitive edge or pursue an interest through online lectures, free courses, and discussion forums, in the adult analog to blended learning. The future seems to offer opportunities to acquire valuable skills that are limited only by the individual's curiosity, dedication, and time.

The technological leapfrogging in developing countries, such as bypassing landlines in favor of mobile phones, is extending into education as well. Areas in which millions lack access to traditional schools are now drawing on online educational resources. In the first decade of the twenty-first century, Asia experienced the greatest growth in online learning. In China, 10 percent of *all university learning* takes place online. Meanwhile, online classrooms provide a way for women in Saudi Arabia to obtain an education without violating societal rules against being in a classroom with male instructors.[19]

The next area ripe for solutions in the education ecosystem is the bridging of the digital and physical learning worlds to replicate the serendipitous sense of community of a bricks-and-mortar school, which a computer alone can't provide. The technical and analytical skills learned online aren't everything; the psychological benefits and soft-skills development of direct interaction matter too, as most schoolchildren will attest. Providing a compelling social component to the online education experience, whether through meet-up groups or team projects, will encourage broader participation in the education ecosystem.

Affordable Housing: An Ecosystem for the Base of the Pyramid

Nearly a billion people live in slums—roughly half of all city dwellers in the developing world. They lack access to basic sanitation and share overcrowded, ramshackle structures. Beyond their general unpleasantness, slums foster disease, sabotage education, and are vulnerable to fires and natural disasters. Globally, at least 100 million people lack housing altogether.[20]

If current trends continue, the number of people living in slums will rise to 2 billion in 2030 and 3 billion in 2050.[21] That's because virtually all the world population growth will be in the cities of developing countries, concentrated in the informal settlements of the poor. To supply shelter for the 40 percent of the world's population that will need affordable housing by 2030 will require the building of 96,150 new housing units every day.[22]

Creating shelter for the poorest citizens doesn't come easy. Not only do these slum dwellers lack money, but they also often live in a form of shadow economy—which discourages mechanisms like the traditional thirty-year mortgage or even rental arrangements. "Housing projects require many different partners, may not have one clear entrepreneur at the helm, often rely on subsidy to be truly affordable, and don't see a finished product on the ground until many months or even years later," writes Acumen's Aden Van Noppen.[23]

Safely housing large numbers of the urban poor in a radically new way requires multiple players to converge in an ecosystem of finance, skilled labor, and legal understanding. The first challenge, however, is simply designing a cheap home. That engineering and business feat demanded its own ecosystem of skilled professionals.

To inspire the necessary collaboration, Vijay Govindarajan and Christian Sarkar, professors at Dartmouth's Tuck School of Business, used an exchange model. They proposed a contest: design a $300 house. And cost wasn't the only constraint. To transform slums, the designs needed to be adaptable to local conditions and simple to construct from available materials. Hardware and construction conglomerate Ingersoll Rand offered prize money for the best designs.

Govindarajan and Sarkar realized the project would require the best minds in business, design, architecture, and academia, as well as feedback from business experts, architects, and nonprofit pros who possessed a rubble-level intimacy with the world's slums.

Open information fed the design process. As the teams prepared their entries, the contestants compared proposals online, and anyone on the internet could critique the plans. Experts were invited to describe the obstacles, both financial and environmental, that the designers would face.

The six winning teams participated in a weeklong prototyping workshop at Dartmouth. One winner designed a house that cut costs through economies of scale. "We realized that by analyzing just one house, we were never going to achieve the goal of $300 per house," says Eric Ho from the Architecture Commons team. "Because of the cost of labor, it's just not possible. So to circumvent it, we had to create a community."[24] This community would need to tap into the principles of the solution revolution, including new forms of investing and finance.

In this model, a hundred families together would apply for $30,000 of microfinance loans. Thus a village would invest in machines to build compressed-earth bricks and special roof tiles, two microenterprise projects that could employ villagers while it created housing for them. At Dartmouth, the Architecture Commons team learned that a working prototype would be customized for a trial run in Haiti, merging the best elements of the winning designs.[25]

Meanwhile, Tata Group, an Indian company known for its $2,500 car, is testing three designs for a $700 house in West Bengal. The prefabricated kit constructs a 215-square-foot home that can be assembled in a week. Though potentially still beyond the reach of the poorest, the design should provide a welcome alternative for the Indian middle and lower-middle classes and should simplify the cost of government housing. Other architects are observing Tata's effort closely to find elements of the design that might scale.

The next layer of the low-cost housing ecosystem is finance and administration. Slum dwellers often lack the legal rights to their homes. Potential builders must consider actual owners as well as the government departments that enforce building codes, fight fires, and must provide shelter for relocated residents. Builders also must coordinate with NGOs, contractors, financiers, and other players, such as academic advisers or volunteer architects. Figure 6-2 shows how all these players and innovations contribute to create affordable housing for people at the base of the pyramid in various countries.

FIGURE 6-2

Affordable housing at the base of the pyramid

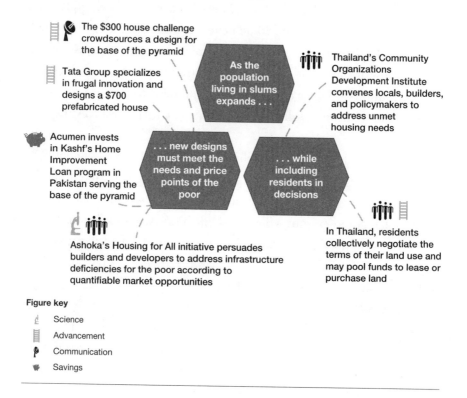

The $300 house challenge crowdsources a design for the base of the pyramid

Tata Group specializes in frugal innovation and designs a $700 prefabricated house

Acumen invests in Kashf's Home Improvement Loan program in Pakistan serving the base of the pyramid

As the population living in slums expands . . .

. . . new designs must meet the needs and price points of the poor

. . . while including residents in decisions

Thailand's Community Organizations Development Institute convenes locals, builders, and policymakers to address unmet housing needs

In Thailand, residents collectively negotiate the terms of their land use and may pool funds to lease or purchase land

Ashoka's Housing for All initiative persuades builders and developers to address infrastructure deficiencies for the poor according to quantifiable market opportunities

Figure key

Science

Advancement

Communication

Savings

Ashoka Egypt is attempting to entice private investors with the potential of a trillion-dollar housing market for the base of the pyramid. It's a hard task. Plenty of businesspeople have been burned in lowest-income housing before.

Ashoka's Rochelle Beck describes the challenges: "Some builders and developers see significant potential profits, but they do not have accurate market information about what their new customers—slum dwellers—need, want, currently spend or can afford for housing. Their traditional marketing and sales forces have little or no experience in slums, nor trusted working relationships with those who do. If a barrier such as ambiguous land title or too few or too expensive home mortgage products [appears,] the perceived risk often is enough to sink their interest."[26]

To protect the enterprise, Ashoka assembles market research to ensure that its housing goes to those who are truly eligible. Tablet technology simplifies a sample census, and census takers photograph families for future reference. Such proof of residency helps prevent latecomer fraud.[27] It also ensures that historic problems of misunderstanding the customer, particularly at the base of the pyramid, are avoided by capturing their wants and needs on the front lines.

Ashoka also acts as a broker, sourcing high-quality construction materials from local builders, assembling potential homeowners into groups to better negotiate with microfinance institutions, and consulting university engineers. One such initiative through Ashoka Egypt has yielded more than ten thousand new housing units.[28]

Ashoka has also been actively trying to create a market for affordable housing in India. Currently, the country's swelling urban populations face a shortage of 24.7 million homes. In India, a pay stub is a standard requirement to finance a home, but 86 percent of the urban population have no proof of income, because they work in the informal economy.[29] The ingrained assumption, of course, is that without a pay stub, a person can't be creditworthy. All the various businesses involved in the housing project have more or less adhered to the rule, sticking to what they knew: the builders focused on building, and the financiers focused on funding those who met the criteria.

To convince everyone of the shared benefit of housing the poor, Ashoka had to develop relationships between the mortgage companies, for-profit housing developers, and local community organizations. The ecosystem for affordable housing works like this: community organizations act as demand aggregators, bringing groups of consumers to for-profit developers, and as design and investment partners. So far, ten thousand homes have been built, representing at least $100 million in sales.[30] And the building continues. Ashoka founder Bill Drayton now considers it "a $340 million market failure that went away."[31] In addition to housing projects in Egypt, Ashoka's ecosystem-building activities for services for the very poor run the gamut from health to agriculture to education.

One community's solution, of course, may not be suited for another. Thailand's Community Organizations Development Institute (CODI) scales a general approach rather than a specific solution. CODI carefully connects the elements a housing ecosystem needs to survive—legal representation, interested developers, and land rights—and then lets the ecosystem operate on its own. Local communities take ownership, and CODI facilitates the processes.

As with Ashoka, CODI begins with intelligence. Recruits identify influential individuals in the community who can share local insights. One case study describes the process: "In the city of Uttaradit, the initiative started with survey mapping of all the slums and small pockets of squatters, identifying those slums that could stay and those that needed to be relocated. This helped link community organizations and began building a community network supported by young architects, a group of monks and the mayor."[32]

Like the funding approach that Govindarajan and Sarkar recommended in Dartmouth's challenge to design a $300 house, the Uttaradit community pools money and labor resources under the control of trusted elders. In this way, the whole community has a stake in the outcome. By becoming a legal entity, the slum community can negotiate with property owners and buy land or secure long-term leases, either collectively or as individuals.

Residents of the Charoenchai Nimitmai community in Bangkok pooled their resources to buy land, while residents in a neighboring community used their new legal status to negotiate a long-term lease. Another community, Kolok Village, stretches along a railroad company's property. The slum dwellers agreed to keep their homes twenty meters from the track in exchange for long-term tenure.[33]

The beauty of this ecosystem is that with proper incentives and formal status under the law, communities begin to develop their own innovations, and solutions emerge from within. By 2012, CODI had housed more than 80,200 households in 745 projects in 249 cities.[34] It's doubtful that anyone sleeping under a proper roof by the train in Kolok understands how much effort went into constructing their homes.

Ending Human Trafficking: An Ecosystem That Saves Lives

Close to twenty-one million people worldwide, a growing share of them children, are trapped in contemporary forms of slavery collectively called human trafficking. Besides child labor, such slavery includes forced labor and sex slavery. Globally, human trafficking is a $32 billion industry.[35]

Modern slavery often begins with the phrase "Want a job?" says Kevin Bales, cofounder of Free the Slaves, a nonprofit working in the modern antitrafficking ecosystem.[36] Trafficking rings recruit marginalized, desperate people, luring them with the hope of work or passage to another country, and then separate them from their support networks. The more marginalized the person, the shorter the reach of those who care. Once at the mercy of their captors—working in an African tin mine far from honest law enforcement or turning tricks in Los Angeles without a passport—victims often feel powerless to find a way out.

Trafficking requires many participants. Recruiters and transporters move humans. Bribed officials turn a blind eye or provide faked documents. Guides transport humans past law enforcement. Informants spy on police. Deep-pocketed investors fund trafficking ventures. "Launderers" clean dirty money. It's an entire black-market ecosystem.[37]

Antonio José dos Santos Filho, a rural Brazilian down on his luck, is typical of the persons who find themselves enslaved in the twenty-first century. He was recruited by an acquaintance who flashed some cash and offered work. Soon Filho rode a bus for two days to the

Brazilian state of Parás. There, armed guards stood watch as he and others cleared rain forest land for cattle grazing. He guessed he was in trouble, but learned for sure when he asked for his paycheck. His bosses told him he owed money for purchases made at the "company store."[38] He would work until he repaid them.

Filho was a slave. He drank the same muddy water the cattle drank. Each night, he slept under a tarp, prey to insects and inclement weather. Luckily for him, authorities found and freed him. Although Brazilian law permits such forced laborers to demand back pay from their former slaveholders, the legal system is complex and frustrating, often causing the victims to give up. But this time the Pastoral Land Commission, in partnership with Catholic Relief Services, a leader in antislavery work, organized forty-two families affected to demand restitution. After a five-year legal battle that the victims could never have afforded on their own, they won 2,670 acres of land and material to build thirty houses.[39]

Sadly, these triumphs are still too few and far between. The lack of coordination across anti-human-trafficking groups does not help. David Rogers of the US Federal Bureau of Investigation admits that "many of us share the goal of eliminating human trafficking, but there are misunderstandings about roles. We need to better understand how to augment—not compete with—each other."[40] The multitude of NGOs focused on the issue brings added complexity. It wasn't until 2009 that a few leaders in this area cofounded an online public database, the Freedom Registry, which now lists more than eight hundred advocate groups active in the United States alone.[41] The registry's success in driving collaboration on anti-human-trafficking work led to the creation of another advocate network in Canada.

Yet even when separate organizations engage, their approaches are sometimes at odds. Some groups attempt legal action, while others maintain a low profile and focus solely on rescuing captives; still others document the horrors with video or photos to raise awareness of the issue.

Groups can fight human trafficking on four fronts, commonly called the four Ps: prevention, protection, prosecution, and partnerships (figure 6-3). *Prevention* includes both warning potential migrants about the dangers of human trafficking, and shaming those who might benefit from it. *Protection* focuses on helping victims escape and rehabilitating them. *Prosecution* encompasses the investigations of trafficking networks. A growing number of countries—134 in 2012—recognize trafficking as an offense that merits legal criminalization; the

FIGURE 6-3

Human trafficking prevention ecosystem

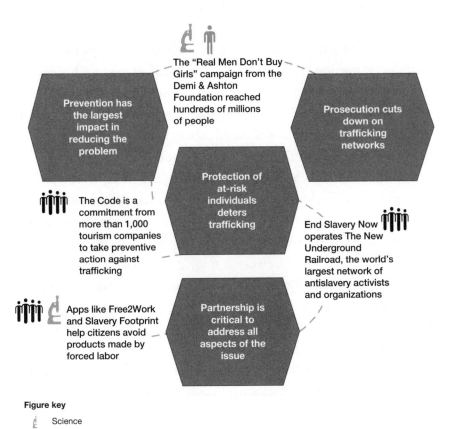

The "Real Men Don't Buy Girls" campaign from the Demi & Ashton Foundation reached hundreds of millions of people

Prevention has the largest impact in reducing the problem

Prosecution cuts down on trafficking networks

The Code is a commitment from more than 1,000 tourism companies to take preventive action against trafficking

Protection of at-risk individuals deters trafficking

End Slavery Now operates The New Underground Railroad, the world's largest network of antislavery activists and organizations

Apps like Free2Work and Slavery Footprint help citizens avoid products made by forced labor

Partnership is critical to address all aspects of the issue

Figure key

Science

number of countries lacking such legislation shrank by half between 2008 and 2012. Unfortunately, according to the most recent UN estimate, global law enforcement averages only one conviction for every eight hundred people enslaved.[42]

Partnership is common among nations but a relatively new phenomenon in the world of grassroots antislavery work. The US State Department, for instance, has stepped up its antitrafficking partnerships in recent years, in 2005 alone supporting more than 265 international programs in about one hundred countries.[43] The European Union also has a vigorous multinational antitrafficking agency. The EU Anti-Trafficking Coordinator is directly responsible for ensuring that EU nations take complementary approaches in fighting traffickers working routes between Eastern and Western Europe, Africa and Spain, and through Albania into Italy.[44]

Most antitrafficking organizations, whether they focus on prevention, protection, or prosecution, are small groups with deep experience in the red-light districts of places such as Kolkata or Haiti. Some, such as Cambodia's Somaly Mam Foundation, are run by former victims.[45] Their personal experience helps them gain the trust of trafficked women, identify trustworthy authorities (as opposed to corrupt police), and cope with local mafias in their efforts to protect women from trafficking. They run women's shelters and use their local contacts to help trafficking victims find work and to head off the desperation that drives some victims to try their luck abroad again or, worse, become recruiters. Because these groups lack legislative clout and other resources, they are often vulnerable to corrupt officials and trafficking networks. These antitrafficking groups are nevertheless bringing good ideas to bear on a daunting problem, but often without a supportive ecosystem.

Consequently, partnership can benefit these small groups as much as, if not more than, partnerships between nations. Larger organizations such as End Slavery Now convene a variety of players and allow grassroots organizations to collaborate and find trustworthy partners in this dangerous business. End Slavery Now also operates the New

Underground Railroad, the world's largest network of antislavery activists and organizations.[46]

Private companies are joining the fight, and in ways that go beyond feel-good CSR campaigns. "Why do I care?" asks Genevieve Taft-Vazquez of Coca-Cola. "If 68 percent of forced labor connects with global supply chains, and we operate in over 200 countries, we know it's in communities where we are, so we have to be vigilant." She adds that her job as global manager of workplace accountability would be made easier with a registry of good and bad labor recruiters, to bring greater transparency to labor sourcing.[47]

The supply chain isn't the only way companies wage battle directly against human trafficking. Companies like Palantir bring technical expertise to tracing networks of traffickers. Palantir techies developed software that stitches together numerous data sources—filed police reports and investigations, citizen-submitted tips, subpoenaed phone logs—across geospatial maps and network diagrams to help prosecutors spot instances of trafficking faster.[48] For the contingent of Palantir programmers who used to work for PayPal, the process bears a striking resemblance to the fraud-detection practices of their former employer. In 2012 the company donated the software to the International Consortium of Investigative Journalists to help journalists analyze the illicit markets for human tissue.[49]

Coordinated, multisector attempts to fight trafficking are growing at the national and international level, from Brazil's National Pact for the Eradication of Slave Labor to the Global Business Coalition Against Human Trafficking. Signatories of the Brazilian pact agree not to buy from suppliers on the government's "dirty" list and to submit to independent audits, to reduce the amount of goods produced with slave labor.[50]

Consumers have also joined the fight, demanding reliable sourcing information. At best, clothing labels once gave you little more than "100% cotton" and "Made in China." Now, consumers can scan QR codes (those little black-and-white squares seen on everything, from magazines to ketchup bottles) to see an item's provenance and care instructions and perhaps to even watch videos of the people who made it. iPhone apps such as Free2Work grade companies on their forced-labor risk factor, and Slavery Footprint, which allows consumers to learn how many "slaves" potentially work for them, also play an important role in raising awareness of the issue. This is both a moral and marketing opportunity, one that many companies have come to recognize. Anvil Knitwear's customers can follow its products through the supply chain via trackmy-T.com. Swiss textile company Switcher has similar labels.

As actress and UN ambassador for human trafficking Mira Sorvino points out, eradicating human trafficking requires enduring effort. "Child labor issues in the chocolate industry were a big deal a decade ago. Consumers pushed companies, companies made commitments to avoid suppliers that used child labor, and many thought that because it was acknowledged, it was solved. Yet there are still 200,000 children forced to work in the chocolate industry."[51] In short, rendering issues of slavery and trafficking obsolete requires persistent action and coordination from all sides.

Complementary Capabilities and the Effective Ecosystem

The issues just raised—modernizing education, providing affordable housing, and eliminating human trafficking—may seem to have little in common. Little, that is, except that societies worldwide have sought to address them for years or centuries—mostly unsuccessfully.

The approaches discussed in this book, however, can yield significant improvements in a wide variety of arenas: new players emerge, partnerships develop, and technologies are harnessed and form the basis for new business models. As markets for solutions grow more diverse and sophisticated, new currencies enable the wider pool of players to benefit from this blossoming of choice, perhaps providing citizen capital instead of money for a service. Exchanges that maximize social outcomes evolve, generating the types of solution ecosystems profiled earlier in this chapter and throughout the book, from the waste reduction ecosystems curated by Recyclebank and Waste Ventures to the emerging car-sharing and ridesharing ecosystems fueled by market innovators like Zipcar and Zimride.

However, these ecosystems are not static. As in nature, the strength and endurance of a solution ecosystem are influenced by diversity and constant adaptation. When Ashoka steps in to clarify land title holdings, it is opening up the flow of information critical to the housing infrastructure, in this case the financing function. When a beaver builds a dam, it alters the ecological environment, allowing new plants and animals to thrive. In the same way, small but critical changes by the convener of a solution ecosystem create new opportunities for other players, encouraging them to evolve and build a new market in the process. (See figure 6-4 for a description of how ecosystems develop.) What wasn't viable before can now thrive, profitably and sustainably.

The natural world is full of such examples. Cheeky clownfish, for instance, score protection in the barbed tentacles of sea anemones. In return for the shelter, anemones snack on the fish's leftovers or on the prey their striped guests attract. When alligators in the Florida Everglades let certain species of birds clean the meat from their teeth, the reptiles can get a better grip on their next meal. And in Copenhagen, some four million honeybees pollinate the city's flowers and plants producing honey, enabling the city's flora to bear fruit and flourish.

While this last example might seem natural, it is actually the result of a human-made social business—one of many positive outcomes in a stunning system of mutual benefit. The City Bee Project, known as Bybi (Danish for "city bee"), is British social entrepreneur Oliver Maxwell's idea to bring millions of honeybees to Copenhagen to create a sustainable honey industry. Working with the city, social organizations, and Danish businesses, the project trains the former homeless and the long-term unemployed to become independent beekeepers. The model benefits at least two groups. The city's disadvantaged gain meaningful work (maintaining beehives on the rooftops of local businesses), and honeybees get safe, urban spaces to pollinate and prosper.

FIGURE 6-4

Fostering a solution ecosystem: From inception to execution

1. Identify

Problems

Existing solutions

Gaps in existing models/markets

Limits and failures of current players

2. Connect

Connect around a central problem

Conveners bring the problem into the spotlight

Ascertain relevant technologies and models to leverage

3. Innovate and incubate

Invest in market-building activities

Convene problem solvers and innovate solutions

Pilot innovative ideas with seed funding

Build and test multiple prototypes

4. Execute and scale

Establish standards and benchmarks

Create an ongoing process to refine solutions

Scale solutions

Beekeepers own and operate the business, while profits from the honey are reinvested into Bybi's social and environmental activities.[52]

This noble, if unusual, experiment aims at a surprisingly sticky problem: honeybees pollinate 70 percent of all plants, representing a third of the food we eat. But because of climate change, new agricultural practices, and mysterious bee diseases, honeybees are dying off in droves across Europe. According to one estimate, bees in England could go extinct as early as 2018 if they continue to decline at the current rate.[53] Their survival, and much of our food, increasingly relies on beekeepers. Meanwhile, an aging workforce threatens to sink traditional beekeeping.

For Maxwell, who has a background in sociology, not beekeeping, it was a problem occurring behind his back. That is, he was little aware of it until the winter of 2009, when he spied a stack of beehives one night while driving home from work and pulled over to talk to the beekeeper. Maxwell was working in Copenhagen developing social enterprises at the time. But after talking with this local beekeeper and discovering the enormity of the problem, the entrepreneur's mind started buzzing with a new idea.

He started meeting with beekeepers and biologists and learning more about the issues. He learned that more bees were needed in the city, that cities offered bees refuge from pesticides, that the next generation of beekeepers were not being adequately trained, and that the demand for local and traditional honey needed to be increased.[54] The solution lay before him in pieces. It just needed to be assembled. So Maxwell brought together development workers from local businesses, city leaders, housing associations, employment projects, and the beekeepers. Each group had knowledge that the others lacked and needs that the others could satisfy working together.

With the diverse groups on board, Maxwell convinced the city to seed-fund the project. Local businesses can now partner with Bybi and "adopt" beehives, providing a workspace for beekeepers and bees on their rooftops. Social organizations, such as Urbanplanen, one of Denmark's largest housing estates, help source the labor. And Bybi provides the bees, the training, and the tools to equip the disadvantaged with new careers as beekeepers. What's more, Maxwell's organization creates a marketing machine for the local honey industry and good business. At the end of each season, Bybi and its business partners produce CSR reports that businesses can use to court investors and customers. They also get their own brand of honey to sweeten their reputation even further.

Within Bybi's ecosystem, bees have a safe harbor, the former homeless and disadvantaged have employment, social organizations meet their goals, top businesses bolster their brands, the city is lusher than ever, and taxpayers don't have to pay a cent for the army of beekeepers working on their behalf. Problem solved.

While each group—the beekeepers with the knowledge, the social organizations with the labor funnel, and the businesses with the vacant rooftops—were integral to the final solution, Maxwell deserves most of the credit. He had the vision and drive to turn a grave problem into everyone's advantage. "I knew there was a story and an opportunity in the problem," he said. "The challenge was to get the right people to meet."[55]

Beekeeping is a centuries-old occupation given a new twist by Maxwell. Other ecosystems, such as the one centered on educational reform, are being refined and redefined by new technologies and business models that public-value innovators are applying in novel, productive ways. But technology is impartial. Human traffickers, for example, use online access and social networks to scale their own destructive operations as well. The same holds true for terrorist and cybercrime networks. It isn't the technology per se that matters; it is the enabling role that technology can play in a solution ecosystem.

Hunger, poverty, and disease thrive on their own. Outpacing the destructive forces that corrode social progress requires a new model. No single enterprise can tackle all the facets of a fast-changing issue. The most effective contributors in an ecosystem are intimately aware of what they can and likewise cannot do well, and they wisely seek out partners with complementary capabilities. Unilever, for example, recognized its role in putting Wheel soap into action, but also where it would need partners.

With health and sanitation, shelter, and even hunger, the solution economy is rewriting the way humans can grapple with the most daunting problems in the world. The technology revolution is enabling new organizations, new currencies, and new solution ecosystems. A new generation of wavemakers is challenging traditional approaches. Coupled with new attitudes among corporate, academic, and governmental thought leaders, they are also producing dramatic results.

But unfortunately the solution economy isn't developing evenly around the globe. In the final chapter, we will examine what government, business, investors, and individuals can do to accelerate the development of the solution economy.

THE ECOSYSTEMS:
IN A NUTSHELL

THE BIG IDEA
The solution economy tears down silos to create ecosystems with a single core issue at their center. In these ecosystems, wavemakers connect with one another in pursuit of a common goal.

TYPES OF SOLUTION ECOSYSTEMS

- **Innovation:** an ecosystem that capitalizes on advances in technology and business practices to deliver novel solutions. For example, far-reaching shifts in the education ecosystem are changing how we learn and who we learn from.

- **Base-of-the-pyramid:** an ecosystem that serves poorer populations typically ignored as consumer markets. For example, safely housing the billions of people who live in slums requires multiple players to converge.

- **Life-saving:** an ecosystem that focuses on interventions and other actions that prevent life-threatening situations. An important life-saving ecosystem in today's solution economy battles human trafficking. This modern form of slavery involves many participants in the crime; fighting it successfully requires an integrated ecosystem.

ECOSYSTEM ACCELERATORS

- A backbone organization often serves as a central organizer or convener.

- Connectors bring together ecosystem members; these members support one another while maintaining substantial autonomy.

- Platforms create simple market conditions and a user culture that facilitates interactions between players.

INNOVATORS

- The social enterprise **d.light**, which provides access to lighting for the base of the pyramid, teamed up with BRAC to provide a distribution mechanism and now has reached ten million people.

- **Udacity** offers open, interactive courseware online as well as traditional brick-and-mortar college services, such as career counseling.

- **Ashoka Egypt** brings private investors to the potentially trillion-dollar housing market for the base of the pyramid. The organization eases the way by sourcing construction materials locally and identifying eligible potential homeowners and sources of microfinancing.

- **Tata Group** is testing three designs for a $700 house. The prefabricated kit constructs a 215-square-foot home that can be assembled in a week.

- Cambodia's **Somaly Mam Foundation** is staffed by former victims and draws on their experience to battle human trafficking locally.

CHALLENGES TO SOLUTION ECOSYSTEMS

- Making connections over certain issues is difficult simply because no ecosystem exists. Wavemakers often have to create an ecosystem from scratch.

- While technology can enable some ecosystems to address social ills, it can also contribute to the ills themselves; wavemakers need to recognize the scope and impact of technology and work to outpace its destructive potential.

QUESTIONS FOR THOUGHT

What ecosystems do you feel that you currently have visibility into? Have your experiences working on one specific challenge provided any lessons that were transferable across ecosystems? What common themes have you observed?

SEVEN

Creating Your Own Solution Revolution

A quick guide to changing the world—seriously

Imagine the world if we were able to double, triple, or even quadruple the number of problem solvers, the diversity of solutions, and the scale of social impacts.

Imagine if every government emulated NASA and opened up its toughest challenges for the world to solve.

Imagine if thousands more investors built off Acumen's patient-capital approach, sharing early-stage funding risk to sow the seeds of dignity and wealth.

Imagine if tens of millions of citizens started building better city blocks and other supportive communities; if every multi-billion-dollar company became a double- or triple-bottom-line business and directed resources to solving society's problems.

Imagine if the number of social enterprises tripled and thousands of them had the size and scale to spread their innovations across continents.

We've started down the road to such a world. The solution revolution is a reality—and it's growing. This growth, however, is uneven. It's flourishing in the United States, the United Kingdom, India, Australia, parts of Africa, and in pockets of Europe. In whole regions of the world, however, the developments described in this book are still quite immature.

The reason is simple: the solution economy grows to fill the space it's given, and certain regions offer habitats more hospitable for a robust solution economy than others. Their governments provide room for creativity, their businesses embrace new measures of value, and their investors trust alternative currencies of return.

What accelerates the solution economy? What constrains it?

Consider two European neighbors: France and the United Kingdom. In the United Kingdom, both Conservative and Labor governments have actively nurtured the social sector for more than a decade. The result is a large and rapidly growing economy of problem solvers and a changing role for government. Instead of shouldering almost sole responsibility for delivery, government increasingly catalyzes solutions. The United Kingdom has fewer civil servants today than at any time in the past seventy years, despite a population increase of 300 percent over the same period. Moreover, the country has experienced a rapid growth in civil society—a 40 percent increase in new charities and a doubling of large charities between 1995 and 2005.[1]

In contrast to the fertile UK landscape of nongovernmental problem solvers, France is pretty barren. Compared with the rest of Europe, France has the fewest philanthropic and charitable foundations per capita. The nonprofit sector is also smaller than most of Europe's and less than half that of the United States (4.2 percent of GDP, compared with 8.5 percent in the United States). And the social enterprise sector is still a new and undeveloped concept.[2]

Some of the differences between France and the United Kingdom can be attributed to long-standing cultural differences. French citizens have long supported the state's large role in the economy and in daily life. But there is more to it than this. In contrast to France, the UK government has devoted significant time and resources to creating conditions for the solution economy to thrive. "You have to get the landscape right," explains Gareth Davies, a key architect of the government's effort. "We spent a lot of time on structural reform, building the institutions necessary to grow the social economy."[3] Steps along the way included opening up services to citizen choice, devolving service delivery to local governments, shifting procurement to payment-for-results models, and creating the £600 million Big Society Capital fund to help finance new entrants into the solution economy.[4]

Some jurisdictions are designed to offer habitats more hospitable to the solution economy. Their governments provide room for creativity, their businesses step up to build social outcomes into business practices, and their investors innovate how social value is measured and exchanged. Some regions uproot thickets of red tape; elsewhere the opposite is happening. Waste Ventures in India, as described earlier, struggles against laws that limit small-scale contractors. With an act as free and simple as changing restrictions, Indian municipalities could gain comprehensive waste cleanup, reduce carbon emissions, and boost a homegrown fertilizer and recycling industry.

On the other side of the planet, Revolution Foods, in Oakland, California, would be vulnerable to shareholder activism if it registered as a regular corporation—the board would face a legal obligation to turn $50 million in revenue into shareholder profit, rather than reinvesting it to serve 120,000 healthy meals per day to schoolkids.[5] Fortunately, recent US laws allowed Revolution Foods to form a B corp, a benefit corporation in which the number of meals served is a valid bottom line.

Think of the ripples emanating from the work of Revolution Foods. The company helps disadvantaged children and the farmers and others who produce healthy food. Children perform better in school, so the education system benefits as well. Private employers later enjoy (and employ) a smarter workforce—and a healthier one. Health-care savings pass both to the students' families and to their communities.

As this example shows, the effects of one benefit corporation spread widely to the greater community. Imagine what the larger solution economy already produces and how much more can be unleashed. It makes a country stronger, for far fewer tax dollars.

Government's willingness to forge partnerships (and vet those partners with accurate metrics), to make data more open, to contract for outcomes, to reduce regulatory minefields, and to convene diverse groups of contributors will hold tremendous sway over the scale of the solution economy within its borders. For instance, legal designations for nonprofits and foundations, along with the accompanying tax exemptions, encourage the proliferation of these organizations.

Some factors important to the solution revolution are more cultural and resist change. These range from citizen expectations of the role of government to societal attitudes on business failure and risk.

Yet across these various cultural contexts, one observation remains the same: today's biggest societal problems are beyond the reach of any individual entity or sector. Collaboration is not just helpful, but essential, for true progress. In many ways, the technologies, business models, and currencies featured in this book offer a more level playing field, enabling the collective strength of all contributors to drive improved public services, wider choices, and better outcomes.

Ignoring the changing ways that solutions are now rapidly developed and deployed presents its own risks. Countries that cultivate connected ecosystems gain the advantage of accelerated growth in the scope and scale of potential solutions, while others that rely wholly on government will increasingly struggle to keep up. As citizens, we know which side we'd prefer. The question is how, as a society, to get there.

Strategies for Growing the Solution Economy

Seeing the potential of the solution economy no doubt provokes questions. What actions can you contribute to the solution revolution? How can you directly benefit? Or if you are a government official, you might be asking, "What can my government do to create a more favorable environment for the solution economy?" If you work at a big company, you might wonder what you can do to promote social innovation at your organization.

In writing this book, we've either developed or come across dozens of actions that business, government, foundations, investors, and social enterprises can take to grow the solution economy (the full list can be found in the appendix). We've distilled these down to six overarching principles—all of them relevant to each of the major players in the solution revolution.

Change the Lens: How Will a Different View Reveal Both Blind Spots and Untapped Opportunity?

More often than not, implementing big change in today's fast-paced world feels like careening down a steep hill in a rail car. Sometimes, it takes your full energy just to make incremental adjustments that keep the wheels on the track. But what if there was a better way to reach your destination?

Just like restricting travel to steel tracks, if you're thinking about solving a big problem solely in terms of current programs, you will confine potential solutions to a flawed status quo. Frequently, legacy programs harden their approaches through a failure to reimagine what might be.

Forget for a moment about how you currently do things. Begin by asking, "What is my goal?" And this time ignore the caveats and parameters that usually filter the question. Think bigger. For instance, thinking "How can we improve schools?" can limit your thoughts to the confines of a brick-and-mortar classroom. Instead, you might ask, "How can we better educate children to prepare them for the workplace of the future?" The latter question opens up a range of possibilities that may not even include schooling as it is traditionally understood.

Focusing on the desired outcome rather than clinging to bygone processes also opens up a whole universe of potential problem solvers. Consider the fight against obesity. If you sat down and made a list of stakeholders that were key to addressing this epidemic, the tally might include doctors and snack food companies, but not the National Football League. Yet it turns out the NFL is an important player in fighting obesity, using its popular brand to encourage youth health and fitness through the Play 60 initiative. The NFL has now donated more than $250 million in airtime and money to youth wellness since the 2007 inception of Play 60, recognizing that children who ignore presidential directives will listen to NFL running backs.[6]

How exactly do you change your lens? Luke Williams, the author of *Disrupt,* defines a disruptive hypothesis as "an intentionally unreasonable statement that gets your thinking flowing in a different direction."[7]

To develop such a hypothesis, Williams suggests exploring the dominant clichés in the area in question and then inverting or denying them. Take the education example. Public schooling evokes in-person teachers, classrooms, textbooks, school facilities, cafeterias, and yellow buses. A disruptive hypothesis might ask, "What would happen if we tried to educate children without *any* of these elements?" The answer might be something like the massive open online courses (MOOCs) profiled in chapter 3.

Also critical to changing your lens is to question assumptions—including your own. Consider the widely held assumption that the disadvantaged cannot afford to pay for products and services. For decades, this assumption blinkered corporate thinking and obscured the opportunity to make a profit in base-of-the-pyramid markets. Now, a range of organizations, both for-profit and nonprofit, have mobilized to serve this population through innovative approaches. While some struggle with this dramatically different business landscape, others, like Unilever and Uganda's LivingGoods, thrive.

A disruptive way of thinking may begin with an organization or individual, but it can't go very far unless others can be convinced to think, and act, differently, too. When Barclays thought about branching out from its traditional clientele and expanding into Ghana, where fully 60 percent of money trades hands and is stored outside the commercial banking system, the bank recognized its blind spot and looked to the real experts of rural finance: Susu collectors. For three centuries, Ghanaians have entrusted the Susu collectors with their sav-

ings, collected daily or weekly, so that it can earn interest. By helping Susu collectors see Barclays in a different light, not just as a bank
to the wealthy, Barclays built trust and from there, a partnership. In
this way, the bank was able to bring low-cost lending capital and savings accounts to a demographic it otherwise would have struggled to
reach.[8]

Sometimes, people discover new lenses after years of staring at the
same place. When he started Social Capital Partners (SCP) in 2001,
Canadian Bill Young focused on finding meaningful employment for
disadvantaged workers via the traditional route with nonprofits. After
five years and a lot of work, SCP had created about five hundred jobs.
It was good—but not good enough for Young.

So he started to look at things differently. What if instead of only
looking to nonprofits, he tried to really engage the private sector?
Young rejiggered his whole model. He would supply cheap financing to businesspeople seeking to purchase a franchise—Young started
with the Canadian quick-lube auto shops Active Green & Ross—as
long as the business agreed to hire from a pool of employees SCP provided from social assistance rolls. SCP then worked with community
hiring agencies to tailor the pool to the franchise's needs. The program
took off—with more than a thousand individuals placed.

Young's model worked so well that Active Green & Ross adopted
it for the parent company without any monetary incentives at all.
And now Young is developing a large-scale program that refocuses
the entire way Canada's community training and placement programs
operate.

Young started out on one path and ended up in a very different
place. Why? Because he was willing to change his lens.

Changing your lens involves looking at institutions in new ways.
Government increasingly is becoming more an enabler, helping to create opportunities for new markets and innovation, rather than a direct
provider.

It also means looking at citizens in new ways, not just seeing what
they want, but also understanding what—with the right incentives—

they would be willing to contribute. Even in the heady world of global diplomacy, former secretary of state Hillary Clinton looked to citizens directly during her foreign tours for partners and creative solutions, which in some cases marked a clean break from traditional government visits: "We do need a new architecture for this new world; more Frank Gehry than formal Greek . . . You can't build a set of durable partnerships in the 21st century with governments alone. The opinions of people now matter as to how their governments work with us, whether it's democratic or authoritarian. So in virtually every country I have visited, I've held town halls and reached out directly to citizens, civil society organizations, women's groups, business communities, and so many others. They have valuable insights and contributions to make. And increasingly, they are driving economic and political change."[9]

Citizens will be the cornerstone of this new architecture. They are empowered to act, whether through apps built from government data, policy input derived from their own analysis, or data visualizations used to advocate for issues they care about. Such knowledge enables greater influence over what services are provided and how they are delivered, signaling a shift in power.

Many foundations are also viewing themselves in a new way, seeing themselves more and more as the "gap fillers" in the solution economy—looking to find where traditional government aid and charity fall short and then targeting those areas. Other organizations would do well, for themselves and the broader ecosystem, to think as creatively about their evolving roles.

Target the Gaps: Develop New Markets by Meeting Neglected Needs

Sixty-five percent of the world's population now lives in countries where being overweight kills more people than does being underweight.[10] In the United States, maps from the Centers for Disease Control and Prevention show obesity metastasizing over the past twenty-five years. Whereas the majority of states once had obesity rates below 10 percent, the widening splotches of color show that today, *all* states have obesity rates above 20 percent—and a majority endure rates above 25 percent.[11]

The problem is also spreading to the developing world. Obesity rates have tripled in Brazilian men and doubled in Brazilian women over the past three decades. China's diabetes rates are now the same as those in the United States. In Russia, one in four women and one in ten men are obese.[12]

A significant number of obese adults and children come from lower-income groups.[13] A lack of opportunities for safe physical activity, limited access to healthy food, and the high cost of fresh produce all contribute.

As the largest grocery retailer in the world, Walmart has enormous influence on the food-access part of this problem. Walmart credits Michelle Obama's Let's Move! campaign with inspiring its own Healthier Food initiative, which commits to opening between 275 and 300 additional stores by 2016 in USDA-designated food deserts—places where access to healthy food is severely limited (on top of the 218 the company has already opened since 2011). The stores will offer produce to more than eight hundred thousand people who today live in food deserts. Walmart has also committed to reduced prices on fresh produce and reformulating thousands of its private Great Value brand products to reduce their fat, sugar, and salt content. And it's a double bottom line for Walmart: penetrating urban markets in the United States could enable the retailer to boost volume by $80 billion a year.[14]

Meeting a neglected need like access to produce is practically the definition of entrepreneurship. Businesses and consumers alike may benefit. While these challenges are daunting, most of the new problem solvers we encountered while researching this book approached gaps in basic needs not as obstacles but as opportunities. Recall Parag Gupta's Waste Ventures. No one else was providing end-to-end solutions for waste removal in poor communities. He improved conditions for waste pickers while satisfying a market need. Or Unilever, which targeted the lack of sanitation in India's poorest villages, selling soap to people who didn't know they needed it and who seemingly had no money to buy it.

Advancements and renewed creativity are transforming deep societal problems into fertile markets for change. Take proper housing for low-income populations. As noted earlier, this tough problem is one of business's greatest opportunities. The same thing can be said for health care and food. The market for serving the very poor in these sectors is an estimated $202 billion and $3.6 trillion, respectively.[15]

Until recently, explains Ashoka's Bill Drayton, the business world was unable to unlock the economic potential of these latent markets. Businesses tended to focus on their traditional demographics and lacked the knowledge to deliver what gap-dwelling customers demanded at a price they could afford.[16] In contrast, citizen sector organizations were deeply in touch with auxiliary markets, but often lacked the necessary business resources such as wide distribution, expertise in manufacturing, and access to financing. Each side saw no role in developing these markets, because it didn't see the other side and viewed the societal issue in different terms. If a project was too lofty for either a business or humanitarian approach, it didn't get done. But all of that is changing.

Like Unilever, more and more businesses are entering difficult, socially important markets with the help of citizen sector organizations. Traditional businesses partnering with social enterprises can build off their respective strengths, unlocking vast markets of public value. Drayton argues that such collaborations—he calls them "hybrid value chains"—can create and expand these markets on a scale unseen since the industrial revolution.[17]

Agriculture profits immensely from business and social sector partnerships. In Mexico, where two million farmers were living on less than $2 a day, Ashoka and local organizations convinced Amanco, a major producer of water conveyance products, to make small-drip irrigation systems for struggling farmers. Community organizations promoted the technology, organized farmers into loan groups, and installed the systems. Farmers' yields began to soar. Meanwhile, Amanco and its collaborators reaped the benefits of a brand-new $56 million-a-year market.[18]

According to Drayton, six hundred of Ashoka's three thousand fellows are pioneering hybrid value chains around the world. He says businesses should "look for walls" preventing partnership.[19] When an obstruction between business and society is torn down to solve a problem, prosperity follows. Drayton says that businesses should look for places where nontraditional services—microcredit services, for example—offer sustainable alternatives to traditionally indifferent commerce, acts of charity, or government services. Partnerships with nonprofits, it turns out, can be profitable and in the company's long-term growth interests. In the words of Drayton and Budinich, "if you're not thinking about such collaboration, you'll soon be guilty of strategy malpractice."[20] While the potential is great, to be successful such partnerships must overcome inherent mismatches in priorities (social versus business) and operational style (the partner's ability to maintain quality, for example).

Besides the gaps stemming from market failures and unmet needs, there are still more gaps among the ecosystem participants trying to address a given issue. For instance, early-stage financing is a major hurdle for most social enterprises. The first investments in a start-up bear the highest risks of failure, referred to as first-loss risk. Few enterprises can front such risk alone, and ironically, the foundations that do have the resources tend to lack an appetite for potential failure. Yet funding experimentation is a critical step to discovery.

In capital markets, such gaps make financiers salivate at the prospect of an arbitrage opportunity; correcting inefficiencies brings pure economic gain to the first movers. While the opportunities for early movers in the solution economy are not always as financially enticing, there is clear value to being the next Acumen or Recyclebank in a new space.

To advance social outcomes, a few bold wavemakers must risk failure in the first plunge to fill gaps. Since the entire ecosystem stands to benefit from this calculated risk taking, creating an environment that encourages exploration—and shortens the recovery time of missteps—can yield major breakthroughs for public gain. Expect some failures with the successes. That's okay. That's innovation.

Rethink Constraints: Focus on an End Goal and Consider Outside Resources

Much to the chagrin of any kids who grow up idolizing astronauts, the start of the twenty-first century has marked an era of cutbacks for NASA. Its space shuttle program shut down in 2011. A year later, Congress trimmed NASA's overall budget appropriation by $648 million.

Now that NASA's Constellation program has lost its funding, prospects look bleak for sending astronauts back to the moon.[21] In 1980, the United States had 100 percent of the global rocket launch capability. This dropped to zero several years ago (but is now inching back up slightly, thanks to private space flight).

The dismal outlook is a far cry from the heady days of the 1960s. It was then, just three years after NASA was founded in 1958, that President John F. Kennedy issued his famous directive that by the end of the decade the United States would send a man to the moon and bring him home safely.

NASA has radically scaled back, but space travel survives. How? In the face of fiscal constraints, NASA has changed its role. For the United States, space exploration is evolving from a government-led venture to a rich collaboration with the private sector.

As NASA has reduced its commitments, a dynamic private-sector space ecosystem has stepped vigorously into the void—with NASA's strong support. Richard Branson's Virgin Galactic, for example, is developing a spacecraft to launch tourists into orbit and perform at least $4.5 million in NASA research contracts, prompting the state of New Mexico to build a $209 million spaceport. Blue Origin, led by Amazon.com CEO Jeff Bezos, is developing space vehicles designed to launch and land on retractable legs. A start-up called NanoRacks arranges for scientists who need zero-gravity environments to place their experiments on the International Space Station.[22]

Many other companies, including Orbital Sciences, XCOR Aerospace, and Boeing, are testing vehicles for space travel. NASA is helping a company called Moon Express Inc. develop robots to search the moon for precious metals. XCOR Aerospace is developing a two-seater *Lynx* vehicle to shuttle passengers to space for $95,000 a trip. Space Adventures has already sent seven people to the International Space Station from a Soviet-era launch facility in Kazakhstan.[23]

One of the most interesting players in the new space ecosystem is SpaceX, of Hawthorne, California. SpaceX holds more than $3 billion in contracts for more than thirty launches, including $1.6 billion worth of contracts from NASA. Its unmanned *Dragon* capsule successfully docked on the space station in May 2012, in what was likely one of many supply runs to come.[24]

Launched in 2002 by Elon Musk, the cofounder of both PayPal and Tesla Motors, SpaceX intends to vastly reduce the cost of space ventures. "Today it costs over a billion dollars for a space shuttle flight," Musk says. "The cost . . . is fundamentally what's holding us back from becoming a space traveling civilization and ultimately a multi-planet species."[25]

Surprisingly, NASA feels no sense of rivalry with these emerging space entrepreneurs. "We have an enlightened self-interest in seeing the industry players do well," explains NASA's Joe Parrish. Not only has NASA welcomed the new players in space, but it has also radically reengineered its own business model to take advantage of outside innovation, an approach that sets NASA apart from most other government agencies. NASA's breakthrough was to change its focus from what it could achieve itself to what outcome it wanted to happen—then find who could help.

"Partnering with U.S. companies such as SpaceX to provide cargo and eventually crew service to the International Space Station is a cornerstone of the president's plan for maintaining America's leadership in space," explains John P. Holdren, assistant to the president for science and technology. "This expanded role for the private sector will free up more of NASA's resources to do what NASA does best—tackle the most demanding technological challenges in space, including those of human space flight beyond low Earth orbit."[26]

NASA shows how an organization can nimbly adapt to resource constraints. It offers powerful lessons for wavemakers who find themselves shifting roles within their solution ecosystems. First, instead of seeing new entrants as a threat, consider potential win-win scenarios that also yield additional public value.

Second, support the development of platforms and exchanges that enable different providers to work together toward solving the big problems that affect everyone. You can't begin to think about ways to combine capabilities with partners unless you know who they are and their specialties, a process that platforms can simplify.

Third, get creative about the resources that you can bring to the emerging ecosystem and that will provide a springboard for new solutions. Perhaps it is funding, or convening a multidisciplinary team of wavemakers, or something as simple as physical space for early-stage innovators to experiment side by side. Pooling these disparate resources will reinforce that there's more support available for problem solving than your own solitary approach. This awareness boosts not only your organization's morale, but also the chance of successfully reaching a solution.

Embrace Lightweight Solutions: Sometimes the Best Solutions Are Also the Cheapest

Chances are, the last online service you signed up for required you to read and enter a somewhat murky-looking set of letters. Those are CAPTCHAs, web programs that filter out spamming robots with the simple, real-human verification test. About two hundred million people solve a CAPTCHA each day.[27] Unbeknownst to them, the nonprofit reCAPTCHA program makes use of those millions of Turing tests to digitize archival print materials. This free, crowdsourced solution double-checks tricky words against multiple human readers to ensure accuracy. In contrast, hiring bored typists for transcriptions, even at minimum wage, would cost astronomical amounts and would offer no such quality control. The better result is far cheaper.

It's a hallmark of the information age: traditional trade-offs dissolve. We no longer always pay the sacrifice of higher costs to get superior results. In fact, superior solutions may emerge for little or no cost, although along the way we may have to sacrifice old models, traditional jobs, and even long-trusted institutions. When we think of solving big problems, especially through government, our minds tend to immediately go to huge sums of money. After all, in today's dollars, the Apollo program would amount to more than $170 billion.[28] But as reCAPTCHA and dozens of other examples in this book demonstrate, today's solutions to even the most intractable problems often don't require the massive spending and heavy infrastructure so associated with the industrial age. Truly innovative solutions deliver results at a fraction of the cost.

A few key strategies have a track record of eliminating the trade-offs between dollar investment and social returns. More lightweight solutions like the following can yield enormous savings over traditional, centrally organized results:

- Leveraging the internet for distribution

- Using tools like peer-to-peer networks to crowdsource solutions

- Encouraging business model innovation

- Helping citizens identify their own needs—something they'll do far more assiduously than any caseworker

- Involving individuals and communities in addressing their own challenges

Today, many governments and private companies utilize these strategies, but typically only as pilot projects or fringe initiatives far removed from the organizations' central "business," because the public agency or company wouldn't trust "outsiders" to handle the project.

The internet, the single most powerful trade-off breaker yet discovered, has decimated numerous traditional business models (music, publishing, news, etc.). This technology promises to revolutionize business even more, because of its most salient feature: the ease of information sharing. Costs in information-intensive activities are not just declining, but are plummeting.

Higher education stands to reap significant savings from the low-cost capabilities in information sharing, if it can work through the financials. Since 1983, the cost of a university education per student rose at almost five times the rate of inflation. US graduates owe about $1 trillion in student debt at last count.[29] Online learning strategies like MOOCs can slash costs and, for poor people in the developing world, can open up unimaginable education opportunities. So too can the low-cost franchise models pioneered by Bridge International Academies and Gyan Shala. Worldwide, the sixty-one million out-of-school children of primary-school age and the seventy-one million out-of-school children of lower-secondary-school age could potentially benefit from the potential to scale education.[30] With the right business model, the outcome can be superior education at a fraction of the cost.

Innovative education solutions that address a learning challenge can readily be scaled to far wider populations or tweaked to tackle entirely different challenges. Online learning approaches that can help a student learn programming in Bangladesh can be modified to help companies in Europe significantly boost the technical proficiency of their workforce for less money.

Lightweight solutions employ the lightest-touch approach to problem solving. Why add complexity if an elegant solution can reach the desired outcome with less intervention? An added benefit with this approach is often lower costs. Take ridesharing. While traffic gridlock chokes some of the world's largest cities, our analysis suggests that shifting about 15 percent of drive-alones to car sharing or ridesharing could save 757 million commuter-hours and about $21 billion in congestion costs annually. To achieve this savings through traditional means would require billions of dollars of infrastructure investment. Ridesharing apps, a tiny fraction of that cost, could engage the millions of commuters needed to generate a sizable impact. The same goes for peer-to-peer education and job training models. All have the potential to hugely reduce the strain on governments, but their impact is highly dependent on all kinds of intangible factors, like marketing, adoption, trust, and societal attitudes that money alone can't buy.

In the health arena, self-help tools can improve health outcomes and lower costs. Self-monitoring, cheap remote consultations, and widely available preventative care information all help cut health-care costs for both consumers and governments. Health-care apps now do everything from monitoring glucose levels in people with diabetes to managing chemotherapy schedules for people with cancer.[31]

By one projection, health-care providers could save up to $5.8 billion by 2014 by using existing mobile health technologies. Another study found that for every dollar spent on wellness programs, medical costs fall by about $3.27 and absenteeism costs fall by about $2.73. This could save billions. The market is responding quickly, with mobile health services slated to reach $4.6 billion by 2014.[32]

Not all lightweight solutions involve sophisticated technology. For years, governments and foundations in Africa have been trying to boost farmers' use of fertilizer. The institutions have poured vast sums

Impact of Lightweight Solutions

CAR SHARING AND RIDESHARING

The combined effect of ridesharing and car sharing would reduce the number of drive-alone commuters by 15.7 million and save 866 million hours annually in the United States.

into fertilizer cost-subsidy programs, but still found that in Kenya, less than one-third of farmers regularly used fertilizer.[33] In one instance, a group of farmers was given free fertilizer one season. Despite experiencing crop yield increases of 70 percent, the majority went back to not using fertilizer the following season. Why?

When asked, the farmers explained that they had spent all the money from the previous harvest, leaving no money to buy fertilizer at sowing time. Farmers in the area explained why they had not bought fertilizer: "When we have the money, they [markets] don't have the fertilizer. When they have the fertilizer, we don't have money."

To rectify this, researchers designed a program in which farmers can purchase a voucher for fertilizer right after a harvest period, to be delivered the following sowing season. ICS Africa, the NGO implementing the program, sold the vouchers at market price, with no subsidized discount, but the program doubled the number of farmers using fertilizer.[34] This low-cost, lightweight approach achieved greater results than a costly, large-scale, international program to subsidize fertilizer use.

As these examples show, technology and innovative, lightweight approaches are breaking the chains that once inexorably linked better results to higher costs. They show a path to overcoming the seemingly unavoidable trade-off between paying more or getting less. In short, a way to achieve that most elusive goal: getting more for less.

Buy Differently: If a Purchase Is a Vote, Are You Driving the Right Outcomes?

Governments and large companies purchase trillions of dollars in goods and services each year from millions of suppliers and partners. One of the fastest ways for these public and private institutions to influence the solution economy is through how they buy. "Procurement is a powerful tool for driving positive social change," explains Jonathan Greenblatt, director of the White House Office of Social Innovation.[35]

FIGURE 7-1

Reaching beyond traditional procurement

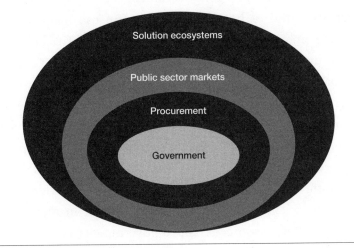

Among OECD countries, government spending averages around 46 percent of national GDP.[36] Figure 7-1 shows a rough depiction of how most governments use their purchasing power. The lion's share of financial resources tend to be in the two innermost rings of the diagram.[37] It's not hard to understand why this is so: in-house provision and one-on-one contracting relationships via procurement are within the comfort zone of most government agencies—and give the perception, if not the reality, of control.

By putting so much attention on the innermost rings in this diagram, governments miss the opportunity to boost public-value creation through the solution economy. Hovering on the periphery, largely out of sight, market innovators, social enterprises, and double-bottom-liners creatively bootstrap new, resourceful solutions to the challenges of their communities. Some solutions never get off the ground, while others, like FareStart, the combination restaurant/soup-kitchen and job-training organization profiled in chapter 1, flourish. Locked into their traditional approaches, governments often ignore this part of the private sector, sometimes even competing with programs that are doing a better job of serving the same citizens. "Social innovation happens on the edges of the network," explains Greenblatt. "The challenge for government is to create the conditions in which this kind of bottom-up innovation can happen."[38] Some agencies are embracing newer, more innovative approaches to accelerate such innovation. Under former Secretary Hillary Clinton, the State Department announced that USAID would embrace an impact-investing approach to development assistance. The agency would look to match funding with private-sector players and foundations. Likewise, the $1 billion India Inclusive Innovation Fund, expected to derive more than 80 percent of its capital from the private sector, represents another radical departure from traditional government grants and contracts.[39] The widespread investor interest in these kinds of partnerships offers resource-strapped governments a compelling opportunity to magnify the impact of the tax dollars spent.

These outer-ring wavemakers can help traditional public institutions address often neglected and misunderstood problems. Consider the innovative waste collection model instituted by Waste Ventures. All the money Parag Gupta raised from private investors and foundations was money that governments didn't have to spend figuring out how to make waste pickers' lives a little better while also solving a waste problem. Governments were also spared the challenge of scaling the model.

Yet most governments, particularly Western governments, don't think through what they could do to help Gupta and innovators like him scale their business models. As a result, governments tend to miss the opportunity for huge amounts of value creation in the outer rings. Yet as described in chapter 6, new ecosystems are quickly evolving to tackle societal setbacks. By neglecting this dense matrix of ecosystems, governments could relegate themselves to peripheral relevance among these agile wavemakers.

Matt Banick and Paula Goldman of Omidyar Network suggest an approach that could apply to governments, foundations, and other funders: "Our experience from the past eight years is that impact investors can massively increase the number of lives they touch by concentrating investments in specific industry sectors in specific geographies, and by investing in *a range of organizations* to accelerate the development of these industry segments."[40] When governments and other large institutions engage with a variety of similar social-sector organizations, for example, they can advance the industry in a very tangible way, helping shave years off the time it takes to bring new models to scale and benefiting millions of people in the process.

Recent actions by the UK government open the door to wider collaboration and investment in social enterprises. The Social Value Act, enacted in January 2013, enables commissioners and public bodies to secure services from the organizations deemed most capable of delivering social impact, criteria that suddenly make social enterprises and nonprofits appear more attractive.[41] As discussed earlier in the chapter, the goal for the UK government and for others that follow suit is to expand purchasing power to the outer rings depicted in figure 7-1— and potentially to shrink reliance on the government-controlled inner rings. Not only would this change give a big boost to the solution economy, but it would also be likely to create greater public value.

Along with promoting social-impact investing and procurement, the public sector can refashion traditional government contracting through myriad other ways. Prizes and challenges, open tendering, and pay-for-success approaches open up the government market to new solution providers, helping to grow the supply side. Competitive markets for public services via citizen-choice models benefit from the same advantages that competition brings to consumers: greater choice of suppliers, greater variety of offerings, and lower prices. These help grow the demand side of solution markets.

Corporate purchasing power can promote social good as well. Consider overfishing. While it was once just an issue for environmentalists, now Costco, Target, and Walmart sell fish that meets the Marine Stewardship Council's standards for sustainable fishery practices.[42] A subset of vocal, informed consumers led large retailers to shift their sourcing strategies, so that the stores now offer a more responsible default setting for the average shopper. Practices like eradicating sweatshop labor and the introduction of cage-free eggs, fair-trade coffee, and organic produce to mainstream consumers demonstrate the power of corporate sourcing strategies.

Unilever's supply chain offers another example. Half of its raw materials are from farms and forests. These sources are critical to its business, but also critical to the health of the world's ecosystem. Because of Unilever's size, how it buys raw materials has a significant bearing on global natural resources. To this end, the company has committed to the sustainable sourcing of raw materials to reduce the pressure on agricultural supplies worldwide. Unilever's sustainable agriculture program defines sustainable farming according to eleven social, economic, and environmental indicators. The company already buys from more than 1.3 million small farmers around the world and has committed to source 100 percent of its agricultural raw materials sustainably by 2020.[43]

The significant buying power of multinationals can help drive the adoption of social and environmental criteria across entire industries. This clout extends into business practices; recall how Patagonia's policy of channeling 1 percent of sales revenue toward environmental causes sent out ripples that encouraged more than a thousand companies to pledge the same commitment.[44] When a company like Coca-Cola requires that the members of its supply chain participate in numerous external audits annually to verify that forced labor is not occurring, workers receive protection that their own national governments may lack the resources to provide.[45]

Choosing to source from small producers or intermediaries that aggregate local suppliers may require some up-front infrastructure development, but can profoundly impact the economic development of remote regions. This style of sourcing falls into a category known as the inclusive business model. Alquería, a large dairy company in Colombia, for example, draws its supply of milk from over sixty-five hundred independent farmers. The company offers these farmers many forms of technical assistance, from bulk procurement of fodder and fertilizer, both of which improve profit margins for suppliers, to millions of dollars dispersed through microcredit financing, since most farmers are ineligible for commercial bank loans.[46]

Altering existing procurement practices is a low-cost way of enhancing social, financial, and environmental outcomes, directly benefiting buyers and consumers in the process. Expect to see increasing innovation in purchasing practices, particularly in the government sector, in the years ahead.

Measure What Matters

The right metrics, Bill Gates says, are a powerful compass for problem solvers, pointing resources to where they will have the greatest impact: "An innovation—whether it's a new vaccine or an improved seed—can't have an impact unless it reaches the people who will benefit from it. We need innovations in measurement to find new, effective ways to deliver those tools and services to the clinics, family farms and classrooms that need them."[47]

Solving society's most intractable problems begins with understanding what actually moves the needle. This allows resources and creativity to be focused where they have the most impact. Requests to support a social purpose are now regularly expected to include a solid demonstration of effectiveness. It may be a donor inspecting a nonprofit on a website like Charity Navigator, an impact investor evaluating a potential loan recipient, a citizen inspecting where his or her tax dollars go, or an investor evaluating socially responsible stocks. How impact is articulated may vary, but providing compelling evidence of *results* is now a make-or-break proposition for organizations seeking financial support.

In theory, it is simple: funding that is contingent on measurable impact should produce better outcomes. In reality, however, decisions about which outcomes to measure and how to measure them present thorny challenges: how do you avoid getting so fixated on measurement that innovation is stifled? What is the right amount of resources to commit to measurement overhead? What is too much?

Unlike in business, social outcomes are more nuanced. Volume measures (such as individuals served) are easy to obtain, but miss critical characteristics of quality. Such quality measures are often elusive, subjective, and difficult to come by. It is far easier to determine how many children are receiving foster care, and nearly impossible to assess the quality of that care in every setting. Attempts to holistically capture various measures of overall impact will certainly raise administrative overhead costs, but such efforts may or may not improve the assessment of actual performance.

On balance, the trend toward greater scrutiny of measures suggests that the complacent acceptance of "activity measures" is disappearing. Better scrutiny is prompting new and better measures of impact.

RARE, a conservation group that deploys its program fellows to areas with biodiversity deemed at risk, is differentiating itself among environmental funders by measuring not only ecological improvements, but also the economic benefits to local communities.[48] The goal is to coach communities on sustainable practices while also looking out for their economic interests.

When RARE is seeking to establish a no-take fishing zone to repopulate overfished areas in the Philippines, it also tries to provide alternative income streams for locals, in some cases by providing honeybee boxes. Prioritizing the well-being of locals not only promotes lasting shifts in behavior, but also reflects a much more comprehensive conservation program than many others that stick to traditional metrics, such as acreage of land preserved.

While organizations like RARE demonstrate the value of unique metrics in conveying the effectiveness of an original approach, speaking a common language with investors does have its benefits. Standard measures enable the development of exchanges, which opens up larger financial channels. A broad coalition of partners, including Acumen, Rockefeller Foundation, and B Lab, established the Impact Reporting and Investment Standards (IRIS) out of awareness that "fragmentation is inefficient and expensive, and also limits comparability."[49] Stakeholders can use IRIS to aggregate sector-wide data and compare it across organizations—the same way the SEC extracts data to analyze public companies. Organizations get an accredited way to assess their social performance and maximize their funds. Investors get transparency.

Innovations like IRIS's web-based platform, which allows organizations to collect, analyze, and report their outcomes quickly and cheaply, as well as social return on investment (SROI) tools, provide a fuller picture of how value is created and can therefore be traded. Innovations in measurement promote systemic approaches to solving social problems, with the knowledge that no single player can fix the world's biggest problems alone. Shared measurement systems help bring disconnected problem solvers together and enhance coordination and impact for funders and funded alike. The Social Progress Index, launched in 2013, represents an ambitious attempt to develop a rigorous way of benchmarking countries' progress in achieving social goals, identifying areas of both strength and weakness.

At the same time, the risk of overly standardized measurement of social impact parallels the arguments against standardized testing: that it diminishes creativity and too often encourages a teach-to-the-test mentality that suppresses innovation. But if standards are easy enough to measure, then additional, distinctive metrics could also be used. While RARE likes to showcase its unique markers of progress, the conservation group covers its bases by capturing more common environmental metrics as well.

Beyond even the most carefully constructed set of measures, there is the feedback of beneficiaries themselves, which offer candid commentary on the social outcomes an organization delivers. Similar to how Yelp's online platform lets users rant and rave about the service at various restaurants and local businesses, platforms like Kiva and Charity Navigator offer similar features for donors and lenders to share their perspectives.

The sooner an organization is aware of a mishap, the more quickly it can course-correct and repair relationships with jilted users. Problems that ferment can quickly produce tarnished reputations that are time-consuming and difficult to repair. For this reason, real-time feed-back is arguably the most valuable test of performance for service-driven enterprises. Real-time feedback, still relatively rare among solution economy organizations, is nevertheless likely to grow with rising consumer expectations. People of all ages are becoming increasingly comfortable with reviewing their consumer experience over social media, whether the feedback comes in the form of restaurant reviews, grades for their professors, or assessments of their doctor's care. Organizations are discovering the benefits of capturing that feedback and reacting to it.

Consider the GlobalGiving Foundation, which connects individuals to more than one thousand prescreened grassroots charity projects around the world. A few years ago, GlobalGiving solicited feed-back from residents in a Kenyan slum. The foundation asked what it was doing right but also where there were delivery gaps or program complaints. However, instead of simply interviewing individuals, GlobalGiving went a step farther and partnered with a UK-based analytics firm, Cognitive Edge. The partner's software helped GlobalGiving turn the raw information of residents into data that could be broken down, analyzed, visualized, and, in turn, inform decisions on where funds should be allocated.[50] Think of it as Monitoring and Evaluation 2.0. Government-funded development projects, including several USAID engagements, are employing similar feedback mechanisms.

Market innovators are similarly using feedback mechanisms to achieve better results. As described earlier, Recyclebank's business model is based on a strengthened feedback loop. When a citizen recycles an empty soda can instead of chucking it in the trash, he or she is rewarded. In turn, the company gleans key insight from the data and analytics collected by the RFID-enabled recycling bins. These detailed metrics about each user can improve services by tailoring them to a community's specific needs—whether the data indicates a need for increased newspaper recycling or more access to eco-friendly products.[51]

Partnerships with data-savvy innovators can also provide the feedback data that many organizations might not be able to otherwise amass. Preserving all 936 of the majestic UNESCO World Heritage Sites scattered across the globe is an ambitious undertaking—one that can benefit from the millions of people who visit these sites every year. While UNESCO may struggle to attract visitors to its website to comment on the condition of World Heritage Sites, a partnership with TripAdvisor gives UNESCO access to the forty-five million visitors who seek and share travel advice on the platform monthly. It's a win-win proposition, sustaining the rare, unique beauty of UNESCO destinations for future travelers, while allowing UNESCO to track in real time the various preservation projects as soon as the need emerges.[52]

Despite the saying "What gets measured, gets done," the measurement of performance is just the start. What will be transformative for the solution economy is applying that insight and feedback to how problems get solved.

In one telling example, as money poured into microfinance, the Bill & Melinda Gates Foundation opted against merely donating to existing microfinance institutions. Instead, it dedicated time and money to understanding the many environmental factors that drive a microfinance organizations' success or failure. The effect? By exposing the weaknesses in the landscape, the foundation had an informed starting point to take action. After identifying a need for more savings vehicles, for instance, in 2010 the foundation dedicated $5.8 million to help microlenders provide savings accounts to even the poorest populations. After observing the positive impact of these grants, the foundation expanded its contribution to the field to $500 million. Just as with a business venture, analysis preceded seed money, and real money came only after proven results.[53]

Measurement, notes Bill Gates, "may seem basic, but it is amazing how often it is not done and how hard it is to get right."[54] Selecting the right combination of measures to gauge impact, and applying them iteratively to track progress, is one of the most powerful ways to accelerate problem solving in the solution economy.

Solution Revolution 2020

This book has chronicled a little-understood revolution that is chang-ing the way public value is created. As the solution economy grows—and it will grow only as fast as it is nurtured—it will change the land-scape dramatically. There will be more alliances between government and the private sector and more mold-breaking alliances across sectors. These shifts stand to reduce gaps in public services and empower in-dividuals and communities to take a greater role in creating their own future. Education deficits that have held back developing nations can be eradicated through greater access to online learning. From housing to obesity, the environment to transportation, a brighter future is in reach if we are savvy enough to grasp it.

Of course, the particulars of tomorrow are impossible to know from today's vantage. But as we scan the solution economy, this promising landscape of breakaway technologies and innovative busi-ness models, we should ask ourselves how much further we can take this. And how many of the old ways of doing business—operating in isolation, ignoring entire classes and groups of people, shrugging off ruinous externalities of the market—are we willing to let go?

If we are smart, quite a lot. Nothing in any economy is static. Technologies and business models keep advancing, and as they do, older modes of service delivery will need to evolve. New problems will emerge. Luckily, the fundamental strength of the solution econ-omy is that challenges become opportunities for progress.

Appendix

Strategies to Grow the Solution Economy[1]

Strategies for Government

Procurement

Open up procurement. Government can use its buying power to shape and create *solution markets*. One strategy is to open public sector procurement to providers that compete with incumbents—including in-house resources. Lowering barriers to entry and simplifying the bidding process for government contracts would allow competition that drives improved services.

Use purchasing power to create demand. Governments have vast purchasing power that can generate *anchor demand* for solutions that address social issues. Once providers find ways to innovatively meet demand, they may be well positioned to extend services to segments beyond government purview.

Create markets for outcomes. Prizes and challenges, social-impact bonds, and pay-for-success approaches dictate outcomes instead of processes. By rewarding new solution providers, outcome-based efforts help to grow the supply side.

Be open to different routes to a desired outcome. Relying on current processes greatly limits imagination. Focusing more on the question

"What does success look like?" opens up a range of new approaches. It elevates the "customer" experience as a critical measure of performance and may entirely reorient service delivery.

Encourage a diverse provider-player mix. Promoting and supporting a diverse range of players increases the mix of solutions and collaborative models that may emerge. Creating platforms for a wide variety of players to offer input, with incentives to pilot potential solutions, activates a wider community around developing solutions to the problem.

Train procurement officials to be smart buyers. Training will enhance their understanding of the solution economy and improve their ability to discern effective solutions from less effective ones.

Policy

Open up public data. In the right hands, public data can produce billions of dollars in value and help assess the true impact of government programs. Making such data public taps the power of vast networks of problem solvers.

Expand citizen choices. A one-size-fits-all approach to public services fails to meet the diverse range of citizen needs. Competitive markets for public services via citizen-choice models benefit from the same advantages that competition brings to consumers: greater choice of suppliers, greater variety of offerings, and lower prices. Greater choice also enables citizens to customize their experience.

Minimize losses by admitting to failure early on. Create a culture that encourages public officials to admit failure early on and, hence, to recover from it quickly in order to encourage productive experimentation of new services and delivery methods. From the outset, clearly define what success looks like to help those in the organization recognize leading indicators of weak performance and course-correct early. One of the main barriers to choice and competition, for example, is deciding how to respond when new, publicly backed ventures fail. The UK government has created a process to determine whether a venture has failed, and then to maintain continuity of service during transitions.

Be judicious about the "smart subsidies" offered to providers and users of market-based solutions. Smart subsidies can improve affordability for the poorest and encourage businesses to cater to this group. Consider the effectiveness of the US food stamp program. However, subsidies are difficult to remove once created and may bring excessive costs, so determine whether the subsidy effectively addresses a long-term systemic issue. Where temporary or cyclical market failures are to blame, explore flexible, less permanent approaches.

Embrace lightweight solutions. Leveraging lightweight strategies—the internet for distribution, peer-to-peer networks, citizen co-creation, and so on—can yield enormous savings and agility over centralized, resource-heavy approaches.

Shift power via co-production and co-creation. Government can leverage a growing network of digitally empowered citizens. Co-creation and co-production focus on developing and delivering new solutions *with* people, rather than for them.

Connect government resources to solvers. From data to distribution networks, from financing to policy expertise, government has a host of resources that can help catalyze and scale solution ecosystems. Improve access to these resources, and encourage citizen changemakers to utilize them for broader public benefit.

Train the next generation of cross-sector solvers. Grow a cadre of leaders adept at solving big problems across sectors. A White House group addressed that question in 2012, developing a set of competencies needed for cross-sector solvers. Once cohorts of solvers are assembled, they should be empowered to try and test new approaches across sectors. Openness to experimentation encourages solvers to openly share what does—and doesn't—work in different contexts, minimizing preventable failures.

Legal and Regulatory Considerations

Avoid overregulating the sharing economy. Despite the usual regulatory instinct to provide safety nets for citizens in an informal economy, remember that most creators of two-sided markets actually share government's goal of helping citizens and find efficient ways to do so. Where possible, work with these organizations to keep abusive or fraudulent users out of the marketplace.

Recognize social enterprises as a new form of business. By creating a new legal designation for businesses that pursue social returns in addition to financial ones, government can encourage a new class of enterprises that deliver services to citizens in a more financially sustainable way than traditional nonprofits. A separate designation widens the range of potential investors, provides greater operational freedom, and makes it easier to track the evolution of the sector.

Finance

Maximize resources through matching. Jointly funding projects with impact investors, foundations, and businesses offers government a compelling alternative to reducing services in the face of budgetary constraints. Moreover, joint action supplies more innovative, customized offerings to citizens. Consider USAID and Skoll Foundation's $44.5 million alliance that brings a venture-capital-inspired approach to fueling innovation in the areas of health, energy, governance, and food security.

See the "Strategies for Investors" section for additional financing actions that government can take to catalyze the solution economy.

Strategies for Business

Align social criteria with the firm's mission and long-term goals. This enables a company's culture and social mission to grow together, rather than feeling like a generic CSR public relations campaign. As Mark Kramer, founder of FSG, says, "social change becomes part of the competitive equation."

Assess daily business decisions against social criteria. Begin by identifying the societal needs, benefits, and harm that a company delivers through its routine business practices.[2] Once social criteria are accounted for, certain daily operating procedures may stand out as greater risks and may warrant a change in procedure.

Adapt the core strengths of a business to social needs. Think about your company's capabilities in the broadest sense. In what ways could the staff members contribute, and how might this enrich their experience? In the process, gaps or complications may emerge that lie beyond the business's current reach. Which individuals or organizations might have faced these hurtles before? This may point to potential partnerships.

Target the gaps. Develop new markets by meeting neglected needs. Wavemakers approach gaps in basic needs not as obstacles but as market opportunities. The base of the economic pyramid and the neglected health-care needs in Western countries represent gaps that numerous organizations profiled in this book target successfully.

Explore reverse-innovation opportunities. General Electric has made reverse innovation a cornerstone of its growth strategy, importing products from emerging markets to create new markets in the developed world.[3] One GE team, for example, developed a pocket-sized ultrasound scanner, so that mobile doctors could perform tests for rheumatic heart disease—a common disease in young people in developing countries. The portability and usefulness of the device also translated to its adoption by practitioners in the Western world.

Make a bold commitment. Directly linking a company's giving and its revenues demonstrates a bold commitment to social values. It's a company's way of saying "my gain is your gain." The makers of KIND healthy snacks, for example, donate to the NGO PeaceWorks with every snack purchased at accessible chains like Starbucks.

Look for ways to *socially* leverage existing infrastructure. Many social problems do not necessarily require new resources, but instead simply need better use of their existing infrastructure. New business models in car sharing and ridesharing, energy optimization, and recycling show how a novel implementation of existing resources can expand opportunities.

Buy differently. Altering sourcing practices can enhance social, financial, and environmental outcomes, directly benefiting buyers and consumers in the process.

Explore how existing business models could be adapted to low-income markets. Reaching out to new segments like the base of the pyramid may require investing in product development, aligning internal processes, potentially updating legacy systems, and even adopting a longer time horizon to recoup up-front investments. Weigh the social and financial opportunities of entering a new segment against these hurtles to determine whether the business can realistically benefit from taking the plunge.

Create measurable milestones of societal success. Consider the long-term view and how the company's net contributions to society can be tracked over that period. Revisit immediate objectives, like quarterly earnings, by asking questions like "Do the actions we are taking to meet this immediate goal help or hurt our social-impact goals?"

Seek donor partners. Coca-Cola, Bayer, Safaricom, and other companies have received funding from foundations and development institutions to serve developing-world populations. Donors can assist organizations by helping to cover otherwise prohibitive up-front costs or by stimulating demand for base-of-pyramid markets.

Build a strategy to leverage open data. As governments open up their data, businesses can incorporate that information into their own services, enhance their own customer data, and use their data analysis to identify opportunities governments missed. As companies set their sights on new segments of the market where they lack certain data, these sources of information can inform business decisions and guide a company's strategy.

Become an integrator in solution ecosystems. Set sights on a quantifiable outcome that the company is well positioned to pursue but that will resonate with a wider audience, and seek out a team of contributors to help your company reach the goal. By originating the goal and being the first to commit, you position the company as an influential backbone of the ecosystem.

Strategies for Investors

Enterprise Level

Team up to increase early-stage funding. Early-stage funding is scarce because of the higher risk threshold. To encourage innovative solutions, donor capital can combine with commercial capital to provide early-stage funding for social enterprises and market innovators. Overall funding levels would likely improve if more organizations would be willing to front a higher proportion of the risk to encourage other investors to start serving early funding needs.

Embrace risk, and acknowledge failures. Working at the frontier of the solution economy in the hope of breakthrough impact is an inherently risky endeavor. Funders need to be comfortable with new models, new markets, and significant, if not high, rates of setback and failure.

Be prepared for the long haul. Recognize that social progress takes longer than commercial success, and be transparent with other investors about this. Conveying the full complexity of challenges helps set realistic expectations and helps cultivate repeat investors.

Reward those demonstrating metrics-driven results with additional funding. Advancements in measurement make it easier to fund approaches that yield demonstrable results. Recognize, however, that some will be tempted to game the metrics. With this in mind, solicit input on performance from various stakeholders, and be familiar enough with the business model to ask the difficult questions.

Contribute not just money, but also skills. Omidyar Network provides executive search services. Nigerian investor Tony O. Elumelu has committed his extensive largesse and business acumen to increasing the competitiveness of Africa's private sector. These resources help social enterprises scale and gain a stronger foothold in new markets. Providing technical assistance that refines a start-up's business model can also position the enterprise for second-stage financing from additional investors.

Ideate, test, perfect, and expand. Test and perfect the solution before scaling it to a larger population. Rapid iteration allows only the best attributes of the new business to become part of the final model.

Fund replication, not just ideation. Too many investors are only interested in funding shiny new business models. Often, a better return on investment can be achieved by replicating successful models—models tailored to local circumstances—in other countries and sectors. A case in point is microfinance, which has been successfully deployed in many regions.

Ecosystem Level

Take a broader view of markets and ecosystems. The impact of any market-based solution, at its fullest potential, will be achieved by a multiplicity of actors in a given market, and not just within the private sector. Philanthropic funders are uniquely placed to take this perspective and work to enhance the conditions for eventual impact at scale.

Tie funding to issue-based movements and campaigns. Instead of providing financing for standalone efforts (e.g., clean water awareness campaigns), tie "category" financing to specific initiatives (e.g., building water kiosks alongside clean water awareness). Funding multiple, interdependent parts of an ecosystem concurrently encourages organizations to work collaboratively toward shared success.

Aggregate supply by organizing a fragmented set of (predominantly informal) enterprises. Often, a contingent of disparate providers is already serving an otherwise marginalized segment of citizens and the task at hand requires upgrading that base en masse. This will make it easier for large companies and international organizations to collaborate toward shared goals.

Provide basic and shared infrastructure. The success of a new enterprise or model often requires foundational infrastructure of some kind. This may be physical infrastructure, like school buildings; social infrastructure, like cooperatives or other aggregation platforms; or knowledge infrastructure, like rigorous analysis and lessons learned from effective market-based approaches. Recognizing what infrastructure is most needed and making it accessible will help set up the funded enterprises for success.

Dedicate grants to priming the market. For example, the Bill & Melinda Gates Foundation committed a $4.8 million grant to Vodacom in Tanzania to help prepare the market for wider M-Pesa money adoption through awareness and education campaigns.[4] Similar to the provision of infrastructure, priming the market encourages the early behavior changes that will be critical to adoption of a new offering.

Spread the responsibilities for risk capital and risk management across a team of contributors. Low-income markets are highly volatile. Donors, investors, and aid agencies are uniquely placed to absorb and share risks. Honest information sharing between early and later-stage investors about the landscape and the enterprise's performance will help manage risk and preemptively address challenges.

Create and back new specialist intermediaries. Such intermediaries would accept funding from a wide range of foundations and aid donors and develop deep expertise in working with firms pioneering new social business models and steering grant funding their way. Today, there is a critical lack of such specialist intermediaries to connect mainstream philanthropic resources to the practice of enterprise philanthropy, in contrast to the two hundred impact-investing funds that have emerged. US foundations, for example, are required to give away five percent of their assets each year to maintain their tax status. "Imagine if they put another five percent in action into the capital markets [via intermediaries] to make smart investments into social enterprises," exclaims the White House's Jonathan Greenblatt. "That's $50 billion. That's creating change at scale. That is how you change the world!"[5]

Cover capital-intensive fixed costs for proven business models. For business models known to work, develop facilities that can support expansion on a much larger scale. This requires funding the fixed upfront capital costs that operators cannot recover at affordable price points (e.g., water kiosks, microgrid generation, microgrid household connections). Also fund the fixed cost of demand stimulation or supplier and agent training—that is, noncapital costs that prevent solutions from operating in a commercially sustainable way.

Notes

This publication contains general information only, and none of Deloitte Touche Tohmatsu Limited, its member firms, or their related entities (collectively the "Deloitte Network") is, by means of this publication, rendering professional advice or services. Before making any decision or taking any action that may affect your finances or your business, you should consult a qualified professional adviser. No entity in the Deloitte Network shall be responsible for any loss whatsoever sustained by any person who relies on this publication.

Introduction

1. Ira Glass, "What Kind of Country," *This American Life*, March 2, 2012, www.thisamericanlife.org/radio-archives/episode/459/transcript.

2. Milton Friedman, "The Social Responsibility of Business Is to Increase Its Profits," *New York Times Magazine*, September 13, 1970.

3. Center for Global Prosperity, *Index of Global Philanthropy and Remittances 2011* (Washington, DC: Hudson Institute, 2011), 10, www.hudson.org/files/documents/2011%20Index%20of%20Global%20Philanthropy%20and%20Remittances%20downloadable%20version.pdf.

4. B Lab, "Impact Investing: Challenges and Opportunities to Scale, Q1 2011 Progress Report," http://giirs.org/storage/documents/GIIRS_2011-Progress-Report-Final.pdf.

5. "Sustainable Living," Unilever, accessed February 6, 2013, www.unilever.com/sustainability/casestudies/economic-development/creating-rural-entrepreneurs.aspx.

6. Matthew Bishop and Michael Green, *Philanthrocapitalism: How the Rich Can Save the World* (New York: Bloomsbury Press, 2008); Rosabeth Moss Kanter, *SuperCorp: How Vanguard Companies Create Innovation, Profits, Growth, and Social Good* (New York: Crown Business, 2009); David Vogel, *The Market for Virtue: The Potential and Limits of Corporate Social Responsibility* (Washington, DC: Brookings Institution Press, 2005); David Bornstein, *How to Change the World: Social Entrepreneurs and the Power of New Ideas,* updated ed. (New York: Oxford University Press, 2007).

7. US Census Bureau, "Census Bureau Releases 2010 American Community Survey Single Year Estimates," September 22, 2011, www.census.gov/newsroom/releases/archives/american_community_survey_acs/cb11-158.html.

8. Deloitte Research analysis, "U.K. Summary of Key Findings from Car-Pooling and Car-Sharing Analysis, 2012—Directline.com."

9. Ibid.

10. According to the Victoria Transport Policy Institute, the cost of congestion in United States is about $0.13 per mile per car. We used this number to calculate the total costs. See also Deloitte, "U.K. Summary of Key Findings."

11. Based on $0.05 per mile in infrastructure costs. Todd Litman with Eric Doherty, "Transportation Cost and Benefit Analysis II," Victoria Transport Policy Institute, January 2009, Roadway Costs, table 5.6.3–3, www.vtpi.org/tca/tca0506 .pdf.

12. Ibid., table 6.3–1, www.vtpi.org/tca/tca06.pdf.

13. "Real-Time Ridesharing," Avego, accessed February 6, 2013, www.avego .com/products/real-time-ridesharing/.

14. Sean O'Sullivan, interview with authors, October 2011.

15. Deloitte, "U.K. Summary of Key Findings."

16. "Delivery of the American Recovery and Reinvestment Act (ARRA)," US Department of Transportation, accessed February 6, 2013, http://flh.fhwa.dot.gov/ policy/arra/.

17. Deloitte, "U.K. Summary of Key Findings."

18. Noah Stevens, interview with authors, August 6, 2012.

19. "Big Society Fund Launches with £600m to Invest," *BBC News*, last modified April 4, 2012, www.bbc.co.uk/news/business-17602323.

20. Suzanne Perry, "Congress Agrees to $50-Million Social Innovation Fund, Cuts Volunteer Fund," *The Chronicle of Philanthropy*, last modified December 9, 2009, http://philanthropy.com/blogs/government-and-politics/congress-agrees-to -50-million-for-social-innovation-fund-cuts-volunteer-fund/11119.

21. "White House Launches Presidential Innovation Fellows Program," The White House, August 23, 2012, www.whitehouse.gov/the-press-office/2012/08/23/ white-house-launches-presidential-innovation-fellows-program.

22. Remarks of Todd Park, White House Forum on Cross-Sector Leadership, Washington, DC, March 20, 2013.

23. "Building an Impact Economy in America," Aspen Institute, Washington, DC, October 2011, www.aspeninstitute.org/sites/default/files/content/docs/pubs/ Building-an-Impact-Economy-in-America.pdf.

24. Ibid.

One

1. "Bill Gates Announces the Winners of the Reinvent the Toilet Challenge," press release, Bill & Melinda Gates Foundation, August 14, 2012, www .gatesfoundation.org/press-releases/Pages/Bill-Gates-Names-Winners-of-the -Reinvent-the-Toilet-Challenge-120814.aspx.

2. "One-one-One with Bill Gates," *ABC News*, February 16, 2005, http:// abcnews.go.com/WNT/CEOProfiles/story?id=506354, 6.

3. "Top Funders: 100 U.S. Foundations by Asset Size," ranking according to most current database as of January 28, 2013, Foundation Center, http://foundation center.org/findfunders/topfunders/top100assets.html.

4. "Who We Are: Foundation Fact Sheet," Bill & Melinda Gates Foundation, accessed February 6, 2013, www.gatesfoundation.org/about/Pages/foundation-fact -sheet.aspx.

5. "Net ODA—DAC Countries—Constant 2010 USD Billion," Organisation for Economic Co-operation and Development (OECD), accessed February 6, 2013, http://webnet.oecd.org/dcdgraphs/ODAGNI/.

6. Matthew Bishop and Michael Green, *Philanthropcapitalism: How Giving Can Save the World* (New York: Bloomsbury Press, 2008).

7. "Philanthropy: Current Context and Future Outlook," Bellagio Initiative, July 2011, www.bellagioinitiative.org/wp-content/uploads/2011/09/Philanthropy _Resource-Alliance_2011.pdf, 19.

8. See Bishop and Green, *Philanthrocapitalism*. See also David Bornstein and Susan Davis, "Social Entrepreneurship: What Everyone Needs to Know Teaching Notes," Ashoka, December 2012, http://ashokau.org/wp-content/uploads/2010/ 12/Social-Entrepreneurship-What-Everyone-Needs-to-Know-Teaching-notes-final .pdf, 12.

9. Despite strong precedents, the foundation devoted some resources toward identifying and calling attention to social-impact measures that had proven effective for some organizations (Melinda T. Tuan, "Measuring and/or Estimating Social Value Creation: Insights into Eight Integrated Cost Approaches," Bill & Melinda Gates Foundation, December 15, 2008, www.gatesfoundation.org/learning/ Documents/WWL-report-measuring-estimating-social-value-creation.pdf, 6). For how the foundation measures the impact of internal funds and disbursed grants, see Fay Twersky, Jodi Nelson, and Amy Ratcliffe, "A Guide to Actionable Measurement," Bill & Melinda Gates Foundation, 2010, accessed February 6, 2013, www .gatesfoundation.org/learning/Documents/guide-to-actionable-measurement .pdf. In addition, the foundation partnered with the RAND Corporation and the University of Michigan's Institute for Social Research to measure teacher effectiveness among numerous other partnerships and was one of the founding organizations of the Global Impact Investing Network ("Foundation Invests $22 Million in Research and Data Systems to Improve Student Achievement," Bill & Melinda Gates Foundation, January 22, 2009, www.gatesfoundation.org/press-releases/Pages/ collect-and-use-data-for-maximum-impact-on-teaching-and-learning-090122 .aspx; Global Impact Investing Network, "Investor's Council," www.thegiin.org/ cgi-bin/iowa/council/member/index.html). For the foundation's expanding reach, see Donna Gordon Blankinship, "Report: Gates Foundation Gave Away $2.5B in 2010," Associated Press, August 3, 2011, http://finance.yahoo.com/news/Report -Gates-Foundation-gave-apf-4031798694.html.

10. John Ydstie, "India Eye Care Center Finds Middle Way to Capitalism," *All Things Considered*, NPR, November 29, 2011, www.npr.org/2011/11/29/ 142526263/india-eye-care-center-finds-middle-way-to-capitalism; "Global Health Initiative: Public-Private Partnership Case Example," World Economic Forum, 2006, 3, www.acumenfund.org/uploads/assets/documents/A%20to %20Z%20Private-Public%20Partnership%20Study%20-%20Global%20Health %20Initiative_R1udShKh.pdf; Dee DePass, "Spreading the Word on Clean Water in Rural India," One Water, www.onewater.org/stories/story/spreading_the_word _on_clean_water_in_rural_india/.

11. The average European VC fund invests $1.6 million to promising enterprises, and the average US VC fund invests $3.3 million, while a venture philanthropy contribution is typically measured in the thousands. This difference is understandable, considering the average European VC firm holds $50 million in assets, whereas half the venture philanthropy organizations in Europe hold less than $8 million.

12. "Financial Information," Acumen Fund, accessed February 6, 2013, www .acumenfund.org/about-us/financial-information.html.

13. Jacqueline Novogratz, "Making a Case for Patient Capital," *BusinessWeek*, October 20, 2011, www.businessweek.com/magazine/making-a-case-for-patient -capital-10202011.html.

14. Yasmina Zaidman (Acumen), interview with authors, January 2012.

15. Warren Buffett, "My Philanthropic Pledge," The Giving Pledge, accessed November 6, 2012, http://givingpledge.org/#warren_buffett.

16. Bishop and Green, *Philanthrocapitalism*. See also Clare O'Connor, "High Roller: How Billionaire Peter Lewis Is Bankrolling Marijuana Legalization," *Forbes*, April 20, 2012, www.forbes.com/sites/clareoconnor/2012/04/20/high-roller-how -billionaire-peter-lewis-is-bankrolling-marijuana-legalization/.

17. Mfonobong Nsehe, "South African Billionaire Patrice Motsepe Joins Giving Pledge," *Forbes*, January 31, 2013, www.forbes.com/sites/mfonobongnsehe/ 2013/01/31/south-african-billionaire-patrice-motsepe-joins-giving-pledge/.

18. "Mohammed Ibrahim: Profile," *Forbes*, last updated March 2013,

19. www.forbes.com/profile/mohammed-ibrahim/.

20. Ibid.

21. "Global Social Investing: A Preliminary Overview," The Philanthropic Initiative, Inc., May 2001, www.global-philanthropy.org/documents/global_social _investing.pdf, 15.

22. Steven Gunderson, "Current Trends in Philanthropy," *Journal of Jewish Communal Service* 84 (winter–spring 2009): 91–95, www.bjpa.org/Publications/ details.cfm?PublicationID=4119.

23. "Europe Fuelling Global Growth of Community Philanthropy, Says International Report," press release, Worldwide Initiatives for Grantmaker Support, November 18, 2010, www.wings-community-foundation-report.com/gsr_2010/ assets/images/pdf/GSR_News_Release_Nov_2010_Final.pdf.

24. "Sustainable and Responsible Investing Facts," The Forum for Sustainable and Responsible Investment, http://ussif.org/resources/sriguide/srifacts.cfm, accessed December 18, 2012.

25. "The Clinton Factor: A Former President's eBay of Giving," *Economist*, September 25, 2007, www.economist.com/node/9857839.

26. "2011 Annual Meeting Topics," Clinton Global Initiative, 2011, www .clintonglobalinitiative.org/ourmeetings/2011/meeting_annual_topics.asp?Section= OurMeetings&PageTitle=Meeting%20Topics.

27. "Sir Richard Branson to Invest $38 Billion to Fight Global Warming," press release, Virgin Atlantic, www.virgin-atlantic.com/en/us/allaboutus/environment/ bransonpledge.jsp; "YUM! In the News," YUM! Brands, September 2011, www .yum.com/company/inthenews/pressreleases/092011.asp; "President Bill Clinton Opens the 2011 Clinton Global Initiative Annual Meeting with a Focus on Generating Jobs for the 21st Century, Sustainable Consumption for Our Planet, 'What Works' for Girls and Women, and Progress of Member Commitments," press release, Clinton Global Initiative, 2011, http://press.clintonglobalinitiative.org/press _releases/president-bill-clinton-opens-the-2011-clinton-global-initiative-annual -meeting/.

28. "Global Competitiveness," World Economic Forum, www.weforum.org/ issues/global-competitiveness; "History and Achievements," World Economic Forum, www.we-forum.org/en/about/History%20and%20Achievements/index .html.

29. Sarah Kessler, "With 500 Million Views, TED Talks Provide Hope for Intelligent Internet Video," *Mashable*, June 27, 2011, http://mashable.com/2011/ 06/27/ted-anniversary/.

30. "Sign the Global Petition Now," Jamie Oliver's Food Revolution, www
.jamieoliver.com/us/foundation/jamies-food-revolution/sign-petition.

31. Analysis of statistics from Clinton Global Initiative. See also "President Bill
Clinton Opens the 2011 Clinton Global Initiative Annual Meeting."

32. Mike Lippitz, "Exploring the Aspen Network of Development Entrepreneurs," *Innovation Excellence,* January 13, 2012, www.innovationexcellence.com/
blog/2012/01/13/exploring-the-aspen-network-of-development-entrepreneurs
-ande/.

33. "Global Shapers," World Economic Forum, accessed December 7, 2012,
www.weforum.org/community/global-shapers.

34. "Sustainable Cities," AVINA Americas, accessed February 6, 2013, www
.avinaamericas.org/impact-strategies/sustainable-cities/.

35. Matt O'Connell, "Conference Hound Joins with BUMP-Network to
Reward Its Members," press release, Conference Hound, January 25, 2012, http://
conferencehound.com/articles/conference-hound/press-releases/conference-
hound-joins-with-bump-network-to-reward-its-members/5329.

36. "Our Founder," DEKA Research and Development Corporation, January 5, 2013, www.dekaresearch.com/founder.shtml.

37. Sarah Adee, "Dean Kamen's 'Luke Arm' Prosthesis Readies for Clinical Trials," *IEEE Spectrum,* February 2008, http://spectrum.ieee.org/biomedical/
bionics/dean-kamens-luke-arm-prosthesis-readies-for-clinical-trials/2.

38. Tim Studt, "To Build a Better World," *R&D Magazine,* August 21, 2006,
www.rdmag.com/Awards/Innovator-Of-The-Year/2006/08/To-Build-a-Better
-World/; Dean Kamen, interview by Stephen Colbert, *The Colbert Report,* Comedy
Central, March 20, 2008, www.colbertnation.com/the-colbert-report-videos/
164485/march-20-2008/dean-kamen; John Abele, "Innovation and Collaboration
for Social Change: Dean Kamen's Slingshot," *Kingbridge Collaboration Blog,* September 25, 2009, www.kingbridgecentre.com/wordpress/?p=81.

39. "The Crisis," Water.org, accessed February 6, 2013, http://water.org/water
-crisis/water-facts/water/.

40. Jessie Scanlon, "Coca-Cola's Freestyle, Dean Kamen, and More," *Business-
Week,* September 30, 2009, www.businessweek.com/innovate/next/archives/2009/
09/coca-colas_freestyle_dean_kamen_and_more.html.

41. Ibid.

42. Paul Solman, "Tech's Next Feats? Maybe On-Demand Kidneys, Robot Sex,
Cheap Solar, Lab Meat," *Newshour,* PBS, April 20, 2012, www.pbs.org/newshour/
bb/business/jan-june12/makingsense_04-20.html.

43. Allan Gerlat, "Traveling Down the Long Green Road," *Waste News,* November 6, 2006, www.highbeam.com/doc/1G1-154155985.html.

44. "USAID Administrator Shah Delivers Remarks at Morehouse College,
Recognizes Coca-Cola for Leadership in Private-Public Partnership," U.S. Agency
for International Development, October 14, 2011, http://transition.usaid.gov/press/
releases/2011/pr111014.html.

45. "Water Stewardship," The Coca-Cola Company, http://www.coca-cola
company.com/videos/safe-water-for-africa-yt9womedqgsry.

46. "Being 'Good' Is Good Business," Deloitte Consulting LLP, 2006, http://
www.deloitte.com/assets/Dcom-Shared%20Assets/Documents/us_cb_good
business_122006.pdf.

47. Katie Kross, "An Authoritative and Candid Insider's Guide to the Essential Knowledge, Skills, and Abilities Needed to Establish a Successful CSR Career" (review of *Corporate Social Responsibility, Health, and Wellness,* by Timothy J. Mohin [San Francisco: Berrett-Koehler Publishers, 2012]), August 1, 2012, www.csrwire.com/press_releases/34432-An-Authoritative-and-Candid-Insider-s-Guide-to-the-Essential-Knowledge-Skills-and-Abilities-Needed-to-Establish-a-Successful-CSR-Career.

48. John Mackey and Rajendra S. Sisodia, *Conscious Capitalism: Liberating the Heroic Spirit of Business* (Boston: Harvard Business Review Press, January 2013).

49. "Rethinking the Social Responsibility of Business," *Reason,* October 2005, http://reason.com/archives/2005/10/01/rethinking-the-social-responsi/singlepage.

50. Michael Porter and Mark Kramer, "Creating Shared Value," *Harvard Business Review,* January–February 2011, 64.

51. Bill Gates, "Remarks of Bill Gates, Harvard Commencement 2007," *Harvard Gazette,* June 7, 2007, http://news.harvard.edu/gazette/story/2007/06/remarks-of-bill-gates-harvard-commencement-2007/.

52. For CSR reporting, see Aman Singh, "CSR + Transparency: Can Voluntary Disclosure Increase Shareholder Value?" *Forbes,* February 14, 2012, www.forbes.com/sites/csr/2012/02/14/csr-transparency-can-voluntary-disclosure-increase-shareholder-value/. For businesses addressing all stakeholders' interests, see John Mackey, "Conscious Capitalism: Creating a New Paradigm for Business," Whole Planet Foundation, 2007, www.wholeplanetfoundation.org/files/uploaded/John_Mackey-Conscious_Capitalism.pdf, 5.

53. "Giving in Numbers: 2011 Edition: Trends in Corporate Giving," Committee Encouraging Corporate Philanthropy, June 2012, www.corporatephilanthropy.org/measurement/benchmarking-reports/giving-in-numbers.html; Margaret Coady, "2011 Trends in Corporate Philanthropy," CECP, June 2012, www.corporatephilanthropy.org/pdfs/2012summit/CGS_Summit_Presentation_FINAL.pdf, 9.

54. "International Partnerships: P&G Pampers," UNICEF, 2010, www.unicef.org/spanish/corporate_partners/index_25098.html.

55. "Shakti Program, India," Unilever, accessed August 12, 2012, www.unilever.com/careers/insideunilever/oursuccessandchallenges/shaktiprogrammeindia.

56. David Vogel, *The Market for Virtue: The Potential and Limits of Corporate Social Responsibility* (Washington, DC: Brookings Institution Press, 2005), 44.

57. Alison Rose, "Giving in Numbers: 2011 Edition; Trends in Corporate Giving," CECP, 2011, www.corporatephilanthropy.org/research/benchmarking-reports/giving-in-numbers.html.

58. Paul Klein, "Why Social Change Is Good for Business," *Forbes,* February 15, 2012, www.forbes.com/sites/csr/2012/02/15/why-social-change-is-good-for-business/.

59. "4th Annual Edelman Good Purpose Consumer Survey," *Edelman Editions,* November 4, 2010, http://edelmaneditions.com/2010/11/4th-annual-edelman-goodpurpose-consumer-survey/.

60. "The Case for Social Enterprise Alliance," Social Enterprise Alliance, accessed February 6, 2013, https://www.se-alliance.org/what-is-social-enterprise.

61. See the following pages, all accessed June 6, 2012, on the FareStart website: "About the FareStart Café @2100," http://farestart.org/cafe/about/index.html; "Youth Barista Training & Education Program," http://farestart.org/training/

barista/index.html, "Barista Student Stories," www.farestart.org/training/barista/stories/index.html.

62. "Social Enterprise: A Powerful Engine for Economic and Social Development," Social Enterprise Alliance, 2011, www.community-wealth.org/sites/clone.community-wealth.org/files/downloads/paper-sea10.pdf.

63. "Bryson: Social Paradigm," *Agenda Ni,* June 6, 2011, www.agendani.com/bryson-social-paradigm.

64. Leila Jana, "The Microwork Revolution," TEDxBrussels talk, uploaded on November 23, 2011, available at www.youtube.com/watch?feature=player_embedded&v=319sQ9s-lyQ.

65. "Social Enterprise Marks 10 Years of Creating Jobs in Developing Countries," *PRWeb,* February 2, 2012, www.prweb.com/releases/2012/2/prweb9157737.htm.

66. "Social Economy Intergroup Considers Perspectives for Social Business," CEDAG-EU, April 4, 2012, www.cedag-eu.org/; FAQs, Social Enterprise UK, accessed February 6, 2013, www.socialenterprise.org.uk/about/about-social-enterprise/faqs; "Small and Medium-Sized enterprises (SMEs)," European Commission, accessed February 6, 2013, http://ec.europa.eu/enterprise/policies/sme/promoting-entrepreneurship/social-economy/.

67. Jo Barraket, Nick Collyer, Matt O'Connor, and Heather Anderson, "Finding Australia's Social Enterprise Sector: Final Report," Australian Centre for Philanthropy and Nonprofit Studies, June 2010, www.socialtraders.com.au/finding-australias-social-enterprise-sector-fases-final-report.

68. Nidhi Chaudhary, "South Asia: A Hub for Social Entrepreneurship," *Echoing Green,* July 31, 2012, www.echoinggreen.org/blog/south-asia-as-a-hub-for-social-entrepreneurship.

69. Deloitte Research economic analysis. The number of social entrepreneurs worldwide was used as a proxy for the number of social enterprises. Entrepreneurship activity was determined using the Global Report on Social Entrepreneurship by Monitor, "Monitor Group's Survey of Social Entrepreneurs," June 14, 2011, http://www.monitor.com/Expertise/Industries/NonprofitandSocialSector/tabid/79/ctl/ArticleDetail/mid/681/CID/20111406162413908/CTID/1/L/en-US/Default.aspx. Analysis is based on the assumption that the number of social enterprises per entrepreneur for the United Kingdom applies to the rest of the world. The total number of employees was determined assuming ten employees per social enterprise.

70. Randall Kempner (Aspen Network of Development Entrepreneurs), interview with the authors, August 2012.

71. "The New Class: B Corp—Does Your Business Have Superhero Status?" Workbar, May 6, 2012, http://workbar.com/bcorp/.

72. Rahim Kanani, "2011 Social Capital Markets Conference (SOCAP): An Interview with Kevin Jones, Co-founder & Convener," *Forbes,* August 24, 2011, www.forbes.com/sites/rahimkanani/2011/08/24/2011-social-capital-markets-conference-socap-an-interview-with-kevin-jones-co-founder-convener/.

73. "About Safaricom," Safaricom, accessed February 6, 2013, www.safaricom.co.ke/about-us; Deloitte Center for Health Solutions, "Retail Clinics: Facts, Trends and Implications," Deloitte, August 14, 2008, www.deloitte.com/assets/Dcom-UnitedStates/Local%20Assets/Documents/us_chs_RetailClinics_230708(1).pdf.

74. Brian Dolan, "2016: 3M Patients Monitored over Cellular Networks," Mobi Health News, February 1, 2012, http://mobihealthnews.com/16162/2016-3m-patients-monitored-over-cellular-networks/.

75. Allen Hammond et al., "The Next 4 Billion: Market Size and Business Strategy at the Base of the Pyramid," World Resources Institute, 2007, www.wri.org/publication/the-next-4-billion.

76. C. K. Prahalad, *The Fortune at the Bottom of the Pyramid: Eradicating Poverty Through Profits,* revised and updated 5th anniversary ed. (Upper Saddle River, NJ: Pearson Education, 2011); "About the Jaipur Rugs Foundation," Jaipur Rugs Foundation, accessed February 6, 2013, www.jaipurrugs.com/about_JRF.aspx.

77. Prahalad, *Fortune at the Bottom of the Pyramid,* introduction.

78. Michael Kubzansky, Ansulie Cooper, and Victoria Barbary, "Promise and Progress: Market-Based Solutions to Poverty in Africa," Monitor Deloitte Group, May 2011, 67, http://www.monitor.com/Portals/0/MonitorContent/imported/MonitorUnitedStates/Articles/PDFs/Monitor_Promise_and_Progress_May_24_2011.pdf.

79. Lester M. Salamon, S. Wojciech Sokolowski, and Regina List, *Global Civil Society: An Overview* (Baltimore: Johns Hopkins Comparative Nonprofit Sector Project, 2003), http://adm-cf.com/jhu/pdfs/Books/BOOK_GCS_2003.pdf.

80. "China Health-Care Spending May Hit $1 Trillion by 2020," *Bloomberg News,* August 29, 2012, www.bloomberg.com/news/2012-08-29/china-health-care-spending-may-hit-1-trillion-by-2020.html; Centers for Medicare & Medicaid Services, "National Health Expenditure Projections 2011–2021," June 11, 2012, www.cms.gov/Research-Statistics-Data-and-Systems/Statistics-Trends-and-Reports/NationalHealthExpendData/Downloads/Proj2011PDF.pdf.

81. "Who We Are," BRAC, accessed November 6, 2012, www.brac.net/content/who-we-are; "Where We Work: Bangladesh: Education," BRAC, accessed November 6, 2012, www.brac.net/content/where-we-work-bangladesh-education.

82. "Who We Are," BRAC; Sir Fazle Hasan Abed, "Guest Post: Sir Fazle Hasan Abed on Frugal Innovation (Jugaad)," *World Affairs Council Blog,* September 10, 2012, http://blog.worldaffairs.org/2012/09/sir-fazle-frugal-innovation/.

83. "1800-1860s," YMCA, accessed February 6, 2013, www.ymca.net/history/1800–1860s.html; "Who We Are," American Red Cross, accessed February 6, 2012, www.redcross.org/about-us.

84. Ann Barger Hannum and John Peralta, "Charity Sector Outweighs Utilities in GDP, on Par with Construction and Finance," Global Philanthropic Limited, http://globalphilanthropic.com/?gpr_news=charity-sector-outweighs-utilities-in-gdp-on-par-with-construction-and-finance.

85. Aisha Ghaus-Pasha, "Role of Civil Society Organizations in Governance," United Nations Public Administration Network, December 2004, http://unpan1.un.org/intradoc/groups/public/documents/un/unpan019594.pdf.

86. Catherine Rampell, "More College Graduates Take Public Service Jobs," *New York Times,* March 1, 2011, www.nytimes.com/2011/03/02/business/02graduates.html?_r=1.

87. Based on analysis of raw data in OECD, *Government at a Glance* (Paris: OECD Publishing, 2011), section 11, part 48, "Government Outsourcing," fig. 48.1, www.oecd-ilibrary.org/sites/gov_glance-2011-en/11/01/index.html?contentType=&itemId=/content/chapter/gov_glance-2011-27-en&container

ItemId=/content/serial/22214399&accessItemIds=/content/book/gov_glance-2011
-en&mimeType=text/html.

88. Stephen Goldsmith and William Eggers, *Governing by Network: The New Shape of Government* (Washington, DC: Brookings Institution Press, 2004).

89. Jane Martinson, "Happy, Touchy-Feely and Driven by God," *Guardian,* February 24, 2006, www.guardian.co.uk/business/2006/feb/24/columnists .guardiancolumnists; "Serco Annual Report and Accounts 2011," July 22, 2012, pp. 7–11, http://www.serco.com/Images/Serco%20AR2011_tcm3-39494.pdf.

90. Scott Drossos, interview with authors, March 2012.

91. Gilad Lotan, "KONY2012: See How Invisible Networks Helped a Campaign Capture the World's Attention," *Social Flow,* March 14, 2012, http://blog .socialflow.com/post/7120244932/data-viz-kony2012-see-how-invisible-networks -helped-a-campaign-capture-the-worlds-attention.

92. "It's a Social World: Top 10 Need-to-Knows About Social Networking and Where It's Headed," ComScore, December 11, 2011, www.comscore.com/Press_ Events/Presentations_Whitepapers/2011/it_is_a_social_world_top_10_need -to-knows_about_social_networking, 2–4.

93. Jeff Howe, "Crowdsourcing: A Definition," *Crowdsourcing blog,* June 2, 2006, http://crowdsourcing.typepad.com/cs/2006/06/crowdsourcing_a.html

94. William Eggers, "XBC: Creating Public Value by Unleashing the Power of Cross-Boundary Collaboration," Harvard Kennedy Ash Center and Deloitte Research, 2011, www.deloitte.com/assets/Dcom-Global/Local%20Assets/Documents/ Public%20Sector/dtt_ps_xbc_060311.pdf.

95. "Our Apps and Projects," Code for America, accessed February 6, 2013, http://codeforamerica.org/projects/.

96. Bill Drayton, "Everyone a Changemaker," *Innovations* (winter 2006): 3, www.ashoka.org/files/innovations8.5x11FINAL_0.pdf.

97. Jennifer Pahlka, "Coding a Better Government," TED Talk, February 2012, www.ted.com/talks/lang/en/jennifer_pahlka_coding_a_better_government.html.

98. Lester Salamon, "Putting Civil Society on the Economic and Policy Map of the World," Johns Hopkins Center for Civil Society Studies, 2010, www.slideshare .net/EuclidNetwork/putting-civil-society-on-the-economic-and-policy-map-of-the -world.

99. Greg Hills and Adeeb Mahmud, "Volunteering for Impact: Best Practices in International Corporate Volunteering," Brookings Institution, September 2007, www.brookings.edu/~/media/research/files/papers/2007/9/volunteering/ volunteering_for_impact.

100. "Milestone Marker: 100 Companies Across U.S. Pledge to Build Nonprofit Capacity Through Skills-Based Volunteering," press release, A Billion Plus Change, May 15, 2012, www.abillionpluschange.org/press_release/milestone -marker-100-companies-across-us-pledge-build-nonprofit-capacity-through.

101. "Philanthropy: Current Context and Future Outlook," 19.

Two

1. See "Municipal Solid Waste (MSW) in the United States: Facts and Figures," annual series, US Environmental Protection Agency, accessed February 6, 2013, www.epa.gov/osw/nonhaz/municipal/msw99.htm; and "Waste (Denmark),"

European Environment Agency, accessed February 6, 2013, www.eea.europa.eu/soer/countries/dk/soertopic_view?topic=waste.

2. Rhodes Yepsen, "Encouraging Sustainable Recycling Behavior Through Financial Incentives," *BioCycle* 48 (December 2007): 34, www.biocycle.net/2007/12/encouraging-sustainable-recycling-behavior-through-financial-incentives/; Center for American Progress, "It's Easy Being Green: It Pays to Recycle," Recyclebank *In the News* blog, July 16, 2008, www.recyclebank.com/corporateinfo/index/presscoveragearticle/id/69?___store=uk&___from_store=us.

3. Ron Gonen, interview with authors, December 2011.

4. Ibid.

5. Mike Olsen, "10 Best Uses for RFID Tags," *Wired,* February 23, 2009, www.wired.com/techbiz/it/magazine/17-03/st_best; Ashok Kamal (Triple Pundit), "Green IT: The Other Clean Tech," August 29, 2011, Recyclebank *In the News* blog, www.recyclebank.com/corporate-info/newsroom/in-the-news/266. Some estimates note decreases in beverage container litter of between 70 and 84 percent, with total litter reduction between 34 and 47 percent from the bottle bill laws. "Litter Studies in Bottle Bill States," Container Recycling Institute, accessed January 10, 2013, www.bottlebill.org/about/benefits/litter/bbstates.htm.

6. "Get Rewards," Recyclebank, www.recyclebank.com/rewards/; "About This Partner: Macy's," accessed February 6, 2013, and Recyclebank, accessed February 6, 2013, www.recyclebank.com/reward/10-off-your-next-50-in-store-purchase-5656.

7. "Recyclebank (Finalist)," Philadelphia Sustainability Awards, accessed February 6, 2013, http://philadelphiasustainabilityawards.org/nominees/recycle_bank.

8. Jonathan Hsu, interview with authors, March 2013.

9. Yepsen, "Encouraging Sustainable Recycling Behavior."

10. "Recyclebank (Finalist)."

11. Yepsen, "Encouraging Sustainable Recycling Behavior."

12. Ibid.

13. "Get to Know Recyclebank," Recyclebank, July 2012, www.recyclebank.com/media/Get_to_Know_Recyclebank_UK.pdf.

14. Supporters claim that it also cut emissions by as much as 16 percent in the first years of operation. Others argue, however, that car pollution was replaced with bus pollution. David Derbyshire, "Congestion Charge Has Had No Effect on Reducing London's Pollution, Finds Study," *Daily Mail,* May 1, 2008, www.dailymail.co.uk/news/article-563269/Congestion-charge-effect-reducing-Londons-pollution-finds-study.html; "London Congestion Charge Cuts CO_2 Emissions by 16%," C40 Cities, accessed February 6, 2013, www.c40cities.org/c40cities/london/city_case_studies/londons-congestion-charge-cuts-co2-emissions-by-16.

15. Vicki Bogan, "Stock Market Participation and the Internet," *Journal of Financial and Qualitative Analysis* 43 (March 2008): 191–212, http://dyson.cornell.edu/faculty_sites/bogan/doc/research/31244854.pdf.

16. "NYSE Group Volume Records: Top 10 Years," NYSE Technologies, accessed February 6, 2013, www.nyxdata.com/nysedata/asp/factbook/viewer_edition.asp?mode=table&key=3003&category=3.

17. Howard Wilcox, "Press Release: Mobile Payments Market to Quadruple by 2014, Reaching $630bn in Value, Although Still Only Accounting for Around 5% of Ecommerce Retail Sales," press release, Juniper Research, May 4, 2010, http://juniperresearch.com/viewpressrelease.php?pr=173.

18. Palash R. Ghosh, "Mobile Phone Service Skyrocketing in Africa, with Huge Potential for Further Growth," *International Business Times,* November 10, 2011, www.ibtimes.com/articles/247111/20111110/africa-mobile-phone-service -subscription-growth-nigeria.htm; Killian Fox, "Africa's Mobile Economic Revolution," *Guardian,* July 23, 2011, www.guardian.co.uk/technology/2011/jul/24/ mobile-phones-africa-microfinance-farming.

19. William Jack and Tavneet Suri, "The Economics of M-PESA: An Update," October 2010, www.mit.edu/~tavneet/M-PESA_Update.pdf. See also Ken Banks, "The Invisible Bank: How Kenya Has Beaten the World in Mobile Money," News-watch National Geographic, July 4, 2012, http://newswatch.nationalgeographic .com/2012/07/04/the-invisible-bank-how-kenya-has-beaten-the-world-in-mobile -money/.

20. "M-PESA Documentary," uploaded January 26, 2009, www.youtube.com/ watch?v=zQo4VoLyHe0.

21. William Jack and Tavneet Suri, "The Economics of M-PESA," revised August 2010, www.mit.edu/~tavneet/M-PESA.pdf; Menekse Gencer, "Amplify-ing the Impact: Examining the Intersection of Mobile Health and Mobile Finance," World Economic Forum and the mHealth Alliance, January 2011, www3.weforum .org/docs/WEF_HE_IntersectionMobileHealthMobileFinance_Report_2011 .pdf, 2–6; Hash, "The Kenyan Mobile Money Ecosystem," *White African,* Decem-ber 8, 2010, http://whiteafrican.com/2010/12/08/the-kenyan-mobile-money -ecosystem/.

22. Fox, "Africa's Mobile Economic Revolution."

23. Ibid.

24. "Africa: Mobile Phones Achieve More Than Aid, Says Industry Chief," all Africa.com, August 4, 2009, http://allafrica.com/stories/200908040141.html.

25. "Our Story," Satellite Sentinel Project, accessed February 6, 2013, http:// satsentinel.org/our-story.

26. Matt Richtel, "Now, to Find a Parking Spot, Drivers Look on Their Phones," *New York Times,* May 7, 2011, www.nytimes.com/2011/05/08/techno logy/08parking.html?pagewanted=all.

27. "SFMTA releases SF*park* Android App," San Francisco Municipal Trans-portation Agency, November 10, 2011, http://sfpark.org/2011/11/10/sfmta-releases -sfpark-android-app/; Will Reisman, "SFpark Hourly Meters Actually Save Motor-ists Money," *San Francisco Examiner,* December 16, 2012, http://sfpark.org/2012/ 12/17/san-francisco-examiner-article-highlights-benefits-of-demand-based-meter -pricing/.

28. William D. Eggers and Joshua Jaffe, "Gov to Go: Boosting Public Sector Productivity by Going Mobile," Deloitte University Press, February 2013, http:// dupress.com/articles/gov-on-the-go/.

29. "SFMTA Approves PayByPhone for On Street Parking in San Fran-cisco," PayByPhone, accessed November 14, 2012, http://paybyphone.com/ san-francisco-news/.

30. "mHealth Technologies: Applications to Benefit Older Adults," Center for Technology and Aging, March 2011, 3, 6, www.techandaging.org/mHealth_ Position_Paper_Discussion_Draft.pdf; Katherine Baicker et al., "Workplace Well-ness Programs Can Generate Savings," *Health Affairs* 29 (February 2010): 304–311, http://content.healthaffairs.org/content/29/2/304.abstract?sid=df003470-6867-4aaf -9b70-2d078c8208c2.

31. "It's a Social World: Top 10 Need-to-Knows About Social Networking and Where It's Headed," ComScore, December 21, 2011, www.comscore.com/Press_Events/Presentations_Whitepapers/2011/it_is_a_social_world_top_10_need-to-knows_about_social_networking, 4–5; Azarias Reda et al., "Social Networking in Developing Regions," 2012, www-personal.umich.edu/~azarias/paper/ictd2012.pdf.

32. Azarias Reda et al., "Social Networking in Developing Regions"; Jenna Wortham, "Public Outcry over Antipiracy Bills Began as Grass-Roots Grumbling," *New York Times*, January 19, 2012, www.nytimes.com/2012/01/20/technology/public-outcry-over-antipiracy-bills-began-as-grass-roots-grumbling.html?page wanted=all.

33. "Cleaning Out Corruption in India," Avaaz.org, accessed February 3, 2013, www.avaaz.org/en/highlights--corruption.php.

34. "Profit with Purpose," *Economist*, January 26, 2013, www.economist.com/news/business/21570763-how-profit-firm-fosters-protest-profit-purpose?fsrc=scn/tw_ec/profit_with_purpose.

35. Jared Keller, "How the CIA Uses Social Media to Track How People Feel," *Atlantic*, November 4, 2011, www.theatlantic.com/technology/archive/2011/11/how-the-cia-uses-social-media-to-track-how-people-feel/247923/.

36. "Crowdsourcing Contest Ends with Partial Victory for MIT Team," TAG Challenge, April 4, 2012, www.tag-challenge.com/news/tag-winner-press-release/.

37. Brett Goldstein, interview with authors, March 2012.

38. Clay Shirky, "It's Not Information Overload. It's Filter Failure," Web 2.0 Expo NY, September 19, 2008, http://blip.tv/web2expo/web-2-0-expo-ny-clay-shirky-shirky-com-it-s-not-information-overload-it-s-filter-failure-1283699; Russ Juskalian, "Interview with Clay Shirky," *Columbia Journalism Review*, December 19, 2008, www.cjr.org/overload/interview_with_clay_shirky_par.php?page=all.

39. Kaylee Thompson, "The Santa Cruz Experiment: Can a City's Crime Be Predicted and Prevented?" *PopSci.com*, November 1, 2011, www.popsci.com/science/article/2011-10/santa-cruz-experiment.

40. Ibid.

41. Charlie Beck and Colleen McCue, "Predictive Policing: What Can We Learn from Wal-Mart and Amazon About Fighting Crime in a Recession?" *Police Chief*, November 2009, www.policechiefmagazine.org/magazine/index.cfm?fuseaction=display_arch&article_id=1942&issue_id=112009.

42. Eric Mills, "An Ounce of Prevention," Officer.com, September 1, 2009, www.officer.com/article/10233299/an-ounce-of-prevention, quotes McCue's summary of the benefits: "The outcomes included a 49-percent reduction in gunfire complaints on New Year's Eve, and a 26-percent reduction in gunfire complaints on the following days. Forty-five weapons were also seized. An unanticipated additional benefit to this operation was a $15,000 reduction in overtime expenses, as personnel were placed where they were needed most and 50 people were able to take the holiday off." See also William M. Pottenger, Xiaoning Yang, and Stephen V. Zanias, "Free Text Conversion and Semantic Analysis Survey: Status Update, January 2006," Lehigh University, January 2006, www.ncjrs.gov/pdffiles1/nij/grants/219548.pdf.

43. Erick Schonfeld, "Knewton Takes Adaptive Learning to the Next Level," *TechCrunch*, December 23, 2008, http://techcrunch.com/2008/12/23/knewton-takes-adaptive-learning-to-the-next-level/; Steve Kolowich, "Technology and the

Completion Agenda," *Inside Higher Ed,* November 9, 2010, www.insidehighered
.com/news/2010/11/09/completion.

44. "Flipping the Classroom," *Economist,* September 17, 2011, www.economist
.com/node/21529062.

45. Michael Nielsen, "The New Einsteins Will Be Scientists Who Share," *Wall
Street Journal,* October 29, 2011, http://online.wsj.com/article/SB100014240529702
04644504576653573191370088.html.

46. "Open Source Cancer Research: Jay Bradner on TED.com," TED Conferences, October 27, 2011, http://blog.ted.com/2011/10/27/open-source-cancer
-research-jay-bradner-on-ted-com/.

47. Ibid.

48. Spencer Reiss, "Cloud Computing: Available at Amazon.com Today," *Wired,*
April 21, 2008, www.wired.com/techbiz/it/magazine/16-05/mf_amazon?currentPage=3.

49. A study by Trend Micro in 2012 demonstrated that cloud providers do
not adhere to the same standards. See Stefanie Hoffman, "Study: Data Security Biggest Cloud Inhibitor," *Channelnomics,* August 30, 2012, http://channelnomics
.com/2012/08/30/study-security-biggest-cloud-inhibitor/.

50. Krishnan Subramanian, "Reaching Africa Through Mobile and Cloud
Computing," CloudAve.com, December 24, 2009, www.cloudave.com/1014/
reaching-africa-through-mobile-and-cloud-computing/.

51. Praekelt Foundation, Young Africa Live website, November 24, 2012,
www.praekeltfoundation.org/young-africa-live.html.

52. "AWS Case Study: Praekelt Foundation," Amazon Web Services, April 21,
2011, http://aws.amazon.com/solutions/case-studies/praekelt-foundation/.

53. "23andMe Goes to Washington," *23andMe* blog, October 17, 2012, http://
blog.23andme.com/23andme-research/in-washington-talking-about-parkinsons
-research/.

54. Gretchen Cuda-Kroen, "Search for Parkinson's Turns to Online Social Networking," *Health News,* NPR, August 20, 2012, www.npr.org/blogs/health/2012/
08/20/158943097/search-for-parkinsons-genes-turns-to-online-social-networking.

55. Robert Langreth "Google's Brin Makes Strides in Hunt for Parkinson's
Cure," *Bloomberg,* May 11, 2012, www.bloomberg.com/news/2012-05-11/google-s-
brin-makes-strides-in-hunt-for-parkinson-s-cure-health.html.

56. "Spotlight on Africa: Mobile Statistics & Facts 2012," Praekelt Foundation,
July 9, 2012, www.youtube.com/watch?v=0bXjgx4J0C4.

Three

1. Adam Richardson, "The Four Technologies You Need to Be Working
With," *Harvard Business Review,* September 12, 2011, http://blogs.hbr.org/cs/2011/
09/the_four_technologies_you_need.html.

2. Adam Richardson, "Zipcar: The Apple of Car Sharing," *Good,* September 17, 2010, www.good.is/post/zipcar-the-apple-of-car-sharing/.

3. Robin Chase, "Robin Chase on Product Failure," presentation at FailCon
France, September 23, 2011, www.slideshare.net/webwallflower/robin-chase-on
-product-failure.

4. Willi Loose, "The Environmental Impacts of Car Sharing," International
Association of Public Transport, June 2009, www.uitp.org/pdf/factsheet_3e_
Umwelt.pdf.

5. Ibid.

6. For Chase statement, see Robin Chase, "Entrepreneurship, Sustainable Mobility and the Digital Revolution," SMART Presentation Summary, University of Michigan, May 18, 2006, www.um-smart.org/resources/speakers/chase.php. For car-sharing statistics, see Juan Ortega, "Car Sharing in the United States," Community Transportation Association of America, April 2006, http://tinyurl.com/an8kybz; "One Thousand World Carshare Cities in 2009," The Commons, last updated October 22, 2008, http://ecoplan.org/carshare/general/cities.htm#latest; "The Ride Revolution," GoLoco, accessed February 6, 2013, www.goloco.org/greetings/guest; and "Rent a Car from Someone Nearby," Getaround, accessed February 6, 2013, www.getaround.com/. For BMW and Mercedes involvement, see Horatiu Boeriu, "DriveNow: BMW and Six Joint Venture for Premium Car Sharing," *BMW Blog*, March 21, 2011, www.bmwblog.com/2011/03/21/bmw-and-sixt-establish-drivenow-joint-venture-for-premium-car-sharing/.

7. Jerry Hirsch, "Avis Will Acquire Zipcar Car-Sharing Business for $500 Million," *Los Angeles Times*, January 2, 2013, http://articles.latimes.com/2013/jan/02/autos/la-fi-hy-avis-buys-zipcar-20130102.

8. Itir Sonuparlak, "New Study: Millennials Prefer Car 'Access Over Ownership,'" *TheCityFix.com*, December 6, 2011, http://thecityfix.com/blog/new-study-millennials-prefer-car-access-over-ownership/.

9. Michael Raynor, *The Innovator's Manifesto: Deliberate Disruption for Transformational Growth* (New York: Crown Business, 2011), 67.

10. "The Bottom of the Pyramid: Businesses Are Learning to Serve the Growing Number of Hard-Up Americans," *Economist*, June 23, 2011, www.economist.com/node/18863898.

11. V. Kasturi Rangan and Katharine Lee, "Bridge International Academies: A School in a Box," Case 9-511-064 (Boston: Harvard Business School, 2010), 5–6, 11.

12. "History/Mission/The Founders," Bridge International Academies, www.bridgeinternationalacademies.com/Bridge_International_Academies/About_Us.html.

13. "Bridge International Academies in Kenya: Quality Schooling for Less Than $4 per Month," Pearson.com, March 7, 2011, www.pearson.com/news/2011/march/bridge-international-academies-in-kenya-quality-schooling-for-les.html?article=true.

14. "Results," Bridge International Academies, http://www.bridgeinternationalacademies.com/results/academic/.

15. Laura Walubengo, "Bridge International Academies Feted at Africa Awards," *CapitalFM*, October 13, 2012, www.capitalfm.co.ke/news/2012/10/bridge-international-academies-feted-at-african-awards/.

16. "Our Model," Bridge International Academies, http://www.bridgeinternationalacademies.com/approach/model/.

17. Rangan and Lee, "School in a Box," 11.

18. "Bridge International Academies Launches Affordable Schools in Kenya," Omidyar Network, December 8, 2009, www.omidyar.com/about_us/news/2009/12/08/bridge-international-academies-launches-affordable-schools-kenya.

19. Rangan and Lee, "School in a Box," 11.

20. Deloitte Research economic analysis, August 2012.

21. "Gyan Shala: Summary," ALYLLU Initiative, accessed February 6, 2013, http://aylluinitiative.org/indiamap/gyan-shala/.

22. "World Development Report 2009," The World Bank, 2009, http://site resources.worldbank.org/INTWDR2009/Resources/4231006-1225840759068/ WDR09_18_GIM04web.pdf, 283.

23. "Where We Work," LivingGoods, accessed February 6, 2013, http:// livinggoods.org/what-we-do/where-we-work/; Monitor Group analysis, "Direct Sales Agent Models in Health," January 2013, 3.

24. Monitor Group analysis, "Direct Sales Agent Models in Health," 3.

25. Tina Rosenberg, "The 'Avon Ladies' of Africa," *NYtimes Opinionator Blog*, October 10, 2012, http://opinionator.blogs.nytimes.com/2012/10/10/the-avon-ladies-of-africa/.

26. Mark Riffee, "iPads Now Helping Marines Unleash Hell," *Wired*, September 16, 2011, www.wired.com/dangerroom/2011/09/death-on-an-ipad/.

27. Rashaun X. James, "Semper FiPad: Marine Corps Aviators Use Popular Tablet in Afghanistan," June 10, 2011, www.cherrypoint.marines.mil/News/ NewsArticleDisplay/tabid/4890/Article/66234/semper-fipad-marine-corps-aviators -use-popular-tablet-in-afghanistan.aspx.

28. Riffee, "iPads Now Helping Marines Unleash Hell."

29. C. Todd Lopez, "'Apps for Army' to Shape Future Software Acquisition," Army News Service, August 4, 2010, www.army.mil/article/43293/apps-for-army -to-shape-future-software-acquisition/. In all, the competition created seventeen Android and sixteen iOS app versions. See also "The US Army Marketplace Application Store," *CTIA Blog*, November 11, 2011, http://blog.ctia.org/2011/11/11/ the-u-s-army-marketplace-application-store/.

30. Digital manuals could save the military millions, and not just in paper costs. Medical forms, for instance, could be filled out via mobile devices. Besides cost and accuracy benefits, this would save time. It takes 15 minutes to fill out the average military medical form on paper, compared with 1.5 minutes on a smartphone. "Connecting Soldiers to Digital Applications (CSDA)," US Army, Army Capabilities Integration Center, http://news.idg.no/cw/art.cfm?id=D934A95B-1A64–6A71 -CE91208A8EA22FF8.

31. Spencer Ackerman, "First Look: Inside the Army's App-Store for War," *Wired*, April 27, 2011, www.wired.com/dangerroom/2011/04/armys-app-store -for-war/. The army will base its store on Apple's strict model rather than Android's open-source platform. The army will verify every application for security and applicability. Once cleared, the apps will be available for download.

32. Budi Putra, "iPhone Can Help Snipers Hit Targets," *iPhone Buzz*, January 21, 2009, www.iphonebuzz.com/iphone-can-helps-snipers-to-hit-targets-215821.php.

33. "KAC Ballistics App for iPhone or iPod," AccurateShooter.com, accessed February 6, 2013, www.accurateshooter.com/gear-reviews/kac-bullet-flight-app/.

34. "'Bulletflight' iPhone App Helps Snipers Hit Targets," Fox News, January 21, 2009, www.foxnews.com/story/0,2933,481004,00.html.

35. Styli Charalambous, "25 Billion Reasons Why Apple Isn't Going Away Anytime Soon," *Asia Times*, March 1, 2012, www.atimes.com/atimes/Global_ Economy/NC01Dj01.html.

36. Wade Roush, "The Big Themes at Y Combinator's Summer 2012 Demo Day," *Xconomy*, August 22, 2012, www.xconomy.com/san-francisco/2012/08/22/ the-big-themes-at-y-combinators-summer-2012-demo-day/.

37. Chris Anderson, "Free!: Why $0.00 Is the Future of Business," *Wired*, February 25, 2008, www.wired.com/techbiz/it/magazine/16–03/ff_free?currentPage=all.

38. "What Is Freemium?" Freemium.org, accessed February 26, 2013, www .freemium.org/what-is-freemium-2/.

39. "Application Directory," Apps for Democracy, accessed October 20, 2012, www.appsfordemocracy.org/application-directory/.

40. Sharon Machlis, "8 More Free Tools for Data Visualization and Analysis," *Computerworld,* April 28, 2011, http://blogs.computerworld.com/18212/8_more _free_tools_for_data_visualization_and_analysis; Peter Burrows, "Nirav Tolia: Hyperlocal Boy Makes Good," *Businessweek,* March 8, 2012, www.businessweek .com/articles/2012–03–08/nirav-tolia-hyperlocal-boy-makes-good.

41. Michail N. Giannakos and Panayiotis Vlamos, "Using Webcasts in Education: Evaluation of Its Effectiveness," *British Journal of Educational Technology,* April 27, 2012, http://tinyurl.com/awv6ceu.

42. Jon Marcus, "Online Course Start-Ups Offer Virtually Free College," *Washington Post,* January 21, 2012, www.washingtonpost.com/local/education/ online-course-startups-offer-virtually-free-college/2012/01/09/gIQAEJ6VGQ _story.html?tid=pm_local_pop.

43. Mary Lou Forward, "Case Study 8: OpenCourseWare," Educause, May 2, 2012, www.educause.edu/Resources/GameChangersEducationandInform/ CaseStudy8OpenCourseWare/250542.

44. Steven Carson (MIT OpenCourseWare), interview with authors, February 2012.

45. "First Course Offered by *MITx* Begins," *MIT News,* March 5, 2012, http:// web.mit.edu/newsoffice/2012/6002x-mitx-begins-today-0305.html.

46. "Harvard and MIT Introduce EdX: The Future of Online Learning," *edudemic,* May 2, 2012, http://edudemic.com/2012/05/harvard-and-mit-to-form-new -online-learning-project/.

47. "Stanford Engineering Everywhere: Courses," Stanford University, accessed February 6, 2013, http://see.stanford.edu/see/courses.aspx.

48. Leonard Medlock and Betsy Corcoran, "YouTube U: The Power of Stanford's Free Online Education," *Fast Company,* March 31, 2011, www.fastcoexist .com/1678792/youtube-u-the-power-of-stanfords-free-online-education.

49. Ibid.

50. Steve Carson, interview with authors, February 2012.

51. "Solar Street Lights Are Functioning in Haiti," *Solar Street Lights Blog,* May 21, 2010, http://www.streetlights-solar.org/2010/05/the-solar-street-lighting -are-functioning-in-haiti/.

52. http://web.mit.edu/fnl/volume/231/miyagawa.html.

53. Liz Gannes, "Watch: Sebastian Thrun Leaves Stanford to Teach Online," *All Things D,* January 25, 2012, http://allthingsd.com/20120125/watch-sebastian -thrun-leaves-stanford-to-teach-online/.

54. Jeff Howe, *Crowdsourcing: Why the Power of the Crowd Is Driving the Future of Business* (New York: Crown Business, 2008); James Surowiecki, *The Wisdom of Crowds* (New York: Doubleday, 2004); Don Tapscott and Anthony D. Williams, *Wikinomics: How Mass Collaboration Changes Everything* (New York: Portfolio, 2006).

55. Erica Hagan, "Putting Nairobi's Slums on the Map," World Bank Institute, January 12, 2009, http://wbi.worldbank.org/wbi/devoutreach/article/370/putting -nairobi%E2%80%99s-slums-map; William Underhill, "Map Kibera," *Design Observer,* July 26, 2010, http://changeobserver.designobserver.com/feature/map

-kibera/14698/; Mark Hay, "More Money, More Problems: The Logic of Slums," *Columbia Political Review*, December 19, 2011, www.cpreview.org/2011/12/more-money-more-problems/; "Kibera UK: The Gap Year Company," Kibera UK, accessed February 6, 2013, www.kibera.org.uk/Facts.html.

56. Hagan, "Putting Nairobi's Slums on the Map."

57. Ibid.

58. The Tanzanian project is now collaborating with the Kenyan project.

59. Michael Levenson, "Send Photo, Get Action," *Boston Globe*, February 2, 2010, www.boston.com/news/local/massachusetts/articles/2010/02/02/residents_use_iphone_to_report_street_level_woes/; "Boston Citizens Connect," *Macworld* app guide, accessed January 21, 2013, www.macworld.com/appguide/app.html?id=323365&expand=false.

60. Sara Jacobi and Cate Lecuyer, "Citizens Connect a Success, According to Boston Officials," *SouthEndPatch,* August 16, 2012, http://southend.patch.com/articles/citizens-connect-a-success-according-to-boston-officials.

61. "'Street Bump' App Detects Potholes, Alerts Boston City Officials," *Fox News,* July 20, 2012, www.foxnews.com/tech/2012/07/20/treet-bump-app-detects-potholes-alerts-boston-city-officials/.

62. Chris Osgood, interview with authors, March 2012.

63. Luis von Ahn, "Massive-Scale Online Collaboration," TED Talks, April 2011, www.ted.com/talks/luis_von_ahn_massive_scale_online_collaboration.html?awesm=on.ted.com_A4Pa&utm_campaign=&utm_medium=on.ted.com-twitter&utm_source=direct-on.ted.com&utm_content=tweetie.

Four

1. Luke Karmali, "Mists of Pandaria Pushes Warcraft Subs Over 10 Million," *IGN*, October 4, 2012, www.ign.com/articles/2012/10/04/mists-of-pandaria-pushes-warcraft-subs-over-10-million.

2. Julian Dibbel, "Recalculating the Global Virtual GDP, Yet Again," *Terra Nova*, June 26, 2007, http://terranova.blogs.com/terra_nova/2007/06/recalculating-t.html.

3. Vili Lehdonvirta and Mirko Ernkvist, "Converting the Virtual Economy into Development Potential: Knowledge Map of the Virtual Economy," executive summary, International Bank for Reconstruction and Development/The World Bank, April 2011, www.infodev.org/en/Document.1076.pdf.

4. Timothy Pratt, "What Happens in Brooklyn Moves to Vegas," *New York Times,* October 19, 2012, www.nytimes.com/2012/10/21/magazine/what-happens-in-brooklyn-moves-to-vegas.html?pagewanted=all&_r=0.

5. Ibid.

6. "On the Origin of Species: Theories on Where Money Comes from Say Something About Where the Dollar and Euro Will Go," *Economist,* August 18, 2012, www.economist.com/node/21560554; Thomas H. Greco Jr., *Money: Understanding and Creating Alternatives to Legal Tender* (White River Junction, VT: Chelsea Green Publishing, 2001), 27–29, http://reinventingmoney.com/documents/MoneyEbook.pdf.

7. "Briton Bay Commercial Fishing," Our Bristol Bay, www.ourbristolbay.com/commercial-fisheries.html, accessed February 6, 2013. See also John W. Duffield, Christopher J. Neher, David A. Patterson, and Oliver S. Goldsmith, "Econom-

ics of Wild Salmon Ecosystems: Bristol Bay, Alaska," *USDA Forest Service Proceedings,* RMRS-P-49, 2007, www.fs.fed.us/rm/pubs/rmrs_p049/rmrs_p049_035_044.pdf.

8. Garrett Hardin, "The Tragedy of the Commons," *Science* 162 (December 1968): 1243–1248, www.sciencemag.org/content/162/3859/1243.full.pdf.

9. Debora Mackenzie, "The Cod That Disappeared," *New Scientist,* September 16, 1995, www.newscientist.com/article/mg14719953.400-the-cod-that-disappeared.html.

10. Elizabeth Bluemink, "Pioneering Nobel Prize Winner Influenced Alaska, Resources," *Anchorage Daily News,* October 12, 2009, www.adn.com/2009/10/12/971399/pioneering-nobel-prize-winner.html.

11. Vincent Ostrom, *The Meaning of American Federalism* (San Francisco: ICS Press, 1991), 163–197, http://pdf.usaid.gov/pdf_docs/PNABM798.pdf.

12. "Acid Rain: The Power of Markets to Help the Planet," Environmental Defense Fund, accessed February 6, 2013, www.edf.org/approach/markets/acid-rain.

13. For example, those used by the Carbon Disclosure Project.

14. Effective public policy can launch new currencies by creating markets that use them. In the United States, many states have established a renewable portfolio standard (RPS), which directs utilities to purchase RECs for some portion of their energy generation each year, with the goal of achieving certain targets down the line. For example, California plans to obtain 33 percent of its energy from renewable sources by 2020, and North Carolina plans to obtain 12.5 percent from renewable sources by 2021. Institute for Energy Research, *The Status of Renewable Electricity Mandates in the States* (Washington, DC: Institute for Energy Research, January 2011), 1, www.instituteforenergyresearch.org/wp-content/uploads/2011/01/IER-RPS-Study-Final.pdf; "100% Green Power Users," Environmental Protection Agency, July 5, 2012, www.epa.gov/greenpower/documents/top100_july2012.pdf.

15. Pierre Omidyar, "How I Did It: eBay's Founder on Innovating the Business Model of Social Change," *Harvard Business Review,* September 2011, 41–44.

16. In exchange for foregoing a couple million dollars in annual charitable tax deductions, ON has considerable flexibility in how it deploys the $442 million it has committed to date.

17. Amy Klements (Omidyar Network), interview with authors, June 2012.

18. Cheryl Dorsey (Echoing Green), interview with authors, June 2012.

19. Omidyar, "How I Did It," 44.

20. Robert P. Chilcott, "Compendium of Chemical Hazards: Kerosene (Fuel Oil)," UK Health Protection Agency, 2006, www.who.int/ipcs/emergencies/kerosene.pdf.

21. "Who We Are," d.light, accessed February 6, 2013, www.dlightdesign.com/who-we-are/. Goals for 2015 are from Susan Phillips (Omidyar Network), interview with authors, June 2012.

22. "Let's Hear It for Our 1,900th Playground!" *KaBOOM! Blog,* November 2, 2010, http://kaboom.org/blog/let%E2%80%99s_hear_it_our_1900th_playground.

23. Kevin Marsh, Evelina Bertranou, and Kunal Samanta, *Cost-Benefit Analysis and Social Impact Bond Feasibility Analysis for the Birmingham BeActive Scheme* (London: Matrix Knowledge, December 2011), 6, www.socialfinance.org.uk/sites/default/files/matrix_be_active_final_report_0.pdf.

24. "The Gigaton War," EV World, October 25, 2010, www.evworld.com/syndicated/evworld_article_1928.cfm.

25. "From Silos to Synergy," Global Impact Economy Forum, Washington, DC, May 4, 2012, www.youtube.com/watch?v=kzspO6U61gE&feature=plcp.

26. "Operation: Green Capital," Carbon War Room, accessed February 6, 2013, www.carbonwarroom.com/sectors/energy-supply/energy-efficiency/green-capital.

27. Todd Woody, "How to Tap a Trillion Dollars for Renewable Energy Investment," *Forbes,* July 23, 2012, www.forbes.com/sites/toddwoody/2012/07/23/how-to-tap-a-trillion-dollars-for-renewable-energy-investment/2/.

28. GIIRS Newsletter, November 2012, http://giirs.org/about-giirs/press/giirs-reports/307.

29. Jason Roberts, "How to Build a Better Block," TEDxOU presentation, February 21, 2012, www.youtube.com/watch?v=ntwqVDzdqAU.

30. Ibid.; see also Allison Arieff, "How To: Build a Better Block," *Good Design,* June 22, 2010, www.good.is/post/how-to-build-a-better-block/.

31. "The Better Block Protect San Antonio TX," Digestible Media, March 6, 2012, www.youtube.com/watch?v=VC5EFcD5aCM.

32. Jessica Day, "Get Creative with Your Rewards," January 7, 2013, http://blog.ideascale.com/2013/01/07/get-creative-with-your-rewards/.

33. "Time Banking: New Economic Model for Those Tired with Capitalism," *Student Environmental Action Coalition,* January 4, 2012, www.seac.org/time-banking-new-economic-model-for-those-tired-with-capitalism/; "About Time-banking," Time Banking UK, accessed February 6, 2013, www.timebanking.org/about/.

34. Deloitte Research analysis. There were 175 projects listed under the VSFS program in 2012–2013. The time and cost savings were calculated assuming seven to eight hours of work each week by the student intern on these projects and a $25 mean hourly wage of a federal worker (source: Office of Personal Management). US Department of State, "U.S. College Students Can Apply Now for Virtual Student Foreign Service eInternships," July 3, 2012, www.state.gov/r/pa/prs/ps/2012/07/194548.htm.

35. Charities Aid Foundation, *World Giving Index 2011* (London: Charities Aid Foundation, December 19, 2011), 22, www.cafonline.org/pdf/World_Giving_Index_2011_191211.pdf.

36. Lester M. Salamon et al., *Global Civil Society: Dimensions of the Nonprofit Sector* (Baltimore: Johns Hopkins Center for Civil Social Studies, 1999), 13, http://politiquessociales.net/IMG/pdf/chapter1.pdf.

37. Lester M. Salamon, S. Wojciech Sokolowski, and associates, *Global Civil Society: Dimensions of the Nonprofit Sector,* vol. 2 (Bloomfield, CT: Kumarian Press, 2004), 3, table 3, http://ccss.jhu.edu/wp-content/uploads/downloads/2011/10/Comparative-Data_2004_FINAL.pdf.

38. "SBTF/USAID: A Partnership—The Future of Digital Volunteers?" *The Standby Task Force,* June 12, 2012, http://blog.standbytaskforce.com/sbtfusaid-a-partnership/.

39. Ibid.

40. Simon Owens, "Can Todd Park Revolutionize the Health Care Industry?" *Atlantic,* June 2, 2011, www.theatlantic.com/technology/archive/2011/06/can-todd-park-revolutionize-the-health-care-industry/239708/.

41. Todd Park, "Welcome," presented at Health Data Initiative Forum 2011, Bethesda, Maryland, June 9, 2011, www.iom.edu/Activities/PublicHealth/Health Data/2011-JUN-09/OpeningSession/Administrator.aspx.

42. Kathleen O'Malley, "Health Datapalooza 2012: Apps Are Making a Difference," *Journal of Participatory Medicine* 4 (June 19, 2012), www.jopm.org/media -watch/conferences/2012/06/19/health-datapalooza-2012-apps-are-making-a -difference/.

43. Todd Park, "Lean Startup in Government," slide presentation, South by Southwest, Austin, Texas, March 13, 2012, www.slideshare.net/500startups/ todd-park-macon-philips-lean-startup-sxsw.

44. For tracking the spread of disease, see O'Malley, "Health Datapalooza 2012." For food desert information, see "About the Locator," US Department of Agriculture, Economic Research Service, accessed February 6, 2013, www.ers.usda .gov/data-products/food-desert-locator/about-the-locator.aspx#Defined.

45. Carleen Hawn, "Government 2.0," *Stanford Social Innovation Review*, fall 2011, www.ssireview.org/articles/entry/government_2.0; James Manyika et al., "Big Data: The Next Frontier for Innovation, Competition, and Productivity," McKinsey Global Institute, May 2011, www.mckinsey.com/insights/mgi/research/technology _and_innovation/big_data_the_next_frontier_for_innovation; David Stegon, "Park: 'Energy Datapalooza' in the Works," *Fedscoop*, July 12, 2012, http://fedscoop.com/ park-energy-datapalooza-in-the-works/.

46. "The Global Positioning System (GPS) Market 2008–2012," TechNavio, April 15, 2009, www.technavio.com/content/global-positioning-system-gps-market -2008–2012-0; Matt Rosoff, "Here's What Google Will Lose When Apple Wipes Google Maps from the iPhone," *Business Insider,* June 8, 2012, www.businessinsider .com/apple-maps-effect-on-google-2012-6#ixzz20WNNL89s.

47. Nicolas Chavent, "Building an OSM Environment, Haiti," Humanitarian OpenStreetMap Team, accessed February 6, 2013, http://hot.openstreetmap.org/ projects/haiti-2; Jeffrey Johnson, John Crowley, and Schuyler Erle, "Haiti: Crisis-Mapping the Earthquake," presented at O'Reilly Where 2.0 Conference, San Jose, CA, March 30, 2010.

48. Alex Howard, "How Data and Open Government Are Transforming NYC," O'Reilly Radar, October 7, 2011, http://radar.oreilly.com/2011/10/data -new-york-city.html; Rachel Stern, "How Open Government Is Transforming New York," presented at the Strata Conference, New York, NY, February 2011, http:// radar.oreilly.com/2011/10/data-new-york-city.html.

49. See Rozell et al., "IOGDS: International Open Government Dataset Search," accessed February 6, 2013, http://logd.tw.rpi.edu/demo/international_data set_catalog_search; Jesse Lichtenstein, "Why Open Data Alone Is Not Enough," *Wired,* July 2011, www.wired.com/magazine/2011/06/st_essay_datafireworks/; Noor Huijboom and Tijs Van den Broek, "Open Data: An International Comparison of Strategies," *European Journal of ePractice* 12 (March–April 2011), www. epractice.eu/files/European%20Journal%20epractice%20Volume%2012_1.pdf.

50. Heather Broomfield, "The Open Data Hotel: Norwegian Hospitality at Its Best!" October 20, 2011, Norway Agency for Public Management and eGovernment, http://data.norge.no/blogg/2011/10/open-data-hotel.

51. "NZ Police Let Public Write Laws," *BBC News,* September 26, 2007, http://news.bbc.co.uk/2/hi/7015024.stm.

52. Lichtenstein, "Why Open Data Alone Is Not Enough."

53. "Transparency and Open Government," Office of the White House, accessed February 6, 2013, www.whitehouse.gov/open/documents/open-government-directive.

54. Jennifer Pahlka, "Coding a Better Government," TED Talk, February 2012, www.ted.com/talks/lang/en/jennifer_pahlka_coding_a_better_government.html.

55. Ibid.

56. Anya Kamenetz, "How an Army of Techies Is Taking Over City Hall," *Fast Company*, November 29, 2010, www.fastcompany.com/magazine/151/icitizen-bonus.html.

57. Jennifer Pahlka (Code for America), interview with authors, May 3, 2012.

58. Markus Mobius and Adam Szeidl, "Trust and Social Collateral," University of Chicago Booth School of Business, May 2007, http://faculty.chicagobooth.edu/appliedtheory/archive/pdf/AdamSzeidlSocialCollateralApril14Spring08.pdf.

59. Muskan Chopra, "Explaining Kiva Zip from a Whitewater Raft," *Kiva Fellows Blog*, July 25, 2012, http://fellowsblog.kiva.org/2012/07/25/explaining-kiva-zip-from-a-whitewater-raft/.

60. Alex Goldmark, "Kiva's Secret Project to Let You Give Peer-to-Peer Loans," *Fast Company*, January 13, 2012, www.fastcoexist.com/1679137/kiva-s-secret-project-to-let-you-give-peer-to-peer-loans.

61. Naomi Klein, *No Logo: Taking Aim at the Brand Bullies* (Toronto: Knopf Canada, 2000), 5.

62. Donald Katz, *Just Do It: The Nike Spirit in the Corporate World* (Avon, MA: Adams Media, 1995), 18.

63. Parag Gupta, interview with authors, July 18, 2012.

64. Amelia Gentleman, "Picking Up Trash by Hand, and Yearning for Dignity," *New York Times*, September 27, 2007, www.nytimes.com/2007/09/27/world/asia/27ragpickers.html?_r=0.

65. Ananda Lee Tan, "Clean Development Mechanism Funding for Waste Incineration: Financing the Demise of Waste Worker Livelihood, Community Health, and Climate," Global Alliance for Incinerator Alternatives, Quezon City, Philippines, accessed February 6, 2013, www.no-burn.org/downloads/Clean%20Development%20Mechanism%20Flyer.pdf.

66. "One Person's Trash Is Another Person's Treasure," Waste Ventures, February 26, 2012, www.youtube.com/watch?feature=player_embedded&v=m2e6BrfnPok#!.

67. Parag Gupta, interview with authors, July 18, 2012. See also "Strategy," Waste Ventures, accessed February 6, 2013, www.wasteventures.org/pages/our-strategy.

68. Linus Kendall, "Two Years and Counting," Waste Ventures, August 2012, www.wasteventures.org/two-years-and-counting.

69. Olivia Solon, "Waste Ventures Gives India's Pickers Access to Carbon Markets," *Wired UK*, January 11, 2012, www.wired.co.uk/news/archive/2012-01/11/waste-ventures.

70. "Changemakers: Waste Ventures," Ashoka Changemakers, last updated August 20, 2012, www.changemakers.com/changeshop/waste-ventures.

71. "Outcomes," Waste Ventures, accessed February 6, 2013, www.wasteventures.org/pages/outcomes.

Five

1. Tom Vander Ark, "How Intelligent Scoring Will Create an Intelligent System," *Huffington Post,* January 9, 2012, www.huffingtonpost.com/tom-vander-ark/how-intelligent-scoring-w_b_1194249.html; Randall Stross, "The Algorithm Didn't Like My Essay," *New York Times,* June 9, 2012, www.nytimes.com/2012/06/10/business/essay-grading-software-as-teachers-aide-digital-domain.html?_r=1.

2. David Strom, "What You Can Learn from Kaggle's Top 10 Data Scientists," *Read Write,* April 12, 2012, www.readwriteweb.com/cloud/2012/04/what-you-can-learn-from-kaggle.php; Liz Gannes, "Kaggle Solves Big Data Problems with Contests—and Now Has Big Funders and $11M on Board," *All Things D,* November 13, 2011, http://allthingsd.com/20111103/kaggle-solves-big-data-problems-with-contests-and-now-has-big-funders-on-board/.

3. Anthony Goldbloom, interview with authors, March 2012.

4. Jason Rhodes, "Competition Shines Light on Dark Matter," White House Office of Scientific and Technology Policy, June 27, 2011, www.whitehouse.gov/blog/2011/06/27/competition-shines-light-dark-matter.

5. "Mapping Dark Matter," Kaggle, accessed December 27, 2012, www.kaggle.com/host/casestudies/nasa.

6. Xavier Conort, email to authors, June 21, 2012.

7. "ASAP Interview with Martin O'Leary," *No Free Hunch* (Kaggle blog), May 13, 2012, http://blog.kaggle.com/2012/05/13/asap-interview-with-martin-oleary/.

8. "Improve Health Care, Win $3,000,000," Heritage Provider Network, accessed February 6, 2013, www.heritagehealthprize.com/c/hhp.

9. "Online Dating Industry Statistics Infographic Video," February 26, 2012, www.youtube.com/watch?v=T0VtT_5Wkh0.

10. John Hagel and John Seely Brown, "Why Most Online Communities Are Failures," *Forbes,* January 18, 2012, http://management.fortune.cnn.com/2012/01/18/why-most-online-communities-are-failures/.

11. Rachel Botsman, "The Case for Collaborative Consumption," TED Conferences, May 2010, www.ted.com/talks/lang/en/rachel_botsman_the_case_for_collaborative_consumption.html.

12. "Kickstarter Stats," Kickstarter, accessed February 6, 2013, www.kickstarter.com/help/stats.

13. Sean Silverthorne, "New Research Explores Multi-Sided Markets," *Harvard Business School Working Knowledge,* March 13, 2006, http://hbswk.hbs.edu/item/5237.html.

14. Thomas Eisenmann, Geoffrey Parker, and Marshall W. Van Alstyne, "Strategies for Two-Sided Markets," *Harvard Business Review,* October 2006, 92–101.

15. Simon Mainwaring, *We First* (New York: Palgrave Macmillan, 2012), 37–38.

16. US Government Accountability Office, *Multiple Employment and Training Programs: Providing Information on Colocating Services and Consolidating Administrative Structures Could Promote Efficiencies* (Washington, DC: Government Accountability Office, January 2011), executive summary, www.gao.gov/new.items/d1192.pdf.

17. UK National Audit Office, "Department for Work and Pensions: The Introduction of the Work Programme," executive summary, January 2012, 6, www.nao.org.uk/publications/1012/dwp_work_programme.aspx.

18. Ashish Sinha, "SkillKindle, an Online Marketplace for Skill-Sharing Secures Angel Funding," *NextBigWhat,* March 15, 2012, www.nextbigwhat.com/ skillkindle-an-online-marketplace-for-skill-sharing-secures-angel-funding-297/.

19. Britney Fitzgerald, "Avi Flombaum, Skillshare Teacher, Earns $100K a Year as Tech Educator, Quits Day Job," *Huffington Post,* August 24, 2012, www .huffingtonpost.com/2012/08/24/avil-flombaum-skillshare_n_1817784.html.

20. "The Re-working of 'Work,'" Institute for the Future, 2011, www.iftf.org/ futureworkskills2020.

21. Fitzgerald, "Avi Flombaum, Skillshare Teacher."

22. "Study Your Way to a New Career," General Assembly, accessed February 6, 2013, http://tinyurl.com/b49z7td.

23. Arun Sundararajan, "From Airbnb and Coursera to Uber: Government Shouldn't Regulate the Sharing Economy," *Wired,* October 22, 2012, www.wired. com/opinion/2012/10/from-airbnb-to-coursera-why-the-government-shouldnt -regulate-the-sharing-economy/.

24. "Statistics," Kiva, accessed February 6, 2013, www.kiva.org/about/stats.

25. Andrea Ordanini, Lucia Miceli, Marta Pizzetti, and A. Parasuraman, "Crowd-Funding: Transforming Customers into Investors Through Innovative Service Platforms," Crowdsourcing.org, July 9, 2011, www.crowdsourcing.org/ document/crowdfunding-transforming-customers-into-investors-through -innovative-service-platforms-/5214.

26. Winston Daryoue, "Liberia's Baby Blues: No Policy for Pregnant School Girls," Inter-Press Service News Agency, July 5, 2012, www.ipsnews.net/2012/07/ liberias-baby-blues-no-policy-for-pregnant-school-girls/; "About Us," More Than Me Foundation, accessed February 6, 2013, https://morethanme.org/about .html.

27. In the years since, More Than Me has focused its attention on its mission of educating women. Education, statistically speaking, delays a girl's marriage by four years. Each year of primary school raises a woman's eventual income by 10 to 20 percent. For more, see Amy Baratta, "More Than Me: Foundation Established by B'ville Native Helps Children in Liberia Get an Education," *Bernardsville (NJ) News,* February 23, 2011, http://newjerseyhills.com/bernardsville_news/news/ article_4a48f10c-3f62-11e0-ac87–001cc4c03286.html?mode=story; Josh Tetrick, "Crowdfunding: How Social Entrepreneurs Are Turning Small Donations into Big Bucks," *Huffington Post,* January 14, 2011, www.huffingtonpost.com/josh-tetrick/ crowdfunding-social-entrepreneurs_b_808613.html.

28. In its first two years, More Than Me won a video grant from Microsoft 7, the Ford Focus Global Test Drive Contest, Global Giving's Facebook photo competition, and a prize from Chase Bank's Community Giving contest. More Than Me directly traded increments of its supporters' energy for money. In this way, it transformed a network of committed people into educations for little girls via Facebook likes and dollars—an odd currency, but for some Liberian woman, currency enough to mean the difference between child prostitution and educated adulthood. See also Tetrick, "Crowdfunding"; "About Us," More Than Me Foundation.

29. Michael Norman, interview with authors, April 2012.

30. Christopher Borrelli, "Who Benefits Most from the Colbert-Bump?" *Chicago Tribune,* July 20, 2011, http://articles.chicagotribune.com/2011–07-20/en- tertainment/ct-ent-0720-colbert-as-political-forc20110720_1_colbert-nation -colbert-report-dutch-bank-dsb.

31. "Directory of Sites," Crowdsourcing.org, accessed February 6, 2013, www.crowdsourcing.org/directory.

32. *Crowdfunding Industry Report: Market Trends, Composition and Crowdfunding Platforms,* Crowdsourcing.org, May 2012, 13–14, www.scribd.com/doc/92871793/Crowd-Funding-Industry-Report-2011; "The Crowdfunding Industry Growing Like Taters, *PR Web,* January 20, 2013, www.prweb.com/releases/2013/1/prweb10340558.htm.

33. Mark Milian, "After Raising Money, Many Kickstarter Projects Fail to Deliver," *BusinessWeek,* August 21, 2012, www.businessweek.com/news/2012-08-21/kickstarter-s-funded-projects-see-some-stumbles.

34. Olga Khazan, "How Popularise Brought Crowdsourcing to D.C.'s Commercial Real Estate Market," *Washington Post,* June 1, 2012, http://tinyurl.com/7d5t7c5.

35. Tristina Sinopoli, "Social Finance: The Key to Innovation City," MaRS Center for Impact Investing, August 2, 2012, http://socialfinance.ca/blog/post/social-finance-the-key-to-innovation-city.

36. Peter Corbett, interview with authors, April 2011.

37. Robin Wigglesworth, "$6.3tn Wiped off Stock Markets in 2011," *Financial Times,* December 30, 2011, www.ft.com/intl/cms/s/0/483069d8-32f3-11e1-8e0d-00144feabdc0.html#axzz2FKny1Oi3.

38. "Report on Sustainable and Responsible Investing Trends in the United States 2012," US SIF (The Forum for Sustainable and Responsible Investment), 2012, executive summary, 12, http://ussif.org/resources/pubs/documents/USSIFTrends2012ES.pdf.

39. Jaideep Singh Panwar and Jenny Blinch, *Sustainable Stock Exchanges: A Report on Progress,* Responsible Research, 2012, 13, www.unglobalcompact.org/docs/issues_doc/Financial_markets/Sustainable_Stock_Exchanges.pdf.

40. In areas such as microfinance, however, repayment rates are typically greater than 95 percent. "Microfinance Basics," Grameen Foundation, accessed February 6, 2013, www.grameenfoundation.org/what-we-do/microfinance-basics.

41. "IRIS Metrics," Global Impact Investing Network, accessed February 6, 2013, http://iris.thegiin.org/iris-standards#m=operationalimpact.

42. Antony Elliott, Gavin Francis, and Geoff Knott, *Financial Planners as Catalysts for Social Investment* (London: Nesta, 2012), 6, www.nesta.org.uk/library/documents/Financialplanners14.pdf.

43. New Economics Foundation, *Developing a Social Equity Capital Market 2006* (London: New Economics Foundation, 2006), 12, http://tidescanada.org/wp-content/uploads/files/causeway/Developing_a_Social_Equity_Capital_Market_2006.pdf.

44. Malaika Maphalala, "Mission Markets Advances Impact Investing," Natural Investments LLC, spring 2011, http://naturalinvesting.com/blog/2011/09/mission-markets-advances-impact-investing/.

45. Paul Sullivan, "With Impact Investing, a Focus on More Than Returns," *New York Times,* April 23, 2010, www.nytimes.com/2010/04/24/your-money/24wealth.html?dbk&_r=0.

46. Sasha Dichter, Robert Katz, Harvey Koh, and Ashish Karamchandani, "Closing the Pioneer Gap," *Stanford Social Innovation Review,* winter 2013, www.ssireview.org/articles/entry/closing_the_pioneer_gap.

47. Harvey Koh, Ashish Karamchandani, and Robert Katz, "From Blueprint to Scale: The Case for Philanthropy in Impact Investing" (Monitor Group, April 2012), 18, http://tinyurl.com/84yn9qv.

48. Gloria Nelund, "Impact Investing for Global Economic Growth," *Wall Street Transcript,* January 9, 2012, www.twst.com/interview/28718.

49. US Securities and Exchange Commission, SEC Filing, EDGAR, TriLinc Global Impact Fund, LLC, accessed February 6, 2013, www.sec.gov/Archives/edgar/data/1550453/000095012312012569/filename2.htm.

50. Gloria Nelund (TriLinc Global), interview with authors, January 11, 2012.

51. "Impact Investing Emerges as a Distinct Asset Class," Rockefeller Foundation, November 29, 2010, www.rockefellerfoundation.org/news/press-releases/impact-investing-emerges-distinct.

52. "Competition Fact Sheet, Wendy Schmidt Oil Cleanup X Challenge," X Prize Foundation, accessed February 6, 2013, www.iprizecleanoceans.org/sites/iprizecleanoceans.org/files/presskit/final/WSOCXC_Fact_Sheet.pdf.

53. McKinsey & Company, "'And the Winner Is . . .' Capturing the Promise of Philanthropic Prizes,'" (McKinsey & Company, 2009), 70–90, www.mckinseyonsociety.com/downloads/reports/Social-Innovation/And_the_winner_is.pdf; Dave Sedgwick, "ePrize," *World Class Care Blog,* accessed February 6, 2013, http://worldclasscare.wordpress.com/tag/eprize/.

54. Tina Rosenberg, "Prizes with an Eye Toward the Future," *New York Times,* February 29, 2012, http://opinionator.blogs.nytimes.com/2012/02/29/prizes-with-an-eye-toward-the-future/?ref=opinion.

55. Sheila Campbell, "Challenges and Challenge.gov," Center for Excellence in Digital Government, U.S. General Services Administration, March 31, 2011, http://siteresources.worldbank.org/INFORMATIONANDCOMMUNICATIONAND TECHNOLOGIES/Resources/D4S3P3-SheilaCampbell.pdf.

56. US Department of Health and Human Services, "OSTP Memo on Prizes and Challenges," accessed February 6, 2013, www.hhs.gov/open/initiatives/challenges/ostp_memo.html.

57. Office of Citizen Services and Innovative Technologies, "2012 Annual Report," General Services Administration, December 2012, 23, www.gsa.gov/portal/getMediaData?mediaId=156463.

58. Luciano Kay, *Managing Innovation Prizes in Government* (Washington, DC: IBM Center for the Business of Government, 2011), 17, www.businessofgovernment.org/sites/default/files/Managing%20Innovation%20Prizes%20in%20Government.pdf.

59. Jenn Gustetic, presentation, South by Southwest Interactive Festival, Austin, TX, March 2012.

60. Joe Parrish and Jason Cruzar (Office of the Chief Technologist, National Aeronautics and Space Administration), interview with authors, February 21, 2012.

61. Robert Lee Hotz, "Science Prize: Innovation or Stealth Ad?" *Wall Street Journal,* May 8, 2009, http://online.wsj.com/article/SB124173078482897809.html.

62. "X-Prize Director Describes Incentive Prizes in an Interview with Sander Olson," *Next Big Future,* June 3, 2011, http://nextbigfuture.com/2011/06/x-prize-director-describes-incentive.html.

63. Sean Mason, interview with authors, January 2012.

64. Tom Gash, interview with authors, January 2012.

65. Antonia Romero, interview with authors, January 2012.

66. Jeffrey B. Liebman, "Social Impact Bonds: A Promising New Financing Model to Accelerate Social Innovation and Improve Government Performance," Center for American Progress, February 2011, www.americanprogress.org/wp-content/uploads/issues/2011/02/pdf/social_impact_bonds.pdf.

67. Randeep Ramesh, "Big Society Bank Aims to Boost Social Enterprise," *Guardian,* February 22, 2011, www.guardian.co.uk/society/2011/feb/22/big-society-bank-social-enterprise-ronald-cohen.

68. Yao Huang (speech, Starting Block Social Innovation Institute 2013, New York, New York, August 4, 2013).

69. The government, which traditionally pays the full value regardless of whether the program works, often helps cover the loss if the target is not met, and is responsible for paying the return on the upside, to encourage investors to shoulder some of the risk.

70. The state invested $4.6 million and has received $34 million in economic value, including savings in welfare subsidies, food stamps, and other subsidies. "Pay for Success Projects and Social Impact Bonds: First Mover States—What Are They Doing and Why?" Nonprofit Finance Fund, June 9, 2011, http://payforsuccess.org/sites/default/files/first_mover_states_sib_webinar_transcript.pdf.

71. Katie Gilbert, "The Latest in Socially Conscious Investing: Human Capital Performance Bonds," *Institutional Investor,* January 10, 2012, www.institutionalinvestor.com/Popups/PrintArticle.aspx?ArticleID=2958534.

72. "I'll Put $2.4m on Recidivism to Fall," *Economist,* August 6, 2012, www.economist.com/blogs/democracyinamerica/2012/08/social-impact-bonds?fsrc=scn/tw_ec/ill_put_2_4m_on_recidivism_to_fall.

73. Antonia Romero, interview with authors, January 2012.

74. Dean James, interview with authors, January 2012.

75. "Potential Social Impact Bonds in Development," Instiglio, accessed February 6, 2013, www.instiglio.org/publications/sib-applications-in-development/; "Social Impact Bonds Go International," Social Finance Limited, May 30, 2012, www.socialfinance.org.uk/sites/default/files/international_working_group_and_director.pdf.

Six

1. "Diarrhoeal Disease," World Health Organization, August 2009, www.who.int/mediacentre/factsheets/fs330/en/index.html; Sandy Cairncross et al., "Water, Sanitation and Hygiene for the Prevention of Diarrhoea," *International Journal of Epidemiology* 39, issue supplement 1 (2010): i193–i205, http://ije.oxfordjournals.org/content/39/suppl_1/i193.abstract; Alyson Paige, "About Soap," eHow, accessed February 6, 2013, www.ehow.com/about_4709726_soap.html.

2. "Hunger: Vital Statistics," United Nations, accessed February 6, 2013, www.un.org/en/globalissues/briefingpapers/food/vitalstats.shtml.

3. C. K. Prahalad and Stuart L. Hart, "The Fortune at the Bottom of the Pyramid," *Strategy and Business* 26 (first quarter 2002), www.cs.berkeley.edu/~brewer/ict4b/Fortune-BoP.pdf.

4. "For Rojamma, Project Shakti Means Being Able to Educate Her Daughter," Unilever, May 9, 2005, accessed February 6, 2013, www.unilever.com/images/es_Project_Shakti_tcm13-13297.pdf.

5. Louis Lucas, "Unilever Extends 'Shakti' Scheme to Africa," *Financial Times,* August 30, 2011, www.ft.com/intl/cms/s/0/732067cc-d012-11e0-81e2-00144feabdc0

.html#axzz1qXV9SHpN; "For Rojamma"; Trefis team, "Unilever Empowers Bottom of the Pyramid Entrepreneurs with Project Shakti," Trefis, September 9, 2011, www.trefis.com/stock/ul/articles/73085/unilever-expands-project-shakti/2011-09-09.

6. Prahalad and Hart, "The Fortune at the Bottom of the Pyramid."

7. "Lifebuoy Launches Lifebuoy Swasthya Chetna," Hindustan Unilever Limited, September 5, 2002, www.hul.co.in/mediacentre/news/2002/lifebuoy -swasthya-chetna.aspx.

8. "Promoting Handwashing," Unilever, accessed March 4, 2013, www.unilever .com/sustainable-living/healthandhygiene/handwashing/; and "Global Handwashing Day," Unilever, accessed February 6, 2013, www.unilever.com/sustainable-living/ healthandhygiene/handwashing/globalhandwashingday/index.aspx.

9. "Diarrhoea Causes Over Three Million Deaths a Year. Handwashing with Soap and Water Can Reduce Diarrhoeal Diseases by Up to 48%," Unilever, accessed February 6, 2013, www.unilever.se/Images/es_Lifebuoy_promotes_handwashing _tcm59-13301.pdf; Grant Tudor, "NextThought Monday: When Mass Marketing Meets Global Health, the Case of Lifebuoy Soap," *Next Billion 2.0*, November 7, 2011, www.nextbillion.net/blogpost.aspx?blogid=2559.

10. "Spread of Water-Related Disease," Nika Water Company, accessed February 6, 2013, www.nikawater.org/the-crisis/.

11. "Lifebuoy 'Swasthya Chetna': Unilever's Social Marketing Campaign," IBS Center for Management Research, www.icmrindia.org/casestudies/catalogue/ Marketing/Lifebuoy%20Swasthya%20Chetna-Unilever%20Social%20Marketing %20Campaign.htm.

12. "Bangladesh: Empowering Women Through Micro-Enterprises," Unilever, 2006, www.unilever.com/sustainable-living/news/casestudies/better-livelihoods/ empowering-women-through-micro-enterprises.aspx.

13. Amit Sahasrabudhe, Holly J. Kellar, Vijay Sharma, and Bill Wiltschko, "Performance Ecosystems: A Decision Framework to Take Performance to the Next Level," Deloitte Center for the Edge, 2012, www.deloitte.com/assets/Dcom-United States/Local%20Assets/Documents/TMT_us_tmt/us_tmt_performanceecosystems_ 060712.pdf.

14. Susan Phillips, interview with authors, May 2012.

15. Jacqueline Novogratz, interview with authors, September 2012.

16. "GAVI's Impact," GAVI Alliance, January 2013, www.gavialliance.org/ about/mission/impact/.

17. Sasha Dichter, interview with authors, September 2012.

18. I. Elaine Allen and Jeff Seaman, "Going the Distance: Online Learning in the United States, 2011," Babson Survey Research Group, November 2011, www .onlinelearningsurvey.com/reports/goingthedistance.pdf.

19. Rebecca Clothey, "Opportunities and Obstacles: Technology's Potential for Expanding Access to Higher Education," *Excellence in Higher Education* 2 (2011): 52, 54, http://ehe.pitt.edu/ojs/index.php/ehe/article/view/29/28.

20. "International Housing Statistics and Research," Habitat for Humanity, accessed February 6, 2013, www.habitat.org/how/why/intl_stats_research.aspx; Gustavo Capdevila, "More Than 100 Million Homeless Worldwide," *IPS News*, March 30, 2005, http://ipsnews.net/news.asp?idnews=28086.

21. "Interview with Janice Perlman," Global Citizens Initiative, accessed February 6, 2013, www.theglobalcitizensinitiative.org/Interviews-with-Gcitizen -Leaders/Interview-with-Janice-Perlman.aspx.

22. United Nations Human Settlements Programme, *Financing Urban Shelter: Global Report on Human Settlements, 2005* (Sterling, VA: Earthscan, 2005), 5.

23. Aden Van Noppen, "Impact Investing in Affordable Housing," in *The BIG IDEA: Global Spread of Affordable Housing,* ed. Scott Anderson and Rochelle Beck (Next Billion and Ashoka Full Economic Citizenship, 2012), 45, http://fec.ashoka .org/sites/fec.ashoka.org/files/The-Big-IDEA-ebook-FINAL.pdf.

24. Eric Ho, email exchange with the authors, March 15, 2013.

25. The teams also consulted several Haitians, each of whom worked closely with NGOs in Haiti. The designers learned that Haitians prefer a certain architecture style and building layout—rooms should ideally provide a *galleria* porch in front and two rooms behind it. The homes would have to withstand earthquakes and hurricanes, possibly requiring expensive refinements to the generic proposals.

26. Rochelle Beck, "Global Spread of Affordable Housing," in *The BIG IDEA: Global Spread of Affordable Housing,* 10.

27. Mayura Janwalkar, "Slumdwellers Not Eligible for Rehab Can Hamper Plan," *Indian Express,* April 26, 2012, www.indianexpress.com/news/ slumdwellers-not-eligible-for-rehab-can-hamper-plan/941545/0.

28. "Creative Solutions for Affordable Housing: Fixing Egypt's Housing Problem the Ashoka Way," Ashoka Arab World, July 6, 2009, http://tinyurl.com/ bbdhh7r; "'Housing for All' Program," Ashoka, 2, http://tinyurl.com/alahdfh.

29. Bill Drayton and Valeria Budinich, "A New Alliance for Global Change," *Harvard Business Review,* September 2010, 56–64.

30. Ibid.

31. Bill Drayton, interview with authors, April 2012.

32. Nick Wates Associates, "Mainstreaming Community-Led Processes for Housing and Urban Poverty Alleviation: The Development of CODI and the Baan Mankong Programme," Communityplanning.net, April 15, 2009, www .communityplanning.net/special/makingplanningwork/mpwcasestudies/mpw CS21.php.

33. Kanokphan U-sha, "The Baan Mankong Program: A New Dimension to Solve the Urban Poor's Housing Problems," Thai World Affairs Center, Institute of Asian Studies, Chulalongkorn University, July 22, 2004, www.thaiworld.org/en/ include/print.php?text=31&category_id=2&print=true.

34. Community Organizations Development Institute, "From Co-ops to CODI: A Glimpse of Thailand's Hidden Legacy," accessed February 6, 2013, www .codi.or.th/housing/CooperativeThai.html.

35. "Global Report on Trafficking in Persons 2012," United Nations Office on Drugs and Crime, 2012, 1, www.unodc.org/documents/data-and-analysis/ glotip/Trafficking_in_Persons_2012_web.pdf; "International Trafficking," Polaris Project, accessed February 6, 2013, www.polarisproject.org/human-trafficking/ international-trafficking.

36. Biiftuu Adam, "Want a Job?" *Slavery in the 21st Century* (blog of the Loyola University New Orleans), November 2, 2011, http://slaveryinthe21stcentury .blogspot.com/2011/11/want-job-children-dying-all-around.html.

37. "Applying Technology, Analytics, and Business Solutions to the Human Trafficking Challenge," panel, Human Trafficking Symposium, Georgetown University, Washington, DC, January 30, 2013.

38. Robyn Fieser, "Trapped in Slavery," Catholic Relief Services, accessed February 6, 2013, http://crs.org/brazil/trapped-in-slavery/.

39. "From Slaves to Homeowners," Catholic Relief Services, accessed February 6, 2013, http://crs.org/brazil/from-slaves-to-homeowners/index.cfm; "Freed Slaves Take on Brazilian Government," *Catholic Exchange,* January 11, 2012, http://catholicexchange.com/freed-slaves-take-on-brazilian-government/.

40. "Applying Technology, Analytics, and Business Solutions."

41. "About the Freedom Registry," Freedom Registry, accessed February 6, 2013, www.freedomregistry.org/aboutus.html.

42. "Global Report on Trafficking in Persons 2012"; "Human Trafficking: The Facts," UN Global Initiative to Fight Human Trafficking, accessed February 6, 2013, www.unglobalcompact.org/docs/issues_doc/labour/Forced_labour/HUMAN _TRAFFICKING_-_THE_FACTS_-_final.pdf.

43. US Government Accountability Office, *Human Trafficking: Better Data, Strategy, and Reporting Needed to Enhance U.S. Antitrafficking Efforts Abroad* (Washington, DC: GAO, July 2006), 8, www.gao.gov/new.items/d06825.pdf.

44. Chris Hilton, "Dying to Leave: The Business of Human Trafficking— Trafficking Routes," *Wide Angle* series, PBS, September 25, 2003, www.pbs .org/wnet/wideangle/episodes/dying-to-leave/business-of-human-trafficking/ trafficking-routes/1428/.

45. Nicholas Kristoff, "Fighting Back, One Brothel Raid at a Time," *New York Times,* November 12, 2011, www.nytimes.com/2011/11/13/opinion/sunday/kristof -fighting-back-one-brothel-raid-at-a-time.html?ref=humantrafficking.

46. "What We Do," End Slavery Now, accessed February 6, 2013, www .endslaverynow.com/?goto=what&section=about.

47. "Applying Technology, Analytics, and Business Solutions."

48. Ibid.

49. "Google Ideas Summit: Illicit Networks," Palantir, July 2012, www .palantir.com/info-summit/.

50. Robyn Fieser (Catholic Relief Services), email to authors, September 2012.

51. Mira Sorvino, keynote presentation, Human Trafficking Symposium, Georgetown University, Washington, DC, January 30, 2013.

52. Elsa Brander, "Bring on the Buzz!—Meet the City Bee Association, Co-penhagen, Denmark," *Stories.coop,* November 3, 2012, www.stories.coop/stories/ video/bring-buzz-meet-city-bee-association-copenhagen-denmark.

53. "British Bees Are Endanger of Becoming Extinct in the Next Six Years," *London Wildlife,* March 5, 2012, http://london-wildlife.com/?p=26.

54. "The Copenhagen City Cooperative," Social Innovation Europe, June 22, 2011, www.socialinnovationeurope.eu/magazine/environment-and-climate-change/ case-studies/copenhagen-city-honey-cooperative.

55. Ibid.

Seven

1. For the number of British civil servants, see UK Civil Service, "Civil Service Statistics: Civil Service Employment Since 1902," CNS Quarterly Public Sector Employment Series, accessed August 23, 2012, http://resources.civilservice .gov.uk/wp-content/uploads/2011/12/Q3-2011-stats-chart.png. For UK population increase, see "History: British Population Animation," BBC, accessed February 6, 2013, www.bbc.co.uk/history/interactive/animations/population/index_embed .shtml. The UK population at the end of the 1940s was 49 million; in 2012, it was

63 million. For growth in UK civil society, see Jacques Defourny and Marthe Nyssens, "Social Enterprise in Europe: Recent Trends and Developments," *Social Enterprise Journal* 4, no. 3 (2008): 202–228, www.emeraldinsight.com/journals. htm?articleid=1752745.

2. OECD Development Assistance Committee (DAC), "Philanthropic Foundations and Development Co-operation," *DAC Journal* 4, no. 3 (2003): 34, offprint, www.oecd.org/dataoecd/23/4/22272860.pdf; Pierre Buhler, Paul C. Light, and Francis Charhon, "The Non-Profit Sector in the U.S. and France: A Compared Analysis," IFRI (Institut Français des Relations Internationals), May 2003, www .ifri.org/?page=contribution-detail&id=4191&id_provenance=88&provenance _context_id=24; Helmut K. Anheier, *Nonprofit Organizations: Theory, Management, Policy* (New York: Routledge), 2005, 76, http://xa.yimg.com/kq/ groups/30802428/172491159/name/01%2Banheier%2B(2005)%2Bnonprofit%2Bor ganizations-%2Btheory,%2Bmanagement,%2Bpolicy.pdf; Laurent Fraisse, "France: The Concept of Social Enterprise," *EMES: European Research Network* 3 (2008): 202–228; "France Takes a Deeper Look at Social Enterprise," *Equal* (newsletter of European Commission), November 2006, http://ec.europa.eu/employment_social/ equal/news/200611-se-avise_en.cfm.

3. Gareth Davies, interview with authors, September 2012.

4. "Big Society Fund Launches with £600m to Invest," BBC News, last modified April 4, 2012, www.bbc.co.uk/news/business-17602323.

5. "Rockstars of the New Economy," in *B Corporations Annual 2012 Report* (Berwyn, PA: B Lab, 2012), 44, http://nicolascordier.files.wordpress.com/2012/10/ bcorp-annual-report-2012.pdf.

6. "NFL Announces 34 Play 60 Super Schools," National Football League, October 31, 2011, http://nflcommunications.com/2011/10/.

7. Luke Williams, *Disrupt: Think the Unthinkable to Spark Transformation in Your Business* (Upper Saddle River, NJ: Pearson Education, 2011), 17–18.

8. Robert Darko Osei, "Linking Traditional Banking with Modern Finance: Barclays Microbanking: Susu Collectors Initiative," UN Development Programme, 2008, www.growinginclusivemarkets.org/media/cases/Ghana_Susu%20Collectors _2008.pdf.

9. Hillary Clinton, "Hillary's Farewell Transcript," *Daily Beast,* February 1, 2013, www.thedailybeast.com/articles/2013/02/01/hillary-s-farewell-speech-read -the-transcript.html.

10. "Obesity and Overweight," fact sheet 31, World Health Organization, May 2012, www.who.int/mediacentre/factsheets/fs311/en/; Michele Cecchini et al., "Tackling of Unhealthy Diets, Physical Inactivity, and Obesity: Health Effects and Cost-Effectiveness," *Lancet,* November 11, 2010, www.oecd.org/els/healthpolicies anddata/46407986.pdf.

11. "Obesity Trends Among U.S. Adults Between 1985 and 2010," US Centers for Disease Control and Prevention, accessed February 6, 2013, www.cdc.gov/ obesity/downloads/obesity_trends_2010.pdf; "Obesity and Overweight for Professionals: Data and Statistics," US Centers for Disease Control and Prevention, accessed January 23, 2013, www.cdc.gov/obesity/data/adult.html.

12. Cecchini et al., "Tackling of Unhealthy Diets," 1.

13. "NCHS Data Brief: Obesity and Socioeconomic Status in Adults: United States, 2005–2008," US Centers for Disease Control and Prevention, December 2010, www.cdc.gov/nchs/data/databriefs/db50.htm.

14. Jundong Song, "Walmart: No Loyalty Card from the World's Largest Grocer?" *89 Degrees Blog,* accessed January 24, 2013, http://blog.89degrees.com/post/Walmart-e28093-No-Loyalty-Card-for-the-Worlde28099s-Largest-Grocer.aspx; "First Lady Michelle Obama Announces Nationwide Commitments to Provide Millions of People Access to Healthy, Affordable Food in Underserved Communities," press release, White House, last modified July 20, 2011, www.whitehouse.gov/the-press-office/2011/07/20/first-lady-michelle-obama-announces-nationwide-commitments-provide-milli; "Wal-Mart Announces Healthy Food Campaign," Sustainable Agriculture, January 20, 2011, http://sustainableagriculture.net/blog/walmart-healthy-campaign/; Elliot Zwiebach, "Big Buildup for Small Wal-Marts," *Supermarket News,* last modified September 27, 2010, http://supermarketnews.com/retail-amp-financial/big-buildup-small-wal-marts#ixzz205Knm2Nh.

15. Bill Drayton and Valeria Budinich, "A New Alliance for Global Change," *Harvard Business Review,* September 2010, 61.

16. Bill Drayton, interview with authors, April 2012.

17. Drayton and Budinich, "New Alliance for Global Change," 58.

18. Ibid., 59.

19. Bill Drayton, interview with authors, April 2012.

20. Drayton and Budinich, "New Alliance for Global Change," 58.

21. John Matson, "Phased Out: Obama's NASA Budget Would Cancel Constellation Moon Program, Privatize Manned Launches," *Scientific American,* February 1, 2010, www.scientificamerican.com/article.cfm?id=nasa-budget-constellation-cancel.

22. For Virgin Galactic spacecraft, see Jesse McKinley, "Spaceport America Eyes the (Near) Future," *New York Times,* September 7, 2012, http://travel.nytimes.com/2012/09/09/travel/spaceport-america-eyes-the-near-future.html?ref=travel; Space.com Staff, "NASA Buys Flights on Virgin Galactic's Private Spaceship," Space.com, October 14, 2011, www.space.com/13280-virgin-galactic-nasa-spaceshiptwo-flights.html. For Blue Origin spacecraft, see Kit Eaton, "SpaceX, Blue Origin, and the Race to Control the Commercial Space Industry," *Fast Company,* September 6, 2011, www.fastcompany.com/1778297/fireworks-or-workhorse-rockets-how-the-commercial-space-business-is-shaping-up. For NanoRacks, see David Zax, "Need a Lab in Outer Space? Try ScienceExchange, the Airbnb of Weird Science," *Fast Company,* December 14, 2011, www.fastcompany.com/1800957/the-airbnb-of-weird-science.

23. W. J. Hennigan, "MoonEx Aims to Scour Moon for Rare Materials," *Los Angeles Times,* April 8, 2011, http://articles.latimes.com/2011/apr/08/business/la-fi-moon-venture-20110408; Jesse McKinley, "Space Tourism Is Here! Wealthy Adventurers Wanted," *New York Times,* September 7, 2012, http://travel.nytimes.com/2012/09/09/travel/space-tourism-is-here-wealthy-adventurers-wanted.html?ref=travel&_r=0&pagewanted=all.

24. Carl Hoffman, "Shooting for the Stars," *Wall Street Journal,* October 27, 2011, http://online.wsj.com/article/SB1000142405297020464450457665349360911651 6.html; "Dragon," Space Exploration Technologies Corporation, accessed August 22, 2012, www.spacex.com/dragon.php.

25. "Space Boost," Science Central Archive, August 25, 2006, www.sciencentral.com/articles/view.php3?article_id=218392842&cat=3_1; "Company Overview," SpaceX, accessed February 6, 2013, www.spacex.com/company.php.

26. John P. Holdren, "Statement by John P. Holdren, Assistant to the President for Science and Technology, on Launch of Falcon 9 Rocket and Dragon Spacecraft,"

National Aeronautics and Space Administration, May 22, 2012, www.nasa.gov/
home/hqnews/2012/may/HQ_12-164_Holdren_SpaceX_Statement_prt.htm.

27. "What Is reCAPTCHA," Google, accessed January 19, 2013, www.google
.com/recaptcha/learnmore.

28. Deloitte Research updated analysis of Glenn Butts and Kent Linton, "The
Joint Confidence Level Paradox: A History of Denial, 2009 NASA Cost Symposium,"
25–26, April 28, 2009, http://science.ksc.nasa.gov/shuttle/nexgen/Nexgen_Down
loads/Butts_NASA's_Joint_Cost-Schedule_Paradox_-_A_History_of_Denial.pdf

29. "Higher Education: Not What It Used to Be," *Economist,* December 1,
2012, www.economist.com/news/united-states/21567373-american-universities-
represent-declining-value-money-their-students-not-what-it.

30. "UNESCO eAtlas of Out of School Children," UNESCO Institute of
Statistics, www.app.collinsindicate.com/uis-atlas-out-of-school-children/en-us.

31. Karthika Muthukumaraswamy, "Please Have a Seat, Your Smartphone Will
Be Right with You," *Huffington Post,* March 31, 2012, www.huffingtonpost.com/
karthika-muthukumaraswamy/health-care-technology_b_1389409.html.

32. "mHealth Technologies: Applications to Benefit Older Adults,"
Center for Technology and Aging, March 2011, 63, www.techandaging.org/mHealth
_Position_Paper_Discussion_Draft.pdf.

33. Esther Duflo, Michael Kremer, and Jonathan Robinson, "Nudging Farmers to Use Fertilizer: Theory and Experimental Evidence from Kenya," National
Bureau of Economic Research Working Paper 15131, July 2009, 5, www.nber.org/
papers/w15131.

34. Ibid., 3.

35. Jonathan Greenblatt, interview with the authors, March 20, 2013.

36. "General Government Expenditures," part 4 of *Government at a Glance
2011,* chapter III, "Public Finance and Economics," OECD, 2011, http://tinyurl
.com/bcqbulo

37. More than one of every four dollars that an OECD-member government
spends goes toward procurement. "Size of Public Procurement Market," part 4 of
Government at a Glance 2011, chapter IX, "Public Procurement," OECD, 2011,
http://tinyurl.com/at3wt5r.

38. Jonathan Greenblatt, interview with the authors, March 2013.

39. Harvey Koh, Ashish Karamchandani, and Robert Katz, "From Blueprint to
Scale: The Case for Philanthropy in Impact Investing," Monitor Group, April 2012,
3, http://tinyurl.com/84yn9qv.

40. Matt Bannick and Paula Goldman, "Sectors, Not Just Firms," *Stanford Social Innovation Review,* September 2012, www.ssireview.org/blog/entry/
sectors_not_just_firms.

41. Celia Richardson, "How the Social Value Act Will Combat the Growing 'Shadow State,'" *Guardian,* December 19, 2012, www.guardian.co.uk/public
-leaders-network/2012/dec/19/social-value-act-shadow-state.

42. Allison Aubrey, "Sustainable Seafood Swims to a Big-Box Store Near You,"
The Salt, NPR's Food Blog, January 20, 2012, www.npr.org/blogs/thesalt/2012/01/19/
145474067/sustainable-seafood-swims-to-a-big-box-store-near-you.

43. "Sustainable Living Plan: Progress Report 2011," Unilever, 2011, 2–5,
www.unilever.com/images/uslp-Unilever_Sustainable_Living_Plan_Progress_
Report_2011_tcm13-284779.pdf.

44. One Percent for the Planet website, www.onepercentfortheplanet.org/en/.

45. "Workplace Rights Implementation Guide," The Coca-Cola Company, April 23, 2012, 5, http://assets.coca-colacompany.com/55/b5/5dcc88f044faa 9e56bf0d0f72a17/SupplierSGPImplementationGuideENGLISH.pdf.

46. "Alquería S.A," International Finance Corporation, August 2012, www1 .ifc.org/wps/wcm/connect/986fd7004d3308238872cdf81ee631cc/Alqueria.2012 .pdf?MOD=AJPERES.

47. Bill Gates, "Bill Gates: My Plan to Fix the World's Biggest Problems," *Wall Street Journal*, January 25, 2013, http://online.wsj.com/article/SB1000142412788732 35398045782617806648285770.html.

48. "RARE Report 2012," RARE, Arlington, VA, accessed February 6, 2013, www.rareconservation.org/sites/rareconservation.org/files/RareAnnualReport 2012.pdf.

49. "About IRIS," Global Impact Investing Network, IRIS (Impact Reporting and Investment), accessed February 6, 2013, http://iris.thegiin.org/about-iris.

50. Suzie Bozz, "Amplifying Local Voices," *Stanford Social Innovation Review*, summer 2011, www.ssireview.org/articles/entry/amplifying_local_voices1.

51. Natasha Singer, "You've Won a Badge (and Now We Know All About You)," *New York Times*, February 4, 2012, www.nytimes.com/2012/02/05/business/ employers-and-brands-use-gaming-to-gauge-engagement.html?_r=0.

52. "What Are UNESCO and World Heritage?" TripAdvisor, accessed March 18, 2013, http://whc.unesco.org/en/news/561/.

53. Patrick Meagher, "Enabling Environments for Microfinance: A Concept Note," Financial Services Investment Project, July 2010, www.fsassessment .umd.edu/publications/pdfs/Enabling-Environments-Microfinanace.pdf; "Bill & Melinda Gates Foundation Awards $5.8 Million Grant to ACCION for Microfinance Development in Africa and India," *PR NewsWire*, January 2010, www .prnewswire.com/news-releases/bill–melinda-gates-foundation-awards-58-million -grant-to-accion-for-microfinance-development-in-africa-and-india-55170757.html; "Financial Inclusion 2.0," *Livemint.com*, December 7, 2010, www.livemint.com/ Articles/2010/12/07205757/Financial-inclusion-20.html; Tavia Grant, "It's Revolutionary, and Ridiculously Simple: What Poor People Really Need Is a Safe Place to Put Their Money," *Globe and Mail*, July 16, 2011, http://tinyurl.com/ckm47cq.

54. Gates, "My Plan to Fix the World's Biggest Problems."

Appendix

1. We teamed up with our Monitor Deloitte colleagues Michael Kubzansky, Anamitra Deb, Ashish Karamchandani, and Harvey Koh to develop these strategies, borrowing in part from various earlier reports, including *From Blueprint to Scale* (2012), *Emerging Markets, Emerging Models* (2009), *Investing for Social and Environment Impact* (2009), and *Promise and Progress* (2011).

2. Michael E. Porter and Mark R. Kramer, "Creating Shared Value," *Harvard Business Review*, January–February 2011, 68.

3. Bill Drayton and Valeria Budinich, "A New Alliance for Global Change," *Harvard Business Review*, September 2010, 56–64.

4. Harvey Koh, Ashish Karamchandani, and Robert Katz, *From Blueprint to Scale: The Case for Philanthropy in Impact Investing* (Monitor Group, April 2012), 16, http://tinyurl.com/84yn9qvOk.

5. Jonathan Greenblatt, interview with the authors, March 20, 2013.

Index

Acknowledgments

If it takes a village to raise a child, it took about that many to complete this book. While our names may be on the cover, in reality many talented individuals contributed to the research, writing, and editing of this book.

Megan Schumann of Deloitte was the book's lead researcher. Involved in the project from nearly the beginning, she contributed significantly to all aspects of the book. Just as important, Megan helped crystallize our thinking about a new way of approaching societal problem solving. Her infectious enthusiasm and intellectual curiosity made the project a pleasure to be involved in. Megan has a very bright future ahead of her.

Two gifted and thoughtful young researchers, both with a deep passion for social change, also were integral to the book's development. Christopher Benz and Nick Hiebert were truly outstanding researchers and helped develop a number of the case studies and modules. We have little doubt that their prodigious talent will someday land each of them on a best-seller list or running an impactful social enterprise.

John O'Leary, the coauthor of a previous Harvard Business Review Press book with Bill, was generous enough to read the manuscript cover-to-cover and provided dozens of helpful suggestions. John's deft touch, wickedly funny sense of humor, and always frank—and often tough—feedback was invaluable.

Dozens of our Deloitte colleagues also played a critical role in the book. Jerrett Myers, Chris Ling, Helen Liu, and Nicholas Fulford from the global team provided research and feedback on multiple drafts. Elizabeth Henry provided critical editing and writing assistance. Mahesh Kelkar, Tomal Biswas, and Abhijit Khuperkar added their considerable statistical skills to the daunting task of sizing the solution economy. Marsha Collins, Amrita Datar, Atul Guljarani, Vikrant Jain, and Owen Sanderson provided top-notch research assistance. Ryan Alvanos and Jon Warshawsky applied their deft editing touch to the introduction. Jonathan Copulsky and John Shumadine were unwavering in their support of the book throughout the extended research process. Evan Hochberg and Dave Pearson connected us to dozens of Deloitte changemakers around the world. Lauren Mistretta, Amy Leonard, Carolyn Vadino, and Amy Pottberg led the marketing efforts. A special thanks to Tiffany Fishman for her contributions to the transportation cases and for keeping the research ship running when we were knee-deep in finishing the book.

Michael Kubzansky, a former colleague from Monitor Deloitte, gave detailed feedback on the manuscript. He and Monitor Deloitte colleagues Ashish Karamchandani, Harvey Koh, and Anamitra Deb helped deepen our understanding of how the solution economy operates in emerging markets like India and Africa. Their pioneering work on impact investing, market-based solutions for development, and business model innovation greatly influenced our thinking.

We have many other Deloitte colleagues to thank. Kishore Rao read the full manuscript and offered some of the most thoughtful feedback we received. Our refreshingly optimistic colleagues at Deloitte's GovLab offered much inspiration and encouragement throughout the process. A special thank you for providing invaluable feedback on chapter drafts goes to Prakash Akshai, Elizabeth Arnold, Coonoor Behal, Nes Diaz-Uda, Devon Halley, Lindsay Hitchcock, Vetan Kapoor, Joe Leinbach, Shrupti Shah, Kara Shuler, Charles Tierney, and Howard Yeung.

Thanks also to other Deloitte colleagues for offering their time and insights: Joe Eshun, David Friedman, Fran Greaney, Mike Kim, Jitinder Kohli, Mette Lindgaard, John Mennel, Caitlin Marie Ryan, Simon Strange, and Namas Vedamoorthy.

A number of good friends from Australia and Canada, who fortunately also happen to be deeply knowledgeable about this space, were kind enough to review the book: Nicholas Gruen, David Mitchell, Gary Sturgess, Martin Stewart Weeks, and David Zussman. Bruce Wright provided extensive editorial assistance. The book is better for your detailed feedback.

Hundreds of wavemakers were interviewed for this book. We learned much from them about what works and what doesn't in cross-sector problem solving. There simply isn't space to thank all of them here, but we would be remiss if we didn't thank the following social innovators for their generous time: Bill Drayton and Tina Choi from Ashoka; Sasha Dichter, Jacqueline Novgoratz, and Yasmina Zaidman from Acumen; Jennifer Pahlka from Code for America; Anthony Goldboom from Kaggle; Premal Shah and Jason Riggs from Kiva; Susan Phillips and Amy Klement from Omidyar Network; and Parag Gupta of Waste Ventures.

Dozens of government officials also helped us sort through how government fits into the solution revolution and all the myriad ways it can accelerate its development. In particular we would like to thank: Gareth Davies of the UK Cabinet Office; Jonathan Greenblatt from the White House; Nick Manning from the World Bank; Edwin Lau from the OECD; Nigel Jacob and Chris Osgood from the City of Boston; Ron Gonen from the City of New York; Joe Parrish, Jenn Gustetic, and Jason Cruzar from NASA; and Christian Bason from Denmark's MindLab.

This is the second book Bill has done with Harvard Business Review Press and the first for Paul. We couldn't have asked for a smoother process and a better team. Jeff Kehoe was once again a top-notch editor and booster. He has an excellent sense of when to be firm ("No, you can't try to change the title for the umpteenth time two weeks before it goes to press") and when to be flexible ("OK, we'll put a box around your chapter summaries"). Jeff did a great job organizing blind peer reviews that offered the candid feedback that helps to take a book from good to great. We will also miss working with the rest of the team at Harvard Business Review Press, including Allison Peter, Erica Truxler, Nina Nocciolino, Erin Brown, and Stephani Finks. We feel grateful to have had such a professional team behind the book from the world's premier management publishing house.

Support from friends and family was so important to both of us. For Bill, Morgann Rose was there through thick and thin. Her immense patience and support never wavered throughout the arduous book-writing process. Morgann's thoughtful questions—and ever-present voice recorder—on many long walks helped Bill break through countless bouts of writer's block. Dave Eggers was always willing to read chapter drafts and offer the kind of editorial insight that money can't buy. His wife Vendela, and Bill's other brother Toph, two more talented writers themselves, were always there to provide feedback on the title and other issues.

Paul's family has been excited and encouraging throughout the project. Janet's support for a truly global project has made the time and travel demands that much more manageable. Kyle's and Kate's active interest in our progress was really encouraging. The Macmillans all benefited from a proven coauthor to lead the way on what was truly a memorable journey.

About the Authors

An author, columnist, consultant, and popular speaker for two decades, **WILLIAM D. EGGERS** is a leading authority on tackling big societal challenges. As a global director at Deloitte Research, he is responsible for research and thought leadership for Deloitte's public sector industry practice. (Deloitte Research is a part of Deloitte LLP).

Eggers's seven books include the *Washington Post* best-seller *If We Can Put a Man on the Moon: Getting Big Things Done in Government, Government 2.0, Governing by Network,* and *The Public Innovator's Playbook.* His writings have won numerous awards including the Louis Brownlow Book Award for best book on public management, the Sir Antony Fisher International Memorial Award for best book promoting an understanding of the free economy, and the Roe Award for leadership and innovation in public policy research.

A former manager of the groundbreaking state government audit, Texas Performance Review, Eggers has advised governments around the world. His commentary has appeared in hundreds of major media outlets including the *New York Times,* the *Wall Street Journal,* and the *Washington Post.* He divides his time between Austin, Texas, and Washington, DC. He can be reached at weggers@deloitte.com or on Twitter at @wdeggers.

PAUL MACMILLAN grew up in Canada's national capital, where he studied public administration at Carleton University and earned an MBA from the University of Ottawa. He has been a management consultant and strategic adviser to government leaders for over twenty-five years. As the global industry leader in the public sector practice at Deloitte Touche Tohmatsu, Macmillan is responsible for the firm's leadership of complex innovations in government organizations around the world. He writes and speaks frequently on topics such as government innovation, public accountability, and advanced analytics.

Macmillan is a founder of the Institute of Public Administration of Canada (IPAC)–Deloitte Public Sector Leadership Awards, which recognize organizations that have achieved bold advancements in public policy and management in Canada. He is also a member of the board of directors of Bridgepoint Active Healthcare in Toronto. Macmillan has contributed his expertise to the OECD Observatory of Public Sector Innovation as a member of its Associate Group.

He lives in Toronto with his wife and two teenage children. He can be reached at pmacmillan@deloitte.ca.